Shakespearean Stage Production

Then & Now

Queen Elizabeth. Engraving by T. A. Dean after the Zucchero portrait which hangs in Hatfield House

SHAKESPEAREAN STAGE PRODUCTION THEN & NOW

CÉCILE DE BANKE

With a Foreword by
Hugh Miller

HUTCHINSON
Stratford Place, London

Hutchinson & Co. (Publishers) Ltd.

London   Melbourne   Sydney   Auckland
Bombay   Cape Town   New York   Toronto

First published 1954

Set in eleven point Monotype Bembo
one point leaded

Printed in Great Britain
by The Anchor Press, Ltd.,
Tiptree, Essex

THIS BOOK IS DEDICATED IN ALL FELLOWSHIP TO
THE MEMBERS, PAST, PRESENT, AND FUTURE, OF THE
SHAKESPEARE SOCIETY AT WELLESLEY COLLEGE
WELLESLEY, MASSACHUSETTS

Contents

PART ONE

Staging

List of Illustrations

Line Drawings In The Text

Foreword

If I could journey out of time and enter the Globe Playhouse in Southwark I should want to meet the Stage Manager to learn from him how the various units of his complex stage are used and to discover the way in which the production of *Hamlet* is made to flow with exhilarating speed and smoothness.

I should ask where Burbage is accustomed to speak the Death soliloquy, that is at what point on the front stage he finds he can best dispense his powers—having in mind the groundlings, friends packing the Penny Gallery and lords crowding the side boxes.

Next, I should mount the platform-stage to get "the feel" of it, clamber to its gallery, under "the heavens" and high above the Open Court, and range the Twopenny Room. Then, behind, to the tiring rooms to hold Othello's robe and Prospero's gown, to handle the stuffs of which the clothes are made: Rash and Baudkin, Linsey-Woolsey, Sarcenet and Mockado, and match them with the fabrics of my day, as I would match Will Kempe's shoe with one of Irving's I have handled.

I would ply my fellow-actors with a hundred questions to fill the gaps in Henslowe's diary. What's the best air for a Wooing dance, for a Lavolta or a Galliard? Will you give me the true measure of a Cinquepace—but slowly, that I may note it? Where are your musicians accustomed to be placed; for they are surely out of sight during the play and yet close enough for the music to be cued accurately? Is that entrance of Edward Alleyn's to music? Come, gentlemen, I have surely warrant for that question for there is a record by one of your number which is extant and runs: "Musique sounds to give enter-breath to the actors and more grace to the action."

It is fitting that everything I ask on this journey should have relation to the craft of my job, for I am now in the very theatre for which Shakespeare wrote and I am touching the actual medium through which his fancy took form and body—a theatre, incidentally, in which the players are the masters. There's little time and much to learn here, and every detail is of immense importance.

Cécile de Banke has written a book which makes my journey really unnecessary. Resisting the attractions of theory and speculation, she unites her patience as a scholar, her skill as an illustrator and her ardour as an artist

13

to produce a complete guide to the playhouse of Shakespeare. The work is a treasure-house of information for the student, the young producer and the craftsman of the stage. If I could think of a single question to which the writer does not give an immediate answer then her magnificent bibliographies direct me to the appropriate authority.

Lovers of Shakespeare owe a debt to Cécile de Banke, for her labour strengthens the hand of all those concerned in the preservation of tradition and in the presentation of his plays in their authentic element—the platform stage.

Hugh Miller

Preface

The conscientious amateur, starting with nothing but enthusiasm on his first production of a Shakespearean play, is quick to realize the need for information that will be of immediate and direct use to him. His first step in search of this will lead him, almost inevitably, to a library, and here, regrettably enough, he may experience his first setback. It is not failure to find the information he seeks, but the overwhelming abundance of it that gives him pause.

What follows? Will he give up all idea of putting on the play when, humbled and dismayed, he catches this first glimpse of how much he does not know? Or will he snap defiant fingers at the loaded shelves and decide to plunge into the job with the text of the play alone to guide him?

The first decision means a loss of valuable experience for himself and his prospective cast and, even more regrettable, supplies one more example of erudition killing inclination.

The second decision has this at least to recommend it, that an attempt will be made that cannot fail to bring a lively awareness of the worth-whileness of the undertaking to the actors and producer. If the results fail to meet the standard of that member of the audience whose censure, according to Hamlet, must in the actors' opinion "o'erweigh a whole theatre of others", there is always the hope that the "others" will, with Theseus, think that "never anything can be amiss when simpleness and duty tender it".

Our bewildered would-be producer is still in the stacks, but let us imagine that, while our backs were turned, he has been reading and has been lucky enough to come across these three facts: that the plays of Shakespeare were, for the most part, written (1) for one particular type of theatre, (2) for one particular group of actors, and (3) for a popular audience from whom a satisfactory box-office return might be expected! Now, suddenly, he knows *what* he wants to know and *why* he wants to know it.

He wants to know what the theatre was like *that Shakespeare had in mind when he was writing the plays.* And he wants to know because the answer to this inquiry may solve the problems of staging stated or implied in the text. In spite of the fact that these plays have been performed on almost every known type of stage during the last three hundred and fifty years, isn't it possible that *only on the stage for which they were written* can their uninter-rupted tempo and certitude of performance be realized?

These plays were written to fit a group of actors whose capabilities and types were known to Shakespeare; surely, therefore, it is reasonable for the producer of today to wish to know something of these men—their training, their acting ability, and, if possible, their physical appearance. Isn't there a chance here of catching a hint as to the *style of delivery, characterization, and technique of business and movement?*

What attracted an audience, composed largely of the illiterate, to return to the theatres of Elizabethan London again and again to support plays of a standard never reached before or since on the English stage? Apart from the appeal made to the ear by magnificent and exquisite poetry, what music delighted them? What appeal was made to their eyes by way of setting and costume? What skill and energy of movement excited them? What illusions astounded them?

As a one-time dismayed producer in the stacks I have attempted in this book to put before those who make similar attempts at inquiry all that pertains to those aspects of Elizabethan staging that will be of direct use to them. I have tried to bring together under one cover the gathered facts and conjectures of the most outstanding Shakespearean scholars, not to save time, be it understood, but, rather, to supply the scholar-player's *immediate need* while pointing to the fields of further inquiry in which he may browse at his own pace in his own good time.

CÉCILE DE BANKE.

Acknowledgments

A book such as this is based largely on the work of others. The extent of my indebtedness to the great Shakespearean scholars is implied in my references to their work, but that is not enough. Beyond such obvious obligation, there is the deeper gratitude I owe them for quickening my understanding of the art of Shakespeare and his fellows. More specifically I wish to thank Dr. John Cranford Adams, whose *The Globe Playhouse* has inspired all my experimentation in Shakespearean stage production for the last few years, and whose generosity has made possible the reproduction of the plans of his reconstructed Globe stage and the photographs of the model based on those plans.

The opinions of scholars on Elizabethan staging are frequently at variance, especially in regard to those aspects of the playhouses that are based on conjecture. Where many divergent opinions are held on some one particular, I have, in every case, accepted that one which, to me, seemed to emphasize the idea of the theatrical effectiveness of the stagecraft of the time.

Looking back over the years of work that have gone to the making of this book, I am deeply appreciative of the interest, help, and encouragement that I have received from members of the Wellesley faculty; of the patient and unflagging courtesy of the Wellesley Library staff under my often, I am afraid, exacting, demands; and I am happily aware of the many vital contributions that have been made to the book by the ardent young scholar-players of my classes. Finally, to Eleanor Blair, kindly critic and loyal friend, I extend my warmest thanks for editorial help and advice.

Beyond the campus, in Canada, England, and the United States, scholars, curators of museums, and heads of publishing houses have made time in their busy lives to answer questions and to match enthusiasm with enthusiasm. To be indebted to all these courteous and kindly people is a privilege and brings added confirmation to my belief in the unfailing generosity of the truly intellectual mind.

Author's Note

The scholar who has decided that in Shakespeare the poet transcends the dramatist argues that in his plays the subtly implicit imagery, the connotative overtones, the packed condensation conveyed in more or less unfamiliar grammar and vocabulary can never be fully appreciated or even comprehended in the swift verbal projection of the actor.

"How," he asks with a touch of pedagogic superiority, "can the actor be expected to know the psychological complexities that affect human behaviour and the reactions of character to the force of external events that are implied in these plays? Only the most painstaking analysis by the scholar of scenes, lines, even single words, can uncover these." And finally, waxing a little waspish, "How can the magnitude of human experience, encompassed here, be revealed by the mediocre intelligence of the average actor?"

Stung by all this the actors might reply: "These plays were created solely for stage presentation. Only in the theatre, where they belong, can the tremendous impact of their dramatic power be felt. To evaluate them from the printed page is comparable to estimating Beethoven's Ninth Symphony from the musical score. You see Falstaff in your mind's eye; come to the theatre and see him in the flesh. The mind's eye was good enough for the remembered likeness of a dead king, but if Hamlet had not *seen* the ghost of that king there would have been no play." And so it has gone on—on one side the scholar reading and analysing the poet Shakespeare, in solitude; on the other, the actor passionately identifying himself with the actor-director-playwright Shakespeare, among the crowds and clamour.

Now, as one standing where there is a fine view of the campus on one side and of the playhouses on the other, I watch, with satisfaction, the subsiding of all this wasteful recrimination. For many years events have tended to break through lines of demarcation and to lessen prejudices and antagonisms.

From the universities have come such men as Harley Granville-Barker and Sir Frank Benson, who have brought scholarly distinction to the professional stage.

In 1938, the students of the Yale University Department of Drama, of which the distinguished drama historian Allardyce Nicoll was then the chairman, constructed a reproduction of an Elizabethan stage within the Yale

University Theatre. On this stage during the academic year 1938–1939, candidates for the M.F.A. produced a series of plays of the period. In 1941, a memorable production of the full-length *Hamlet* was staged.

At the University of Illinois, Elizabethan plays are being presented on a reproduction of Shakespeare's Globe, as recently reconstructed by that eminent scholar, John Cranford Adams, in his book *The Globe Playhouse*. Inspired by this same book, Ronald Watkins and Maurice Percival in England are producing Shakespeare at Harrow with a correctness and distinction that the professional theatre is watching with respect.[1]

It is true that, while there are still scholars and actors of Shakespeare's plays who are not completely reconciled, they are at least willing to exchange a mutual nod of recognition of each other's endeavours and achievements. In the meantime there are the young amateur actors coming from university and college theatre workshops whose scholarly knowledge and trained acting ability are likely to bridge the gulf completely, combining and exemplifying, as they do, the best of both approaches in a new type of interpreter—to wit, the scholar-player.

This book is dedicated to a specific band of scholar-players, but they may be considered as representing all such groups who seek to present the plays of Shakespeare in a manner that reflects the very age and body of this time.

---

[1] Since the writing of this book Ronald Watkins's admirable work, *On Producing Shakespeare*, with delightful illustrations by Maurice Percival, has been published in London by Michael Joseph.

Part One

Staging

Elizabethan & Jacobean Staging of Shakespeare's Plays

There was nothing that Shakespeare and his players wanted to do that they could not do; their stage was an instrument magnificently equal to every demand that could be made upon it.

John Drinkwater, *Great Lives*

IT IS usually with surprise that we learn how much is known of the Elizabethan repertory theatre. We know, for instance, the place, name, and date of the building of all but one of the professional theatres that existed during Shakespeare's lifetime, and a good deal about the innyards which served intermittently as theatres before, during, and after Shakespeare's professional career in London. We know, from contemporary maps and "views" of London, the appearance of the exteriors of four of the public playhouses, and there are extant four illustrations of interiors—although it is doubtful if any of these latter give us an authentic reproduction of the type of stage for which Shakespeare wrote his plays. Finally, we know the admission charges and receipts; the seating and standing accommodation for the audience; the most important personnel of Shakespeare's acting company; and something of the playwrights, landlords, lessees, managers, and financial backers of most of the London theatres of the day.

Of the physical construction of the stage itself we know least, but, from the wealth of scholarly deduction that has resulted from careful study of documentary evidence, it has been possible to arrive at a fairly definite idea of its component parts, and thence to an assembling of those parts into a stage that meets all the production needs indicated in Elizabethan plays. ·

Often as Shakespeare must have chafed at the inadequacy of this theatre to supply the vast spectacles that his imagination saw—as he did in *Henry V*, I, 1—yet, on the whole he must have found it workable. It remained for his wonderful sense of "good theatre" to make it a vehicle for practical and theatrical effectiveness.

In all the thousand years of English stage history, that of 1576 is the most significant. This was the year that saw the first permanent professional theatre built in England—indeed, the first public theatre in all Europe. The builder was James Burbage. As a one-time carpenter turned actor, and at this time manager of an excellent band of actors, Burbage was particularly qualified to build a playhouse for the delight of the public and, at the same time, to provide efficient headquarters for a company of players. His professional experience provided an understanding of the needs of audience and actors, and his carpenter's skill enabled him to construct a building to meet those needs.

There is much to be said for the pluck and sagacity of Burbage, for the undertaking called not only for expenditure of his entire savings from years of hard work and fitful fortunes, but also involved the entire fortune, down to wearing apparel, of his brother-in-law, John Brayne. It is, of course, possible that the enterprise might never have gone beyond the stage of wishful thinking had not circumstances forced it into actuality.

Events Leading to the Building of the Theatre

Up to 1576, a convenient place in which to present their art had been the professional actors' most pressing need. Apart from the Great Halls of the houses of the nobility, where they played very infrequently, the players found few places suitable and none adequate for their purpose. The reputable troupes under the patronage of the nobility met with abuse and prohibitions in the provinces, and, had they not worn the livery of their patrons and carried letters of guarantee, it is doubtful if they would have found even the makeshift accommodation of schools, town halls, market halls, and even village greens so grudgingly allowed them. The troupes in London were in even worse plight: they were compelled to use the yards of inns for the presentation of their plays.

The square yards, surrounded on three, and often four, sides by the walls of the inns, were primarily for the use of carriers with their teams and wagons, and only on those days when they had returned to the country to restock produce or pick up goods for carriage were the innyards available to the actors. Frequently, the innyards would be closed to the actors by civil authority as a precautionary measure against the spread of the plague, which raged with virulence during the summer and intermittently throughout the rest of the year. Added to these inconveniences, the audience, which included the drunken and dissolute hangers-on of the inn bars and tap rooms, not infrequently created such disturbances that the actors were brought into ill repute with the Common Council. Not that this seems to have caused them concern, for there is no doubt that royal and aristocratic patronage had caused the actors to be contemptuous of civil threats and penalties. In 1573, however, the Puritans succeeded in electing a Lord Mayor and in securing control of the Board of Aldermen, with the result that the actors found themselves facing not only restrictions that were part of legitimate reforms for the maintenance of order and the protection of health, but also a fanatical moral prejudice against everything connected with the performance of plays. At a meeting of the Common Council on December 6, 1574, a special ordinance[1] was passed which included a censorship of plays, compulsory licensing of inns and proprietors of inns where plays were performed, the closing of "playing-places" during the hours of church services and "*at any other time thought fit*", the power to revoke the licences of the inns, and the power to exact a big amusement tax from the innkeeper for the support of the poor. The severity of this ordinance forced the actors to two decisions: they must find a place other than the inns in which to give their performances, and the place must be in a locality that was not under control of the Common Council. The idea of building their own "playhouse" may have come from Burbage. At any rate it fell to his lot to raise funds and to find a suitable location in which to build.

In selecting a site, James Burbage had four choices. There were two areas in the City itself which were free from interference from the Common Council. Known as the "liberties", these were the partially ruined monasteries with their grounds that had originally belonged to the White Friars and the Black Friars before their confiscation by the Crown during the Reformation. Outside the City walls were two other areas, one to the south, across the Thames, known as "the Clink" on Bankside, and one to the north, known as "the liberty of Holywell". It was in this last, in April, 1576, that Burbage leased a site. Not only was this location cheaper than the other three, but, being adjacent to the recreation grounds of Finsbury Fields, it had the advantage of being associated with pleasure seeking and holiday-making. Here he erected a building that was to be used exclusively for the purpose of popular entertainment; that was to be a repository for costumes, properties, and scripts of plays; and that was to be headquarters

---

[1] Full details of the Act can be studied in "Documents of Control", to be found in Chambers, (Sir) Edmund K., *The Elizabethan Stage*, Vol. IV, Appendix D.

for his company of actors. Here, by the autumn of 1576, although the building was by no means complete, the actors were presenting plays.

INFLUENCES DETERMINING THE ARCHITECTURAL PLAN OF THE THEATRE

When Burbage started to plan his playhouse, he had two sources of information from which to draw ideas. One consisted of the known features that had been, for hundreds of years, effective in the presentation of any kind of spectacle, whether religious, military, or civic; and the other, the structural elements in public and private buildings in which actors had performed up to this time and which they had found to be theatrically effective. Combining the best from both sources, Burbage built a theatre that served as a model for all those built in London in the next eighty-seven years and which determined, to a surprising extent, the structural plans of theatres down to our own times. The Theatre, as it was called, was an instant success, and a very short time later another playhouse, the Curtain, rose in its immediate neighbourhood. This proving equally successful, others followed in quick succession. Before Shakespeare retired to Stratford in or about 1611, there were no less than thirteen playhouses in the small metropolis, to say nothing of the five innyards which continued to serve as winter quarters for many acting companies, including Shakespeare's own.

In 1599, the ground lease of the Theatre ran out, and it says much for the soundness of its structure that, after it was dismantled, its sturdy timbers were used in the erection of a new theatre on the south side of the Thames. This theatre, built in the Clink on Bankside, was none other than the famous first Globe.[1]

In 1599, William Shakespeare, Will Kempe, John Heminges, Augustine Phillips, Thomas Pope, and the two sons of James Burbage, Richard and Cuthbert, had formed themselves into a syndicate to finance the erection of the Globe playhouse and had employed Master Builder Peter Streete to carry out its construction. With the exception of Cuthbert Burbage, all the members of the syndicate were actors, and, under the circumstances, it is safe to guess that the Globe stage met all the requirements of Shakespeare and his fellows. Not only were they in a position to demand what they wanted, but they could actually supervise the construction of the acting area, an opportunity afforded to few actors, and one of which they doubtless took full advantage.

---

[1] It was burned down in 1613 and replaced by what is now known as the "second Globe".

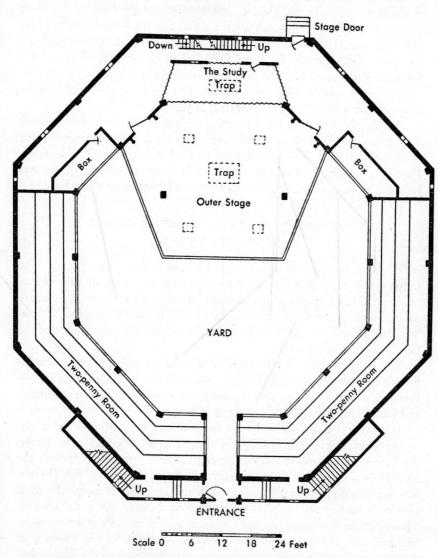

Reconstructed plan of the Globe: first level (From John Cranford Adams, *The Globe Playhouse*, Harvard University Press, Cambridge, Mass., 1942. Courtesy of Dr. John Cranford Adams and Harvard University Press)

Up to 1599, Shakespeare was writing plays for the type of stages he found in innyards, in the Theatre, and, possibly, in the Curtain. But with the building of the Globe with a stage practically made to order, he could take for granted more effective means of stage production and could call for more elaboration in his stage directions, both for new plays and for revivals of old ones. He was now approaching the height of his creative ability, and it was the Globe that saw the first performances of his greatest plays and the years of his most stupendous productivity.

For the above reasons the following analysis of the component parts of a typical Elizabethan theatre will refer, in general, to those found in the Globe, and will be based on John Cranford Adams's work, *The Globe Playhouse*, which gives us the benefit of his scholarly research into, and judicious deductions on, this most famous of all Elizabethan theatres.

Component Parts of the Elizabethan Theatre— Origin and Survival

1. *An enclosed space in which to erect a stage and house an audience.* The simplest way for a crowd to view any spectacle is to get round the object, or objects, of their attention; hence the circular sites of the "dancing grounds" of primitive peoples, the circular form of prehistoric temples, such as Stonehenge, and the circles and semicircles of the vast auditoriums of the Greek and Roman theatres.

The Roman occupation of England saw the introduction of the amphitheatre into the country, and it is possible that the Cornish "rounds" at Perranzabulo and St. Just, and the amphitheatres at Colchester, Silchester, and Cirencester exemplify the Roman influence.[1]

In medieval times not only did the audience stand around the horse-drawn floats on which short religious plays were performed, but, we know, the longer miracle plays were presented in the Cornish rounds with the audience on all sides of the performers. Burbage, in building the Theatre, was, without doubt, directly influenced by the survival of the amphitheatrical plan in the structure of the bear-baiting rings on the south side of the Thames. These circular buildings ensured the seating of a capacity audience in an enclosed area, and this was sufficient recommendation for the adoption of the plan in the building of all except one (the Fortune) of the Elizabethan theatres. The possibility that the Globe theatre was octagonal rather than circular is suggested by many authorities, a suggestion possibly based on contemporary pictorial representations. In further support of the idea,

---

[1] It is thought by some antiquarians that these were early British remains of places of worship but that the Romans revived their use for gladiatorial spectacles.

John Cranford Adams points out that straight beams rather than curved ones could be used in an octagonal structure, thereby ensuring a more compact and stronger building at less cost.

In the Elizabethan theatre, the idea of the audience surrounding the players persisted in a modified form. The main part of the acting area consisted of a platform stage jutting out into the auditorium round three sides of which the audience could gather. In the wall behind the stage, as in the innyards, a certain number of spectators could be seated in the balcony on the second level of the building. In later theatres, this audience area, known as "the lords room", was incorporated into the acting area, and the fops and lordlings, who had previously occupied it, sat on the sides of the stage itself.

The ground plan of the modern theatre—an elongated, horseshoe-shaped auditorium with the stage across the end—is derived from the Greek and Roman amphitheatre by way of the public theatres of Elizabethan London.

2. *Entrances to and exits from the theatre for audience and actors.* If illusion, that indispensable element in dramatic presentation, is to be maintained, the less the identity of the actor infringes on that of the character he portrays the better. This was realized in the classical theatres of Greece and Rome and was no doubt responsible in part for the adoption of the conventional masks worn by all actors. But the actor, particularly the leading actor, became an increasingly important figure in his own right. Today the "star" system actually publicizes the personal life, traits of character, and idiosyncrasies of personality of the "leading" man or woman and deliberately fosters an interest in the actor that far exceeds that in any part he plays. However, in one respect the need for a certain amount of illusion is still realized, and this is seen in the attempt to prevent any mingling of audience and actor in the theatre itself; hence the isolation and careful guarding of the stage door.

In the innyards there was a wide passageway leading from the street to the yard, through which the carters drove their teams, and in many of them there was another passageway on the opposite side of the yard, making possible an exit into another street. The actors, on the days when they used the yard, would be able to close the big door that stood at the entrance of one of these passageways and use only the small wicket door cut in one side of the big door. In this way they could control the taking of the entrance money as the audience passed through in single file. Furthermore, by locking both big and wicket gates on the other side of the yard, the actors could keep this entrance for their exclusive use. When the yard did not possess an exit passage, the actors doubtless entered through the inn itself.

Burbage followed this plan in the Theatre, and, when that playhouse was dismantled in December, 1599, and the timbers re-erected in the building of the Globe, the two doors, one for audience and one for actors, at opposite sides of the building were maintained. Today one exit for a large audience— it is estimated that the Globe held over two thousand persons—would be condemned by the fire and public-safety laws.[1]

The audience entering an Elizabethan theatre would find themselves in a passage where the "gatherer" stood, box in hand, to receive the entrance fee of one penny which was demanded of all who entered, regardless of what part of the house they were going to occupy.[2] In this passage, or hallway, on one or both sides, staircases ran up to the galleries. It is possible that one short stairway on one side led to the second gallery, and a longer one on the opposite side to a third gallery. At the top of these stairways, gatherers waited to receive further payment for the sitting or standing room desired.

This general plan is seen today in the box-office where money is paid, in the narrow door through which people, passing one at a time, give their tickets as a check on their payment, and in the foyer beyond, where staircases run up to the balconies and upper circles.

3. *Sitting and standing accommodation for the audience.* A crowd standing on level ground round some focus of attention soon realizes that visibility is possible only to those standing in the first few rows, and some elevation is sought by those behind these rows. In the street, people tiptoe, get on each others' shoulders, climb trees, statues, or lamp-posts, go up to windows on higher levels, or occupy stands especially provided for spectators. The need of elevation for the audience was met in the very earliest Greek theatre by the simple expedient of arranging the seating on a hillside, and, later, when the Greeks came to build their great theatres at Epidaurus and Athens, they continued to choose hillside sites. The Romans, on the other hand, chose flat ground and built outer walls of great height with the tiers of seats within rising from the ground level to the height of the walls. This last architectural plan has been the one that has persisted down to modern times.

In the Cornish theatre at Perranzabulo there are seven rows of turf seats rising one above the other with a wide space at the top where spectators could stand.

The spectators of the cycle plays—that is, a privileged few on the street level—were seated on stands, or "scaffolds",[3] and, of course, spectators

---

[1] It is remarkable that, when the Globe caught fire in 1613 during a performance of *Henry VIII* and burned to the ground in "one short hour", the audience and actors escaped unharmed.

[2] Double the price was demanded for the first performance of a new play.

[3] Called "bleachers" in the United States.

also sat at second- and third-story windows in buildings lining the route of the pageants.

In 1495, a stationary miracle play was performed in a quarry at Shrewsbury, where, no doubt, the sloping sides offered excellent visibility.

The bear gardens used wooden scaffolds rising from the level of the bear pit to somewhere near the height of the outer walls, but Burbage in planning his auditorium was directly influenced by the two galleries of the innyard, which offered greater safety and comfort, and his plan gave us the tiers of seats on separate floor levels in the theatres of today. The bear-garden seating survives, appropriately enough, in sports stadiums, circuses, and, in part, in the grandstands of racecourses.[1]

In the innyard there was no means of seating anyone on the ground level under the first balcony as this part of the building was taken up by stables, coach-houses, harness rooms, and storerooms, but there is reason to believe that stands were erected in front of these rooms at the sides of the yard, and it is here that Burbage may have got the idea of a first gallery raised some few feet above the yard level. Rising above this first level were second and third galleries, and these, after the fashion of second and third stories in Elizabethan houses, had a "juttey forwards", or overhang, of ten inches on each level, which not only served the original purpose of preventing seepage of rain into the uprights supporting the structure, but gave better seeing and hearing facilities to those seated farther from the stage. Finally, the top gallery had a thatched[2] roof. Within these galleries were tiers of benches with standing room at the highest level at the back, and partitions of varying heights divided the tiers into sections. The small sections with high partitions immediately adjacent to the stage in the first and second galleries were known as "gentlemen's rooms", while the larger sections with lower partitions that were farther from the stage were known as "two-penny rooms". It is doubtful whether there were "rooms" of any kind on the third level. This third gallery and the unpartitioned parts of the first and second floors were, possibly, the "penny" and "two-penny" galleries often referred to. In the modern theatre, the gentlemen's rooms have become boxes situated near the stage on the first-, second-, and even third-floor levels, while the equivalent of the two-penny rooms is to be seen in the boxes running round the second balcony in opera houses such as the Metropolitan Opera House in New York and Covent Garden in London, and in the boxes at the back of the dress circle in some provincial theatres in England.

---

[1] Amphitheatral seating is to be found in a few small repertory theatres in England and Germany, and is an essential feature of the auditoriums of the arena theatres of today.

[2] In the later theatres, as a fire-prevention measure, the thatch was replaced by tile.

The first gallery, which seems to have been about thirty inches above the floor of the yard, had wooden palings with spikes on the top to prevent the people in the yard from climbing over. This gallery was entered from the yard by means of small flights of steps, placed, possibly, between the various-priced sections. But in view of the need for the palings, we must conclude that these entrance steps could be closed off by small gates just before the play started.[1]

The open space below the first gallery was still called the "yard", as it had been in the inns. Halfway across this space the platform stage projected, and here, surrounding it on three sides, the poorer patrons stood throughout the performance, exposed to rain and shine. It is possible that in the yard itself the amphitheatre survived in a modified form, for John Cranford Adams contends[2] that the brick-paved yard sloped down to the stage on all three sides, thus allowing the audience seated in the first gallery to see over the heads of the audience standing in the yard, and, furthermore, facilitating drainage after rainstorms, supposing that there was a sink at the lowest level. The yard area has become the orchestra stalls, stalls, pit stalls, and pit of the modern English theatre. In most theatres the floor of the auditorium still slopes down to the stage, but the audience is now seated, and, instead of the "groundlings" and "stinkards" of the yard, who paid only a penny to see the performance, we have the more exclusive members of the audience occupying these seats, which, together with those in the boxes, are the most highly priced in the house.

4. *Platform stage.* George Bernard Shaw once said that the first actor was the man who conceived the idea of standing on an upturned bucket to address his fellow-men. He realized, Shaw explained, that by elevating and isolating himself at the same time, he obtained the attention that his ego demanded.

Apart from the physical necessity of being seen and heard, the psychological value of elevation was realized from earliest times and was first used by priests for ritualistic purposes. The hill or rock used for the purpose later became the elevated chancel and altar platform, and these, in turn, served as a stage for the first liturgical dramas of the tenth century.

The stage of the Greek theatre was a platform running across one end of the amphitheatre, and it was here that the actor spoke his lines while the chorus chanted and danced in the circular "orchestra" below. In the Roman theatre this stage was very much deeper and the orchestra became a half-circle. A survival of this is seen in the curved orchestra pit of many modern theatres.

The pageants of the medieval cycle plays were two stories high. The

---

[1] These gates are, I think, indicated in De Witt's drawing of the Swan.
[2] Adams, John Cranford, *The Globe Playhouse*, pp. 37–41.

Dr John Cranford Adams

Dr John Cranford Adams' model of the Globe playhouse, now in the Folger
Shakespeare Library, Washington, U.S.A.

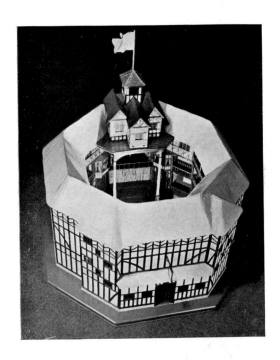

Two views of Dr John Cranford Adams' model of the Globe

Dr John Cranford Adams

lower level was enclosed and used for a dressing-room; thus the stage on the upper level had considerable elevation. Something of the effect of this may be seen in the Punch and Judy show. Again, street theatres (stationary floats) had to have considerable elevation in order to be on a level with the horse-mounted monarch or the distinguished visitor in whose honour they were erected.

There are many types of platforms shown in extant pictures of outdoor performances by strolling players, but the one most frequently depicted is that which was made by resting boards on barrels. In the innyards there may have been a permanent platform at one end for the use of the carriers in unloading their wagons, but it is more likely that the temporary stage of the board-and-barrel type had to be erected whenever the players gave a performance. This movable type of stage continued in those theatres that were not used exclusively for dramatic performance, since they could be easily dismantled whenever the whole yard at the ground level was needed for other types of entertainment—animal shows and fencing demonstrations being cases in point. The theatres used exclusively for dramatic performances built stages that were permanent and that were far more complicated in structure. The Globe stage was, it has been established, 43 feet wide, 29 feet deep, and 4 feet 5 inches in height, and projected halfway into the area of the yard. The extreme width may be accounted for by the fact, already stated, that the best-paying patrons occupied the sides of the stage. To offset this width it is possible that the platform tapered toward the front and so did not take up as much yard space as would at first appear. This stage was boarded in below, topped by a low railing, and covered, in part, by rushes, later replaced by matting.

5. *Traps.* Machinery for raising demoniac personages from "below",[1] which had been such a popular feature of the medieval stage, was an indispensable part of Elizabethan production, and stage directions in plays of the time indicate that there were as many as five traps in some platform stages, a small one at each of the four corners, capable of carrying one person, and one long narrow one across the centre which could bear as many as eight persons and, at the same time, elaborate and heavy properties. The noise of the elevating machinery must have been considerable, for we find that the use of traps was always accompanied by "music", "thunder", blasts from wind instruments, or rolling of drums. Trap-doors, or "star traps", are still to be seen on the British stage, but their use is limited almost exclusively to pantomime productions.

[1] It is interesting to note that the Greek theatre at Eretria and the Cornish round at Perranzabulo both have an underground passage leading from the side to the centre, where a pit no doubt represented the entrance to the underworld in classical times, and, in the case of the Cornish theatre, "hell's mouth" in medieval times.

6. *Background for the stage with entrance and exit doors.* The first background known in the history of the stage seems to have been a small wooden hut erected behind the orchestra of the Lycurgos Theatre of Dionysus in 465 B.C. In 425 B.C., this was replaced by a stone façade of a supposed temple or palace. As time went on, this background, or *"skene"* as it was called, became more and more decorative, until, in the Roman theatre at Aspendos, we see the height of elaboration in the *frons scaenae* of the classic theatre

When medieval drama moved from the interior of the church to the great West Door, the large centre door, flanked on either side by the two smaller doors, was used as a background; and when the next step was taken and drama moved into the street, the wagon stages of the street theatres, although open on three sides, often had as background a scenic façade of columns framing three curtained alcoves. It is possible that Burbage, as a carpenter, often helped to build such stages, and he was also no doubt familiar with the curtained alcove stage used in the universities for classic tragedies and with the row-of-shops background used in classic comedy.[1]

Another type of background with which Burbage was familiar was the wonderful carved "screen" with its two big doors situated at one end of the Great Hall in the houses of the nobility, the universities, and the Inns of Court, where he and his fellows occasionally presented their plays. Small wonder then that when he came to build his theatre he used as a background to his platform stage a façade which, although in part determined by the three galleries of the auditorium, resembled a three-storied Elizabethan house topped by a gabled attic rising above the roof of the third gallery, and that he had on the ground floor—that is, the stage level—in either end of this façade *two doors* (having small barred windows, or wickets), and between them a *curtained alcove* (see page 27).

A glance at John Cranford Adams's diagrams comparing the Theatre of 1576 with the Globe of 1599 (p. 35) shows the expansion of the background in the latter to include the two sloping sides of the octagon adjacent to either end of the stage. This accounts for the alteration in the position of the doors, which, instead of being on a line with each other, as they had been in the Theatre, were situated in the extended sides at the Globe and so actually faced one another.

These two doors were a traditional part of the British stage until recent times. Long after they ceased to be of practical use they flanked the modern picture-frame stage, and were even used as a decorative device in the proscenium itself. The survival of these doors both for architectural decoration

---

[1] An interesting survival of this "shop" background for comedy is the act drop painted to represent a street of mean shops and houses used as a background for comedians on the English music-hall (vaudeville) stage.

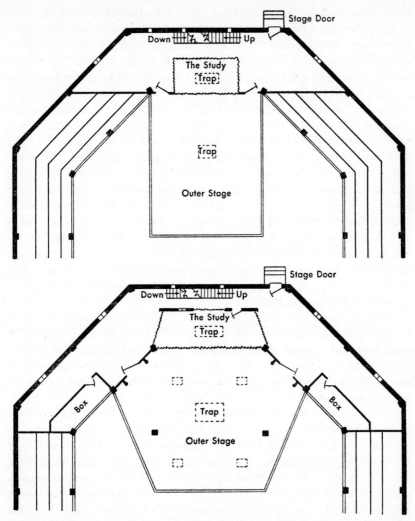

Evolution of the platform and tiring house: first level. Theatre (1576) and Globe (1599) plans compared. (From Adams, *The Globe Playhouse*. Courtesy of Dr. John Cranford Adams and Harvard University Press)

and for practical use is evident in the Memorial Theatre at Stratford-on-Avon.

7. *Curtained alcove.* The signifying of *place* on the English stage was, in the beginning, simple and unaided by scenery as we think of it today. In Church drama, acceptably enough, the rood loft was Heaven, the altar

steps or chancel, Earth, and the crypt, Hell. For other localized scenes, such as rooms in the houses of certain characters or council halls in palaces, spaces between the pillars of the nave were curtained and a definite place could be suggested. Unlocalized places, such as "on the road", or "in a street", were indicated by the simple expedient of walking in the nave or in uncurtained spaces between the pillars.[1] This method of presenting localized and unlocalized scenes was adopted in the cycle plays, where each pageant represented a definite place, the action of the play in unlocalized scenes taking place in the street below. Again in the arena stage of the longer stationary miracle plays, a series of platforms, both curtained and uncurtained, was erected in a circle and represented definite locations, while the unlocalized scenes were played in the open spaces between. On the university stages, the curtained alcoves were labelled with names of persons who, supposedly, occupied the houses, shops, or palaces of the alcoves represented. In these alcoves, localized scenes took place, the unlocalized scenes taking place on the platform in front of the closed curtains of the alcoves. In the street theatres, a curtained alcove in the centre of the scenic background was frequently used for the purpose of revealing a figure or figures against an interior background.

That Burbage was familiar with most of these types of staging is substantiated by the fact that, when he came to build his own theatre, he combined and adapted them into a satisfactory and effective whole, the outer platform stage being used for unlocalized scenes and a curtained alcove at the back of the platform, together with that part of the stage adjacent to it, which we shall call the "middle stage", for localized scenes.

The measurements of the inner stage at the Globe have been estimated as 20 to 25 feet wide, 10 to 12 feet deep, and 12 feet high. This alcove, according to John Cranford Adams, resembled a room with a window in the back wall to the audience's left, a door to the right which, when open, revealed the foot of a staircase leading to the second story, and a curtained alcove in the centre (see p. 65). It will be seen that this arrangement resembles the box set of the modern theatre, but instead of side walls the Elizabethan set had curtains with an overlap wide enough to enable an eavesdropper to listen to characters speaking on the inner stage. The curtains in front of the inner stage, of the rod-and-ring type, ranged from silk tapestries in the indoor, or "private", theatres to imitation tapestry painted

---

[1] A survival of this custom is to be found in the Quarto 2 stage directions for *Romeo and Juliet*, I, 4. Benvolio calls, "Strike drum." Then follows, "They march about the Stage and Servingmen come forth with Napkins." This shows that, while the masquers were marching round the forestage on their way to the house of the Capulets, the preparations for the ball and banquet of the following scene were taking place at the same time on the middle and inner stages.

on cloth in the cheaper public theatres. The latter survives in the painted act drop still to be found in many provincial theatres. The predominant colour of this curtain had a symbolic significance, it is believed, being blue when comedy was presented, and black or a sombre colour when the play was a tragedy (see p. 74 and chart on p. 153). There seem to have been rods running from the front to the back of the inner stage on which curtains, "traverses", could be hung when the localized scene represented a row of shops, adjacent rooms, or tents, etc.

Behind this curtain the "hired men" brought on properties and set the interior scenes while the play continued on the outer or middle stages. When the curtains were drawn, the interior scene was played entirely in this alcove, provided that few characters were introduced. When the scene involved many characters in a supposedly large room or hall, then a few appropriate properties placed on the middle stage could, when the inner-stage curtains were opened, link the two stages into one. This double stage would be used, for instance, in the ballroom scenes in *Romeo and Juliet* and *Much Ado about Nothing*, and in the trial scenes in *The Merchant of Venice*, *The Winter's Tale*, and *Henry VIII*. When occasion called for curtains behind an interior scene, these were, doubtless, hung against the back wall of the inner stage, but, owing to the rather obscure position of this stage, a very important interior scene would be played farther forward, in which case beds, thrones, etc., would be "thrust out"[1] from the inner stage and its closed curtains would then be the arras backing the scene.

In the floor of the inner stage there was a long narrow trap-door, known as the "grave", which could be used for ghostly apparitions rising beside beds, or, when a ladder was placed, for descents to a vault or underground prison. When it represented a pit or stream into which a character was hurled, a mattress was, let us hope, placed below the open trap to break his fall. When a character had to stand in an excavation, as in the case of the Gravedigger in *Hamlet*, a low platform must have been provided for him.

When the first indoor theatres were built and used,[2] their smaller auditoriums and more effective means of artificial lighting allowed for the more frequent use of the alcove stage. From 1606 on the area of the platform stage began to shrink and the alcove stage to become deeper and wider. The theatre of the Restoration with its picture-frame stage had a small forestage, but by the middle of the eighteenth century it had shrunk to a margin

---

[1] This is a stage direction often found in plays of the period. It refers to the pushing on of heavy properties either by way of doors or through the inner-stage curtain.

[2] Although the first indoor theatre was built by James Burbage in 1577 in the monastery of the Black Friars, its use, as such, was prohibited until 1600. In 1608 it became the winter quarters of Shakespeare's company.

beyond the proscenium arch, known as the "apron", the only function of which was to hold the footlights. The nineteenth century saw the increasing popularity of such forms of entertainment as melodrama, musical comedy, and, later, revues, all of which called for the alternation of full-stage scenes with forestage scenes in order to maintain the uninterrupted action and speed necessary for their successful presentation. But the space needed for front-stage acting did not result in a marked projection of the stage beyond the proscenium arch; the act drop was merely set farther upstage. In recent times the tendency has been to increase the forestage, and many plays, especially those between 1920 and 1930, called for ramps, platforms, bridges, and flights of steps projecting beyond the proscenium arch.

8. *Curtained balcony stage*. Action taking place on two or more levels, either separately or simultaneously, was provided for on the Greco-Roman stage, and, as we have seen, three levels were used in Church drama. There is a description of a cycle-play pageant having "hell's mouth" on a stage beneath a stage, and in the street theatres the background frequently represented a castle, with figures, real or pictorial, appearing at windows of different levels as well as on the battlements. In the Great Halls, the screens with the two massive doors were almost always topped by a minstrels' gallery, and this was, without doubt, used by the players. In the innyards, the second floor with its gallery was above the back of the platform stage, and this must have been used as an acting area. The framework of the Elizabethan theatre, with its three floor levels, which continued round the entire building, gave three levels to the background of the stage, and it was merely carrying out a long-established tradition to make the second level an acting area. It came about, then, that above the inner stage and jutting out ten inches beyond it, there was a curtained balcony having removable railings in front and revealing, when the curtains were opened, an interior similar to the one below, except that the door was on the left and the window on the right.

It has been usual to consider that this balcony stage was used most frequently in the early chronicle plays where it served to present castle battlements, city walls, etc., but John Cranford Adams suggests that all interior scenes which would have been "upstairs" in Elizabethan houses and public buildings were also played on this level. Apart from bedrooms this could include prisons, the upper deck of a ship, private rooms in taverns, a place from which royalty might view a masque or play, upper halls of a palace, and a room for a lady and her attendants. The floor of the balcony seems to have been strewn with rushes and to have had an opening of the trap-door type. (For the position of this trap-door see Dr. Adams's conjectural plan, p. 40.)

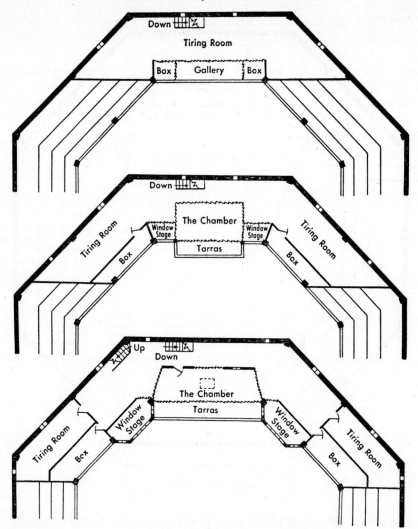

Evolution of the tiring house: second level. Theatre (1576), Rose (1592–1595), and
Globe (1599) plans compared. (From Adams, *The Globe Playhouse*. Courtesy of
Dr. John Cranford Adams and Harvard University Press)

The decline of the use of this upper stage was rapid after the opening of
the private theatres, and we find that it no longer existed in the theatre of
the Restoration. However, it has had a sensational revival in modern times,
for during the 1930s two stages, one above the other, in which action

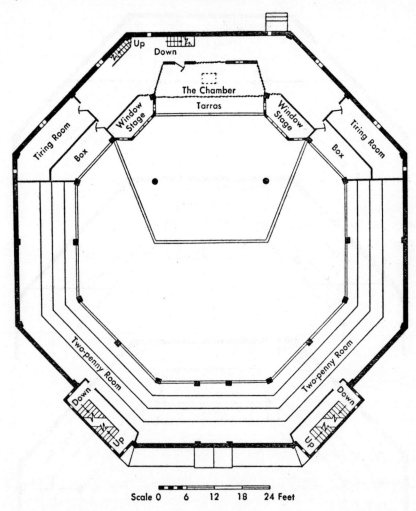

Reconstructed plan of the Globe: second level. (From Adams, *The Globe Playhouse*. Courtesy of Dr. John Cranford Adams and Harvard University Press)

occurred simultaneously, were used in many productions. A more recent use of the two-level stage was seen in Jo Mielziner's setting for Arthur Miller's play *Death of a Salesman* at the Morosco Theatre in New York.

9. *Tarras*. When the curtains were closed on the balcony stage, there remained a narrow space—about three feet—between the line of these curtains and the balustrade. This space, known as the "tarras", extended

the whole width of the balcony, and it is probable that this, and not the balcony proper, represented city walls, battlements, etc. When the curtains were opened, this space would be included in the area of the then "discovered"—or uncovered—interior scene (see p. 40).

10. *Window stages.* The slanting sides of the Globe, containing the doors, allowed for two other units in the acting area. These were the bay windows on the second level immediately over the doors. These bays contained windows opening on three sides, one narrow one opening towards the audience, two or four opening towards the opposite side of the stage, and one opening towards the balcony stage. When the windows were open, one or two actors could stand in the bay and be seen, down to the waistline at least, in any part of the auditorium. With curtains at the back, these bays formed small stages in themselves. Jutting out above the doors and supported by slender columns, they formed penthouses or porches below, giving, with the window above, the effect of a very convincing house unit for such scenes as Jessica's elopement in *The Merchant of Venice*, II, 5 and 6. If the wing curtains on one side of the balcony stage were open, this window stage could then be a window-recess extension of the balcony stage, such as might have been used in the balcony-bedroom scenes in *Romeo and Juliet.*

11. *Gallery for Musicians.* The third level of the structural plan of the Globe allowed for yet another stage unit (see p. 42), but as the visibility at this height would be poor for all save the audience in the third gallery, it is doubtful whether this level was used for acting with any frequency. But one use for this area must have occurred to Burbage, prompted by his familiarity with street theatres. The background of these stationary floats was frequently an elaborately constructed castle, and it was the custom to place the musicians and choristers high up on the battlements. Doubtless this custom prevailed where, as often happened, the real castle-like city gates were used. The highest place in the theatre then was obviously the place for the musicians, who, stationed in this small window gallery behind opaque curtains, could furnish incidental music. As we shall see later (p. 212), it was a particular type of music required for a particular purpose that was played by invisible musicians on this third level.

This gallery might also have been used effectively for single actors at certain moments in the action of a play, and we can imagine its being used as the crow's nest of a ship, a watch-tower from which a signal might be given, or for a celestial or supernatural figure to watch and direct the actions of mortals below. John Cranford Adams has given a lively description of Prospero directing the actors and musicians in the apparition scene in *The Tempest* from this height, proving the position of the sorcerer in the

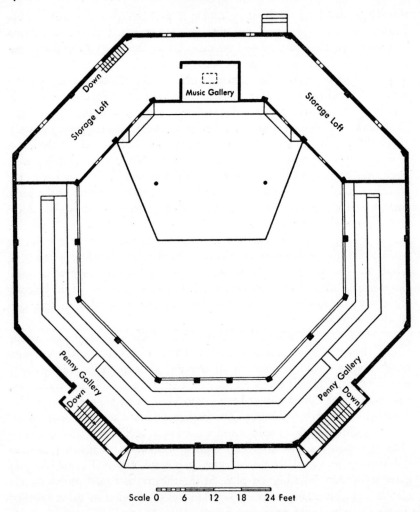

Reconstructed plan of the Globe: third level. (From Adams, *The Globe Playhouse*.
Courtesy of Dr. John Cranford Adams and Harvard University Press)

musicians' gallery to be not only theatrically effective, but most advantageous for the stage management of a very complicated scene.[1]

12. *Overhead shelter for actors.* Consideration of weather conditions must always have been a primary one in open-air theatres, and shelter from sun and rain for audience and actors must have been a major problem.

[1] Adams, John Cranford, *The Globe Playhouse*, pp. 319-22.

In a picture showing the reconstruction of the *frons scaenae* at Aspendos there is a sloping canopy roof which might have afforded some shelter for the actors. There is a hint also of awnings that could be drawn over the top of the Roman auditorium.

In medieval times the deep porches of the church doors and the canopies over the top of the pageants served to give protection to the actors and their magnificent costumes. But what of the actors in the innyards? No such provision was available, it seems, and rainstorms during a performance must have been something of a calamity for all except the audience seated in the galleries.[1] In building his playhouse, Burbage realized that here was an opportunity to meet this need for shelter—for his actors, at least.

When Philip Henslowe, Burbage's contemporary and rival manager, built the Fortune theatre in 1600, he stipulated in the contract that the stage was to be a replica of the Globe stage with "a shadowe or cover over saide stadge", but added that the "posts" of the frame and stage were to be "square and wrought palasterwise". From this, from the De Witt drawing of the Swan, and from the stage directions and allusions in Elizabethan and Jacobean plays, it is clear that running from the ceiling line of the third level of the tiring house, that is, the minstrels' gallery, to halfway over the platform stage was a shelter for the actors known as the "shadowe". This was supported below by two stout pillars which were usually round above, rested on square bases, and were possibly painted to resemble marble columns. The ceiling of this structure, which would be visible from below, was often painted to resemble a star-spangled sky,[2] a fact which accounts for its being referred to as the "heavens". The actual position of the pillars is still a matter for conjecture, but, since they supported the "shadowe" and this in turn ran forward from the flat back section of the tiring house, their position on a line with the ends of this section and halfway down the platform stage, as seen in Dr. Adams's reconstruction plans (p. 27), seems to be the most likely.

Apart from its usefulness to the actors as a shelter from rain and sun, the "shadowe" had an important structural function, supplying, as it did, part of the framework upon which rested the superstructure, or "huts".

13. *The "huts"*. Machinery for the lowering of actors from above, together with the "cars", "clouds", or "birds" in, or on, which they were seated, had been a feature of all stages from the earliest times. Such machinery, in order to preserve some degree of illusion, had to be invisible, and, until other methods were invented, was situated above the stage in what was

---

[1] In the magnificent motion picture *Henry V* there is an amusing scene of a rainstorm in an Elizabethan theatre.

[2] A device constantly used in the street theatres.

known as "the huts". If we keep these necessities in mind, the purpose of the superstructure of the Elizabethan theatre is not hard to guess, or to prove. By using the strong, well-supported frame of the "shadowe" in front and the uprights of the tiring-house wall behind, it was possible to erect a superstructure which extended part way over the "shadowe" in front and over the ceiling of the minstrels' gallery behind, and rose well above the level of the roof. Here was housed the simple hand-worked machinery for lowering and raising actors and heavy properties, such as a throne of state, down to and up from that part of the stage immediately in front of the inner stage. The "huts" also provided storage for sound-effect properties, such as cannon balls to roll up and down an incline for thunder, small cannon which could be fired,[1] and fireworks that would be "let off" where "salutes", din of battle, etc., were required.

A door at one side of this superstructure opened on to a small platform upon which a man could stand to hoist the "house" flag to the top of the staff in the morning to indicate that a play would be presented that day. From here he also sounded the three blasts of the trumpet that announced the commencement of the play. These two methods of attracting attention to the performance were both carry-overs from the innyards.

The "huts", as seen in maps and "views" of sixteenth- and seventeenth-century London, show considerable variety in their structure. Some were rectangular with gabled roofs and had two windows facing towards the auditorium;[2] some seem to have had two gables forming a widespread M with two windows in each gable,[3] while the famous Visscher "View of London" (1616) shows the Globe as having two rectangular "huts" with a tower rising above them.[4] See also the diagram on p. 45.

14. *Bell tower and flagstaff.* The tower mentioned above, apart from being an excellent place on which to mount the flagstaff, also served to house one of the most effective properties used in Shakespeare's plays—the big bell, whose tolling, clashing, and chiming must have been heard across the Thames in the City itself.

15. *Dressing-rooms, property room, and wardrobe room.* The backstage area at the Globe seems to have been extensive. Even if we exclude the excavated "hell"—as we shall have to, considering the marshy ground on which the theatre stood—there were still plenty of dressing- and property rooms behind the tiring-house façade, behind the gentlemen's rooms on

---

[1] It was the firing of such a cannon that caused the fire at the first Globe in 1613 and led to the use of tile instead of thatch for the roofing of later theatres.

[2] This type is seen very clearly in the De Witt drawing of the Swan theatre.

[3] See the conjectural reconstruction of the Globe in Adams, Joseph Quincy, *A Life of William Shakespeare*, facing p. 286.

[4] *Ibid.*, facing p. 280.

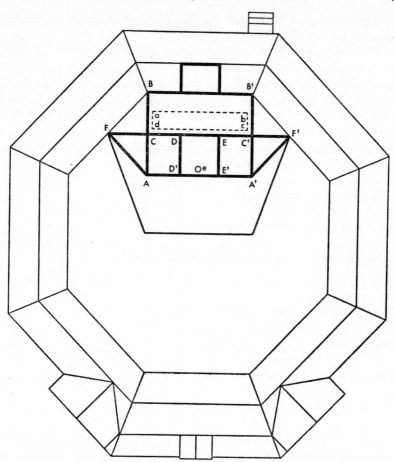

Reconstructed plan of the Globe: superstructure. (From Adams, *The Globe Play-house*. Courtesy of Dr. John Cranford Adams and Harvard University Press)

The stage posts, 32 feet high, are spaced 24 feet apart (A and A')—the spacing of the corner posts of the frame (B and B'). They stand 17 feet forward of the scenic wall in line with the pair of corner posts marking the ends of the gentlemen's rooms. A beam (A-A') 24 feet long spans the stage posts. Beams 17 feet long, affixed at right angles, cross from the top of each post to the corresponding corner posts of the tiring house (A-B, A'-B'). Into these principal beams framing the base of the stage heavens secondary beams are secured to serve as sills for the huts (C-C', D-D', and E-E'). Supplementary beams (A-F and A'-F') are required to ensure a rigid frame. The transverse hut used for descents rises over the rectangle based on B, B', C', and C. The forward hut used for pyrotechnic displays rises over the rectangle based on D, E, E', and D'. (The rear hut rises over corresponding beams supported by the playhouse frame on the other side of the transverse hut.)

The projecting under side of the superstructure is then supplied with a wooden ceiling (except for the large trap opening—marked *a, b, c, d*—and the small forward aperture—marked *e*), and the parts of the upper side not occupied by huts are roofed. Gutters "Carrie & convey the water frome the Coveringe of the saide Stadge to fall backwardes."

the first and second floors, and over the gentlemen's rooms on the third floor. See pp. 27, 40, and 42.

16. *A swinging sign.* One other feature of the Elizabethan playhouse that came directly from the inns was the swinging sign, with the name of the playhouse and a descriptive painting on both sides of the suspended wooden panel. Such signs may still be seen outside inns all through England. It has been recorded that the Globe had a "figure of Hercules supporting the Globe, under which was written '*Totus mundus agit histrionem*' ", and it is believed that there is a direct reference to this in *Hamlet*, where, referring to the popularity of the child actors, Hamlet asks:

"Do the boyes carry it away?"[1]

and is answered by Rosencrantz:

"Ay, that they do, my lord; Hercules and his load too."

---

[1] I.e., carry all before them.

II

Modern Staging of Shakespeare's Plays

BOTTOM: "Are we all met?"
QUINCE: "Pat, pat; and here's a marvellous convenient place for
our rehearsal."

A Midsummer Night's Dream, III, 1

THE APPROPRIATE setting for a Shakespearean play will be a question
of primary importance to a producer and a band of scholar-players. Fortunately, they have direct access to a source of practical information for the
construction of a typical Elizabethan stage. With John Cranford Adams's
The Globe Playhouse in hand they have all measurements and plans for every
level at once available, and these, in turn, can be adjusted proportionately
to the acting area under consideration. Again, the experience of the Illini
Theatre Guild of the University of Illinois, the members of which have
actually constructed a stage based on these plans and measurements, will
be of inestimable value. Facing p. 65, photographs of this stage will be
found, one taken during construction and showing the scaffolding, and one
of the completed stage. From Professor Joseph W. Scott, the Technical
Director of the Illini Theatre Guild, we have the following details:

The pipe scaffolding requires about two days to erect. The cost varies from four
to five hundred dollars. The façade of the stage is constructed in standard units of
scenery and is attached to the pipe scaffolding. The forestage is extended out over the
orchestra pit and the first two rows of seats.

This construction of standard units allows for quick setting and a minimum space in storing.

47

In an educational institution the cost of such a valuable asset as an Elizabethan stage could possibly be undertaken by the budgets of interested and contiguous departments, such as those of English, Drama, and Speech. Again, the cost might be sustained by institution funds allocated to extracurricular projects. If part, or all, of the labour can be supplied by a group of players, the cost can be kept to a minimum. This is by far the most satisfactory way for players to become familiar with the stage on which they are to act. If the subsidizing has been in the form of a loan, this can be paid back by box-office returns on performances and, possibly, by fees paid by other institutions for the hire of this equipment.

Such a stage, as Dr. Adams's plans make clear, constitutes the *ideal* stage, but lack of this ideal should not prevent amateur groups from presenting Shakespeare's plays. Aided by their own resourcefulness and ingenuity, they can convert a far simpler setting into an adequate substitute. Stage business will have to be modified, of course, but it should not be impossible to follow the plan of Elizabethan presentation in a setting that meets only the general requirements of Shakespearean stage directions.

First then to consider the presentation of the plays of Shakespeare on a stage based on Dr. Adams's conjectural plans, and the use of the separate and combined units in staging as suggested by the plays themselves; then to suggest the construction of a simple substitute for this stage and to consider any modification of staging that will be necessary, but which, at the same time, will not impair dramatic effectiveness.

Let us suppose that we are standing on the stage of John Cranford Adams's reconstructed Globe theatre. We walk to the edge of the forestage and look back at the acting area. No less than eight units: forestage, middle stage, inner stage, balcony stage, two window stages, the tarras, and the musicians' gallery. We now turn to the play we are about to produce. How shall we set the scenes so that we can use these units to the best advantage? This play was written for this type of stage, and a study of the text should, in almost every case, indicate the location of every scene, or—since the Elizabethans did not think in "scenes"—of every episode in the play.

All unlocated scenes that take place in streets, on plains, or in forests, etc., are obviously played on the forestage—that part of the platform that is actually in the auditorium. All semi-located places, such as the courtyard of a castle, in front of a house or palace, where a background of some kind is needed, or where doors are of importance to the action of the scene, will be set on the middle stage—that part of the platform encompassed by the three sections of the "tiring house". In scenes of battles, pageantry, and the like, these two areas can become one in order to give greater freedom of movement to the crowds. Interior scenes taking place in downstairs rooms in which few people take part will be played on the inner stage. Interior scenes in which a great many characters take part can be played on both the inner and middle stages. Interior scenes that would be on a second-floor level in Elizabethan castles, palaces, or houses, and in which few people are concerned will be played on the balcony stage. Scenes played by one or more persons on the second level who talk to others below will use either one of the window stages and the middle stage, or the balcony and middle stage. All out-of-door scenes that occur at an elevation—on city walls, on battlements, or in an antechamber adjacent to an upstairs apartment, etc.— will take place on the tarras. If greater elevation is required, a single person can appear at the window of the musicians' gallery.

Although some scenes will be played in single units, it will be found that by far the greater number of scenes are played in combinations of the units; moreover, changes from one unit to another may occur *within* the now-designated "scenes" showing the original episode divisions.

Examples of Single-unit Settings

Forestage[1]

3 *Henry VI*, V, 2, 3, 4, 5; *As You Like It*, III, 2, 3, 4, 5; *Othello*, I, 2. Scenes that are supposedly "before" a building but which do not require the background, if very important, should be played on the forestage. Examples of this would be *Othello*, III, 4, and IV, 1.

Middle Stage

1 *Henry VI*, II, 1, and IV, 1; *The Taming of the Shrew*, II, 1, and III, 2; *Hamlet*, II, 2; IV, 3, 5; and V, 2.

Inner Stage

Henry VIII, II, 3; *Romeo and Juliet*, I, 3; II, 3; and III, 4; *Much Ado about Nothing*, I, 2; III, 4; and V, 3.

Balcony Stage

Romeo and Juliet, III, 5, and IV, 3; *Hamlet*, III, 4.

[1] For use of the forestage for soliloquies, see p. 128.

TARRAS

The Winter's Tale, II, 2; *Richard III*, III, 5; and all scenes on city walls and battlements.

Examples of Combined-unit Settings

MIDDLE AND FORESTAGES

The Merchant of Venice, IV, 1; *The Winter's Tale*, III, 2; *Othello*, I, 3; *Henry VIII*, V, 3; *Henry V*, I, 2; *A Midsummer Night's Dream*, I, 1.

MIDDLE AND INNER STAGES

The Merchant of Venice, II, 7, 9; III, 2; *A Midsummer Night's Dream*, II, 2.

MIDDLE STAGE AND BALCONY

Macbeth, I, 7.

Romeo and Juliet, IV, 5. (The Nurse, by Juliet's bed on the balcony, is joined by Capulet and Lady Capulet. Friar Laurence and Paris arrive below and then go up to the balcony, leaving Peter and Musicians below.)

Antony and Cleopatra, IV, 4. (Antony and Cleopatra on the balcony; Antony calls to Eros to arm him; Eros, who is on the middle stage, goes through the inner-stage curtains, and reappears on the balcony. Captains and Soldiers enter on the middle stage, and Antony and Eros come down and join them. Cleopatra watches from the balcony as they all exit through one of the side doors below.)

Antony and Cleopatra, IV, 13.

Hamlet, III, 1. (Hamlet could appear on the balcony in the opening of this scene and so overhear the conversation taking place on the middle stage. See illustration of Yale production, facing p. 64.)

MIDDLE STAGE AND TARRAS

3 Henry VI, V, 1.

Richard II, III, 3. (Enter on the walls, King Richard and attendants, lines 61–83.)

Richard III, III, 7. (Richard and the two Bishops enter on the tarras; the Mayor and crowd are below.)

MIDDLE AND WINDOW STAGES

Romeo and Juliet, II, 2; *The Merchant of Venice*, II, 6.

MIDDLE STAGE AND MINSTRELS' GALLERY

1 *Henry VI*, III, 2 (Joan of Arc); *The Tempest*, III, 3 (Prospero).

BALCONY AND A WINDOW STAGE

Romeo and Juliet, III, 5. (Romeo and Juliet are on the window stage; the Nurse enters on the balcony stage; Romeo descends to the middle stage and exits.)

INNER, MIDDLE, AND FORESTAGES

Much Ado about Nothing, II, 1 (possibly spectators on the balcony); *Henry VIII*, II, 4; *Romeo and Juliet*, I, 5.

INNER AND MIDDLE STAGES, AND BALCONY

Romeo and Juliet, IV, 4 and 5 continuous; *Macbeth*, II, 1, 2, and 3 continuous.

INNER, MIDDLE, AND WINDOW STAGES

The Merchant of Venice, V, 1. (Lovers on a grassy bank on the inner stage, other characters on the middle stage, Musicians in the window stage.)

Sometimes, in spite of scene divisions indicated in the text, there is no change of setting. This occurs when the action implied in the text is obviously continuous. This has already been indicated as occurring in *Romeo and Juliet*, IV, 4 and 5, and in *Macbeth*, II, 1, 2, and 3.

There are a number of scenes during which the action shifts from one locality to another or in which another unit is added to the original setting. Sometimes the change is clearly indicated in the text; at others it is dictated by technical necessity; again it may be a matter of aesthetic fitness.

Changes of setting during a scene which are clearly indicated in the text occur in *Henry VIII*, II, 2. Here the scene starts on the middle stage, but when Norfolk opens the curtains to discover the King, the scene continues on the inner stage. In the same play there is a change which, although it is not specifically indicated in the text, is obvious enough. It takes place in Act V, scene 1, which opens on the tarras. After Gardiner and the Page have made their exit, the curtains of the balcony stage must certainly open to discover the King and Suffolk playing chess.

The most obvious example of adding a unit to the setting is seen in *The Tempest*, V, 1, when Prospero with a wave of his hand causes the curtains to fly apart in order to reveal Ferdinand and Miranda playing chess in the cave (inner stage). An unusual transition in *Romeo and Juliet* (between scenes 4 and 5 of Act I) has already been discussed (see p. 36, footnote 1).

When two inner-stage settings follow one another, each representing a different kind of interior, it is obvious that stage-hands must have time to effect the change if the action is to be continuous. Two excellent examples of meeting this problem occur in *A Midsummer Night's Dream*, IV, 1, and in *As You Like It*, I, 3. In the former, the scene starts with the lovers lying asleep on the forestage, while on a grassy bank on the inner stage Bottom, Titania, and the Fairies play their scene, at the conclusion of which they also sleep. Oberon and Puck, who have been watching the scene from a window stage, now appear on the inner stage, and Titania is released from the charm, upon which the Fairies, scorning the ass-headed Bottom, who still lies sleeping on the grassy bank, come on to the middle stage and exit through one of the side doors. The curtains now close. A horn is heard. Theseus and his train enter by the door opposite from the one through which the Fairies made their exit, wake the lovers, and all exit. Bottom now rolls out from under the curtains, wakes, and discusses his "dream", after which he also exits and the curtains open to reveal Quince's House.

In *As You Like It*, I, 3, the scene opens on the inner stage, where Rosalind and Celia are exchanging confidences. The Duke and his lords enter by one of the side doors on to the middle stage, the girls come downstage and join them, the curtains close, and the scene continues on the middle stage. In the meantime, the stage-hands are setting up a grassy bank, trees, and shrubs for "the Forest of Arden"—as part of the scene which follows.

The question of aesthetic fitness is a matter for careful consideration. A close study of the text not only will point to the change of emotional emphasis which calls for a change of setting, but, more than likely, will also reveal the original end of one episode and the beginning of another. In *Much Ado about Nothing*, IV, 1, a scene of near-tragedy has been played on the inner-outer setting of a church. When all exit except Beatrice and

Benedick, the curtains close to hide the altar and church properties, and the near-comedy scene that follows should be played on the middle or forestage.

In *The Merchant of Venice*, IV, I, the tremendous and passionate trial scene has just ended. The Court has risen, and the Duke and the officials have passed off the stage with impressive dignity. The curtains close, hiding the dais and the Duke's throne of justice, and Portia, Nerissa, Gratiano, Antonio, and Bassanio play out the high-comedy scene of the refusal of the gift rings on the middle stage.

It can be seen by these two examples that the change in emotional key is most delicately modulated by this kind of stagecraft. It points to the subtle yet simple means of increasing dramatic suggestion which this type of stage affords.

There are three scenes where the whole acting area might be used with fine effect. Two of these occur in *Henry VIII*. One is the coronation scene in Act IV, scene I, and the other, the final christening scene in Act V, scene 4. In both scenes, spectators in balcony and window stages and a herald in the musicians' gallery, or heralds in the window stages and a male choir in the musicians' gallery, would greatly add to the effect of excitement and interest aroused by the pageant passing below.

In *A Midsummer Night's Dream*, when all the wedding festivities have ended and all have gone to bed after the "iron tongue of midnight" has tolled twelve solemn strokes from the bell tower, the Fairies appear to bless the "house". They are everywhere with their gleaming lights! Puck is at one moment in the minstrels' gallery, the next—or nearly the next, for it is a long way—is popping up through a trap on the forestage; Titania and Oberon appear on the tarras to bless the bridal chambers; fairies sweep and garnish the inner stage, others appear in the window stages. Slowly, almost imperceptibly, their numbers begin to diminish until only Puck is left, lit by the embers of the dying fire, to bid "good night".

Types of Scenes & Suggested Staging

HISTORIES[1]

Unlocated Exteriors on Forestage (77 *scenes*): Open Country; Between Camps; Camp; Field of Battle; Forest; Garden; Plain; Street; Road; Public Way

Located Exteriors on Middle Stage (24 *scenes*): Before Tavern; Before City; Before Castle; Before Pavilion; Court of Guard; Innyard

[1] These stage directions are taken from the three-volume edition of the plays published by the Oxford University Press, New York, 1932.

Located *Exterior on Tarras and Middle Stages* (17 *scenes*): City Walls, with or without gates below

Located *Interiors on Inner Stage* (15 *scenes*): Room

Located *Interiors on Middle Stage, or Middle and Inner Stages* (62 *scenes*): King's Palace; Antechamber; Presence Chamber; Council Chamber; Hall; Room of State; Apartment in Palace

Located *Interiors on Balcony Stage* (11 *scenes*): King's Apartment; Queen's Apartment; Room, or Private Room in Tavern

Alcove on Inner Stage or Balcony Stage (1 *scene*): Falstaff discovered "fast asleep behind the arras"

COMEDIES

Unlocated Exteriors on Forestage or Fore- and Middle Stages (71 *scenes*): Street; Park; Open Place; Forest; Another Part of the Forest; Mart; Wood; Field; Without the City Walls; Camp; Garden; Country near the Sea; Public Place; Seaport; Part of the Island; Another Part of the Island

Located Exteriors on Middle Stage, or Middle and Inner Stages, with or without Door and Window-stage Units (41 *scenes*): Park with Pavilion and Tents; Before Pavilion; Garden before House; Court (yard) in Palace; Before an Abbey; Before a House; Room with Dark Chamber Adjoining; Avenue to House; Wood with Bower; Before an Alehouse; Orchard before House; Lawn before House; Lawn before Cottage; Lawn before Palace; Road near Cottage; Before Cell; Street before Prison

Located Interiors on Inner Stage (1 *scene*): Room

Located Interiors on Middle Stage, or Middle and Inner Stages, or Middle, Inner, and Forestages (61 *scenes*): Room; Room in Palace; A Monastery; Anteroom; Hall in Palace; Apartment in Palace; Court of Justice; Hall in House; Room of State; Inside a Church; A Chapel; A Prison

Located Interiors on Balcony Stage (12 *scenes*): Bedchamber; Room of Queen's Apartments; Room at Inn; Prison; Ship

Second-floor Interior on Tarras (1 *scene*): Outer Room of Prison

TRAGEDIES

Unlocated Exteriors on Forestage (43 *scenes*): Street; Public Place; Camp; Between Two Camps; Heath; Forum; Forest; Open Country; Platform

Located Exteriors on Middle Stage, or Middle and Inner Stages, or Middle, Inner, and Balcony Stages (74 *scenes*): Before the Capitol; Outside the Castle; Before the Castle; Before the Palace; Before the City; Court (yard) within a Castle; Under the Walls of the City; Lane by Wall; Camp with Open Tent; Woods with a Cave; Woods with Cavern; Orchard

Located Interiors on Balcony Stage (28 *scenes*): Room (for a few characters); Cell; Bedchamber

Located Interior on Middle Stage, or Middle and Inner Stages, or Middle, Inner, and Forestages (82 *scenes*): Room (for large number of characters); Hall; Council Chamber;

Hall of State; Temple; Church; Senate House; Within the Castle; Tomb; Grave; Shipboard (middle stage for *Antony and Cleopatra*; balcony or middle stage for *Pericles*); Prison (middle stage for *Cymbeline*); Bedchamber for final scene in *Othello* (middle stage)

Elevated Exterior on Tarras (4 *scenes*)*:* Walls; Aloft

Simplified Form of Staging

A director having the choice of a proscenium-enclosed stage in a theatre or a bare platform in a hall will do well to choose the latter, for here, at the outset, the platform stage approximates more closely to the acting area of the Elizabethan playhouse. The proscenium in a theatre tends to divide the forestage from the middle stage so sharply that the actors will have the feeling of stepping *off* the stage *into* the auditorium every time they pass out of its frame. Again, the heavy line of the arch in the foreground will cause the inner stage to appear to recede, considerably diminishing its importance. However, as there is sometimes no choice in the matter and the director finds himself in either one of these playing places—or even in a hall that is a combination of both—the adjustment to both types of stage will have to be taken into consideration.

FORESTAGE. This extension of the acting area is of the utmost importance. If the platform stretches right across one end of the hall from wall to wall, the extension should not start from the extreme outside edges but should be placed so as to leave enough room for at least two lines of seats at the sides (as in the right-hand diagram below).

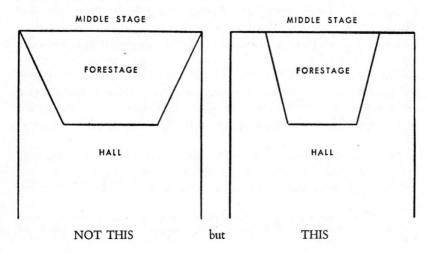

MIDDLE STAGE   MIDDLE STAGE

FORESTAGE   FORESTAGE

HALL   HALL

NOT THIS   but   THIS

This forestage should project into at least one-third of the audience area —one-half would be more correct, but it is doubtful whether a business manager can be persuaded to "sacrifice" as much seating space as this, especially if the hall is not very large. The construction should be strong, firm, and, if possible, *creakless*, and may consist of trestles and boards arranged so as to give the tapering effect towards the front as seen in the diagram. It should be enclosed on all three sides below the floor level with wallboard or curtaining and, if an authentic Elizabethan touch is required, topped by a very low balustrade.

In the case of the picture-frame stage in a theatre, the forestage will start from the boarded-over footlight trough and should extend into the auditorium in the same way as suggested above for the hall stage (see p. 65). This will necessitate the removal of seats that are permanent fixtures and will run into considerable labour and expense, giving an additional reason for the choice of a hall that has movable chairs—if there is a choice.

The height of the forestage is, of course, determined by the height of the platform or stage. In a theatre there is likely to be a rake to the floor of the auditorium which will help the audience seated in the rows at some distance from the stage to see very well, but will necessitate some neck-craning for those seated immediately round the forestage as the actors will be considerably above eye level.[1] In a hall where the floor of the auditorium is flat and the platform low it is possible that the fairly low forestage will give better visibility to the audience as a whole.

CURTAIN. There was no front curtain in the Elizabethan playhouse, but the curtain in front of the inner stage at the back of the middle stage was of the utmost importance. These characteristic features can be carried out in a modern theatre by the simple expedient of taking the act drop down and rehanging it upstage, leaving a depth of ten feet between this curtain and the back wall of the stage. On a platform, a frame of piping set in heavy wooden bases will be needed to carry this curtain. The stage curtain and the one used on a platform must be of the rod-and-ring type with a centre opening and infallible and smooth-running mechanism with which to pull the two halves straight back to the sides. The width of the opening will be, by these means, adjustable to the requirements of the scenes revealed on the inner stage.

The curtaining should be, of course, opaque and of fairly heavy material. In colour it should be neutral—stone grey, beige, taupe, or smoke blue, for instance. Such tones will leave a wider choice of colour to be used in utility

---

[1] The Globe stage is said to have been 4 feet 5 inches high, but the audience in the yard stood and, even then, as John Cranford Adams suggests, there may have been a rake to the floor of the yard.

properties, such as hangings and cushions, and will not limit the use of brilliant and daring colour combinations in costuming, which would certainly be the case with a curtain of vivid and definite colour.[1] It would also be advisable to use the same curtaining to enclose the space below the fore-stage, if boards are not used, the uniformity of material and colour serving to integrate the component parts of the setting.

MIDDLE STAGE AND ENTRANCES AND EXITS. One of two things can be done to enclose the sides of the middle stage and provide equivalents for the side doors in the Elizabethan playhouse. Four frames supporting curtains can stand, two to a side, with the downstage ones in front of, and slightly overlapping, the upstage ones, thus supplying masked entrances; or fourfold screens can be used—made of light wood and with supporting feet at each end. These enclosing sides should correspond in height to that of the frame that supports the centre curtain. It would be as well if the material used to drape these frames, or to cover these screens, were of a darker colour than that used for the centre curtain, in order to lead the eye up to the inner stage and so to give it greater prominence. For instance, if the centre curtain were beige or taupe, then dark brown would be an effective colour to use at the sides. In placing these, care should be taken to give a considerable spread towards the front in order to avoid hiding the inner stage from the audience seated at the sides of the forestage.

In a theatre, "backstage" will be hidden by the proscenium walls, but on a platform masking will be needed. Screens or curtaining set on a diagonal with the sides should serve adequately (as in the right-hand diagram below).

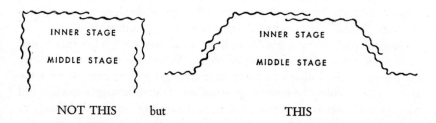

NOT THIS   but   THIS

INNER STAGE. With the centre curtains drawn back, the reserved space behind becomes the inner stage. Where space is limited the depth of this unit, as determined by the position of the curtain, can be as shallow as eight feet without endangering dramatic effectiveness. The width of the "discovered"—or uncovered—scene will be determined by the size of the

---

[1] The writer has been struggling for years to adjust costume colouring to a ruby-red velvet curtain!

opening between the curtains: they can be drawn to frame a narrow scene in which one character is revealed, or drawn back as far as they will go to show an interior in which three or four characters, furniture, etc., are discovered.

The interior can be as simple or elaborate as means allow. It can consist of another curtain hung flat against the back wall—preferably of a grey-blue colour to give depth—against which, with different furniture or even with changes of cushions and tablecloths only, all interior scenes can be represented. It can have two or more curtains of different colours that can determine separate scenes more definitely—or even only different strips hung panelwise over the permanent curtain. It can be enclosed by high screens papered to represent a panelled interior, with further sets to suggest fairy bowers, caves, tombs, etc. Or it can be a scenic unit having the window, alcove, and door, as seen in the conjectural Globe setting (facing p. 65).

BALCONY AND WINDOW STAGES. The balcony and window stages are, fortunately, the units most easily dispensed with, since they are the parts of the stage most infrequently used, and in a simplified stage they will be the last things to include, involving, as they do, the heaviest expense. The lack of them will call for all sorts of ingenious substitutes. A Juliet has appeared on a balcony by the simple process of standing on a table behind a fire-screen covered with vines and ivy. With the curtains drawn only far enough to reveal this one figure and a dark-blue tablecloth to suggest depth below the jutting balcony and, incidentally, to cover the legs of the table, the effect was convincing enough to be acceptable to a very discerning audience. A Jessica has looked out of an upstairs window by standing on a step-ladder and parting two sections of material hung in the top quarter of an upstage screen. A Richard III with his "two Bishops above" has been suggested by the hearing of his voice off stage while those on stage, presumably "below", *looked up* to a high point off stage at the side.

It goes without saying that without a balcony stage adjustments will have to be made in the locating of scenes. When, for instance, a balcony or "above" scene follows an inner-stage scene, it will be necessary for the actors either to play the inner-stage scene on the middle stage or, while still playing the inner-stage scene (that is, still carrying on the dialogue), to step out on to the middle stage, thus allowing the stage crew to close the curtains and set the inner stage for the "balcony" scene that follows.

Here then are the minimum requirements for a simplified Elizabethan acting area:

1. A forestage
2. A middle stage with enclosed sides and two exits
3. A curtain of the rod-and-ring type
4. An inner stage

But even these simple requirements can be modified. So long as the actors keep in mind the general characteristics of the stage for which Shakespeare wrote his plays, they can give a creditable performance on a bare platform. The simplest setting can be as effective as the most elaborate in the presentation of a great play provided the actors have the power to move the imagination of the audience to an *unconscious* acceptance of any, or no, scenic representation.

III

Lighting on Elizabethan & Modern Stages

MOON: "This lanthorn doth the horned moon present."
A Midsummer Night's Dream, V, 1

IT HAS been proved beyond doubt that in Shakespeare's time performance in public theatres took place in the afternoon and, in the case of the Rose and Swan theatres, at 3 p.m. in summer and at 2 p.m. in winter. Most scholars are agreed that the performances lasted for two and a half hours, a little longer perhaps when the play was followed by the jig, a popular solo song with patter and dance, which survives in the low-comedy turn of the music-hall today.

Let us start by realizing that by far the greater part of the performance, in fair summer weather, was lit by daylight coming from overhead. It would be wrong, however, to think of this as the dim light seen from the bottom of a well. We have to remember, in spite of most of the contemporary exterior views of the theatres, which seem to prove the contrary, that these buildings were much less in height than they were in width. In the case of the Globe, for instance, the walls were not much higher than 35 feet, while the width of the building was 58 feet. Once the erroneous idea of the high narrow building is corrected we can see that, given fair weather, the forestage would be well lit as long as the light lasted.

But what of overcast and stormy weather, and the short afternoons of autumn and winter? And what of the other parts of the stage that were not under the open sky? Again what of the lighting of scenes that were supposedly taking place at night?

Little or no provision seems to have been made to meet seasonal and poor-weather conditions. We hear Webster complaining that the failure of his *The White Devil* was due to the fact that it was given in winter and presented "in so open and black a theatre". And yet, as great an authority as Sir Edmund K. Chambers believed that some "primitive" attempt at illumination was made "in form of cressets, or baskets of tarred and flaring rope".

When the actors performed on the part of the stage that was under the "shadowe", there would certainly be a reduction of light, but this would not be very considerable since the "shadowe" was nearly as high up as the roof of the top gallery. Scenes on the alcove and balcony stages, however, would be very dimly lit if the actors had had to depend wholly on daylight. It is therefore not surprising to find in many Elizabethan and Jacobean plays stage directions in which the parting of the curtains to disclose interior scenes is the cue for the entrance of pages carrying lighted candles, which they evidently held throughout the scene. (This was a service performed no doubt by the "tiring men" and was considered a menial task, as implied in "cannot even hold a candle to him".) There is frequent mention of candles being placed on tables on the alcove and balcony stages, but whether the candle bearers were present also on these occasions is unknown. (Notice the candle bearers lighting the players in *Hamlet*, p. 64.) To these simple devices may have been added a few lighting effects borrowed from the Court masques, such as setting lamps behind bottles of coloured water or placing tin reflectors behind lights. In the private theatres the use of revolving reflectors to dazzle the eyes of the audience while scenic properties were set up or removed may also have been introduced; if so, they also were suggested by their use at Court for similar purposes.

Besides the intricate and powerful artificial lighting of the modern theatre this light seems feeble and wholly inadequate, and yet it never seems to have curtailed the use of these inner stages. Nor did the playwrights restrict the time of their scenes to daylight hours. Sir Arthur Quiller-Couch draws attention to Shakespeare's constant use of darkness to aid spectacular effect. To quote a few examples:

In *Romeo and Juliet*

the tragic action really starts under a moonlit balcony and ends in a vaulted tomb. . . . *Hamlet* opens on the dark battlements of Elsinore. . . . *Othello* opens with the mutter of voices in a dark street, and ends by the bedside lit by one candle: the total impression of *Lear* is of a dark heath upon which three or four men wander blindly, lit only at intervals by flashes from the dark elements. . . . What, again, is the scene that gives quality to *Julius Caesar* but the brooding night in Brutus' garden? . . . What, again, . . . retrieves *The Merchant of Venice* from tragedy . . . to comedy but the Fifth Act, with placid night shimmering towards dawn . . . as Portia . . . says in four words what concludes all?

> **"It is almost morning."**

As to *Macbeth*, Shakespeare saw the whole play as "a thing of night".[1]

When we consider that the daylit theatre did not prevent the playwrights from demanding the most subtle and difficult light effects in their scripts, we see that realism, as we understand the term on the modern stage, had no place in the Elizabethan public theatre. But we must also remember that this lack of realistic representation was the poet's chance to create his own day and night.

There was a strange and what must have been traditional attempt to indicate night and darkness on the outer stage by the symbolic use of torches, lanterns, cressets, and candles. The arrival of characters carrying these in broad daylight seems to have been viewed by the audience with complete composure. But isn't there a suggestion of sly laughter at this custom in the arrival, in *A Midsummer Night's Dream*, of one of the rustic players with a lantern and bush of thorn who "comes to disfigure, or to present, the person of Moonshine"?

In considering this prevalence of night scenes in plays of the period, we have to take into account the fact that many of them were written for Court presentation, where they would be performed at night and where, we know from the accounts of the Revels Office, the artificial light was brilliant, and, more important still, since it consisted almost entirely of candelabra and chandeliers, was *capable of being extinguished when required*. The same would be true of the lighting in the private theatres, in the Inns of Court, and in the palaces and mansions of royalty and nobility, where the companies under royal and noble patronage sometimes performed.

The greatest scenic importance of modern stage lighting on an Elizabethan stage is its capability of focusing attention on any of the single units when they are used in isolation and of increasing and decreasing illumination during scenes. But modern lighting must be used with discretion. Though no producer today would be so pedagogic as deliberately to forego the use of all the wonderful and effective lighting devices that he has at hand, he would do well to remember that the limited lighting equipment of the Elizabethan theatre was directly responsible for some of the loveliest descriptions of light and darkness in the English language, and that garish or over-theatrical lighting of the scenes where such poetry occurs detracts from a full realization of their beauty. He should also realize that certain types of lighting known to have been used in Elizabethan times can be

---

[1] Quiller-Couch, (Sir) Arthur, *Shakespeare's Workmanship*, pp. 45–8.

wonderfully effective. Fire laws no longer allow the use of "naked" light, but electrical devices can be transformed and disguised in such a way as to prevent their use from being incongruous on an Elizabethan stage. For instance, attempts should be made to reproduce the flickering, murky light from cressets, which can be hung on the pillars of the "shadowe" to illuminate the dagger scene in *Macbeth*; again, when the alarm bell rouses the sleeping castle, torches, with a savage fluttering flare, carried by the entering servants, would increase the horror of the scene in a way that could not be realized by either the diffused light of borders and floods or the concentrated light of "spots".

After the duel in the semi-darkness of the graveyard in the last act of *Romeo and Juliet*, where Romeo wishes to identify his victim, if he takes a shuttered lantern left by his servant Balthasar and, kneeling, opens it, the light falls naturally and directly on the dead face of the young Paris, and the very simplicity with which the pitiful disclosure is made increases the tragedy as no focusing of a "baby spot" at the "psychological moment" can hope to do. If the traditional exit of Fortinbras's men bearing the dead Hamlet on their shields were to be lit only by the tossing flare of torches, leaving, as they pass out of sight, a totally dark stage, we might find the only appropriate ending for the greatest of all tragedies.

IV

Properties & Sound Effects

Quince: "I will draw a bill of properties, such as our play wants."
A Midsummer Night's Dream, I, 2

THE PROPERTY master of a Shakespearean production will find his task of collecting scenic, utility, and acting properties far from difficult. Scenery will be simple, and furnishings required by the action of the play and by the actor will be few and fairly easy to come by. For the sake of the ambitious stage carpenter and his crew who wish to make their own furniture, a glance at similar tasks required of their fellow craftsmen of three hundred years ago will be interesting, and, very possibly, profitable.

Elizabethan Production

James Wright, in his *Historia Histrionica*, published in 1699, extols the plays and actors of "the last age" by pointing out that they could "support themselves merely from their own merit, the weight of the matter and goodness of the action, *without scenes and machines*".

That scenery, as we think of it today, was little more than symbolic painting on coarse canvas—"painted cloths"—is pretty certain, but we must conclude that it was guesswork on Wright's part that excluded scenic properties and mechanical devices from the Elizabethan theatre. From contemporary descriptions of the street theatres, from Henslowe's note-books, from Dekker's *Gull's Horn Book*, and from the stage directions in the plays themselves, it is certain that these aids and embellishments were elaborate, ingenious, and, to an Elizabethan audience, effective. Nor were

64

A reproduction of an Elizabethan stage within the Yale University Theatre (1941), showing two scenes from *Hamlet*

Pipe scaffolding and completed reproduction of Dr John Cranford Adams' Globe
playhouse, by the Illini Theatre Guild at the University of Illinois (1948)

these innovations. The classical theatres had introduced "machines" in which gods and goddesses descended from "above", and, as already mentioned, had provision for arrivals from and departure to the "underworld" below.

In England, as early as 1236, street pageantry included such scenic splendours as castles, columns painted to represent marble and jasper, angels descending on wires, gigantic puppets, Noah's ark, a great dragon spouting fire, a desert with trees and a well, God appearing in a cloud, Lucifer going down to Hell, and the sudden springing up of a fountain with fine flowers all about it. The list of scenic properties used in the cycle plays and the elaborate representations on the painted cloths that enclosed the pageants on three sides is no less astonishing.

There is no doubt that certain scenic effects and properties that had become traditionally associated with any kind of spectacular entertainment would certainly be looked for in the public theatres, and good showmen like Burbage and Henslowe knew that such expectations must not be disappointed if they were to attract popular audiences to the playhouses.

To the traditional scenic effects and properties novelties must have been constantly added. These may not have emanated from the public theatres themselves. The street theatres, which had engaged the services of artists and skilled craftsmen, may have offered a few suggestions, and certainly the close association of Shakespeare's company with the Court masques must have inspired much that was ingenious and magnificent in the way of *décor*, and have even influenced the actual style and forms of the plays themselves.

There is no doubt that the rising tide of classicism must have at least lapped the doorsills of the Globe and a glance at this influence will be rewarding.

Renaissance art, which originated in Italy, had, in architectural forms, been influenced by Vitruvius, and this, in turn, influenced the settings of the private theatres that were being built at the ducal courts. Italian artists were attached to the English Court as early as the reign of Henry VIII, and by the end of the sixteenth century not only were English scholars visiting and even residing in the Italian ducal courts, but English architects, such as John Shute and Inigo Jones, were studying in Rome. To Rome also went John Lyly, and it is easy to see how these two men, Lyly and Jones, who later held such important posts, influenced theatrical production through the performances they created for the English Court. The classical influence spread to the presentation of classical drama in grammar schools, universities, and the Inns of Court, and graced the performances given by the Boys of St. Paul's and the Children of the Chapel Royal.

In 1566, "classical houses" were constructed for a performance of *Palamon and Arcite* at Oxford, and classical "palace doors" in a production of *Jocasta* at the Inns of Court. That there was a mingling of the romantic with these classical elements is evident for along with classical "doors" went a garden of magnificence and beauty where flowers could be gathered. Many properties are mentioned that suggest the medieval art of illuminated manuscripts and tapestries. That this mingling of styles was seen at its worst in the public theatres there is little doubt. The jumbled and incongruous styles in the costuming of pseudoclassical plays bear this out (see pp. 143–144). We can conclude, then, that this influence was apparent in public-theatre performances, although not to any great extent. The suggestion of George R. Kernodle that the classical elements seen in the street theatres influenced the interior decoration of the playhouses[1] has led to reconstructions of Elizabethan stages that are over-elaborate and lacking in the sturdy quality that we associate with all Tudor design. John Cranford Adams's restrained treatment of the decorations suggested by the extant Fortune contract are far more acceptable, and the realization of their quiet worth is experienced to the full on careful examination of his beautiful model of the Globe theatre in The Folger Shakespeare Library in Washington, D.C. (see illustrations opposite pp. 32 and 33).

There is no doubt that most of the scenic innovations at the Globe were direct importations from the Court entertainments where, as early as 1527, fixed and movable scenery was being used. Further evidence is found in the similarity of properties listed in the Revels Office's books and the account books and diary of Henslowe. In both are to be found monsters, beasts, "serpentes", birds and fish, grassy banks, artificial flowers, "mosse", and rocks. One item in the Revels Office list starts a train of conjecture. It consists of numbers of life-sized figures—savages, soldiers, and bands of men—carved in wood, which passed across the stage during the intervals and were propped on stands at the side of the stage during the masque. Now, if the King's Men were privileged, as the student players at the universities were, to borrow elaborate scenic properties from the Revels Office, were these strange figures ever used in crowds, battles, processions, and the like at the Globe? Again, if they (the King's Men) had access to valuable and ingenious properties after 1603, does that account for the increased elaboration of the staging and scenic properties called for in Shakespeare's last plays—Cymbeline, The Winter's Tale, The Tempest, and Henry VIII?

To summarize, medieval survivals and contemporary innovations in scenic properties and effects, going hand in hand with splendour of costuming, must not only have compensated for the lack of actual scenery, but have provided a spectacle of wonder and beauty for the eyes of the Elizabethan audience.

[1] Kernodle, George R., From Art to Theatre, Fig. 47, p. 152.

The early chronicle plays, possibly written for innyard presentation,[1] call for little beyond such warlike properties as gates, walls, scaling ladders, and tents, and leave waving banners, marching and countermarching of soldiers, martial music, the clash of arms, and the firing of cannon to suggest the excitement, glory, fury, and clamour of war.

Early comedies, such as *The Two Gentlemen of Verona* and *The Comedy of Errors*, also call for very simple stage effects, and the idea that Shakespeare wrote *Love's Labour's Lost* before he came to London or had actual contact with the professional stage is supported by the fact that this play has only one location throughout, scenes being merely nearer or farther from the "tents" or "pavilion" in the background.

Starting with these simple beginnings, the stage directions, stated and implied, in the plays between 1595 and 1603 show increasing demands for scenic properties. From 1603 to 1613, to the demands for even more elaborate scenic properties there is added an increased emphasis on grandeur and ingenuity in staging and action. Finally, spectacles, masques, and pageantry begin to take a place of first importance, so ushering in the decline from the greatest period of English drama.

Modern Production

SCENIC PROPERTIES

Walls and Gates. The above discussion will serve to show that little will be required in the way of scenic properties in the early chronicle plays, that is, *Henry VI, Parts I, II*, and *III*. There is, however, one important item that must be considered, and that is the wall,[2] with gates inset or attached, that covers the front of the inner stage in the siege, parley, and battle scenes. Owing to the weight and bulk of this property there is no possibility of its quick setting-up or removal, and it is suggested that after its first appearance it remain throughout the rest of the play. If it is set behind the curtains, it can be covered whenever a change of scene is required. In this case all interior scenes will, of course, be played on the middle stage.

On the Walls. Overhanging the wall is the tarras, and, with the balustrade removed and a low crenelated border placed at the front edge, this becomes the top of City Walls or ramparts of City Gates. Against this the

[1] It must be remembered that, although the suggested dates of these early plays are a decade later than the building of the Theatre and the Curtain, the winter season still found the company using the innyards.

[2] This wall presents an unsolved problem. In *1 Henry VI*, II, 1, French soldiers in their shirts "leap over the Walls", and in *King John*, IV, 3, Arthur "leaps down" from the Walls. In spite of the fact that many Elizabethan actors were also acrobats it is difficult to imagine them jumping down 12 feet without injuring themselves.

scaling ladders can be placed in sieges, and upon it soldiers, governors, and mayors of the cities can appear to fight or parley.

Rose Hedge. In *1 Henry VI*, II, 4, there are roses that are plucked from "this thorn", "this briar", and "the tree", all of which, no doubt, refer to a property hedge placed so as to run upstage from the centre of the forestage, with white and red roses growing on either side. Such placing not only will make the grouping and business easier, but will give symbolic emphasis to the division of the Yorkist and Lancastrian factions. In a similar way, the wall that runs from the middle stage up to the centre of the curtains of the inner stage in *Romeo and Juliet*, II, 1 and 2, serves to divide Juliet and the boundaries of the Capulet orchard from the roistering young Montague kinsmen and supporters. Romeo's climbing of this wall is one of the most significant and symbolic actions leading to the ultimate tragedy.

Mole Hill. In *3 Henry VI*, I, 4, the dreadful scene of the mockery and murder of York takes place on a "mole-hill", and it is on a "mole-hill" again in Act II, scene 5, that the King sits to watch the symbolic scenes of civil strife. This is, surely, that same grassy bank or mossy bank that turns up so often in lists of Elizabethan properties. In both scenes this hill should be placed at the foot of one of the pillars.

Hedge. In *All's Well That Ends Well*, IV, 1, and in *Twelfth Night*, II, 5, a hedge is called for, and, since it is described in the latter play as a "box tree", one resembling the dark-green close-set foliage of box would reasonably do for both.[1]

Trees and Shrubs. Trees and shrubs on the playhouse stages were real, as they were in the Court banqueting hall when entertainments were presented, an easy matter for the property masters of the playhouses with the country close at hand on every side of the City.

In *As You Like It* it is possible that trees were fastened against the two pillars before the play began.

In a modern professional production property trees would be used, but it is well for amateur players to remember that real pines, firs, or hemlocks are more effective, and that, placed in tubs of wet sand, they will keep fresh for two or three weeks. The same applies to small shrubs and boughs of greenery.

Arbour. An arbour, or summerhouse, will be needed in *Much Ado about Nothing*, II, 3, and III, 1. If we judge by the descriptive lines, this must be a three-sided affair of latticework covered with vines and creepers. It could come up on the centre trap, as it undoubtedly did at the Globe, or it could be "thrust out"[2] between the inner-stage curtains.

---

[1] This hedge and the rose hedge above should have castors to aid in their quick handling.
[2] See p. 37, footnote 1.

Tents. Tents are often needed in the histories, and, though the inner stage can serve for some tent scenes, others require that the tents be brought on and set up on the fore- or middle stages. Pictures of tents of the period show them to be mostly square in shape, and these will be easy to assemble if heavy wooden bases with deep holes are used. In these holes poles can be stood upright and crosspieces dropped into slots at the top. All that is then needed for their completion is drapery long enough and deep enough to cover back and sides, with, possibly, an extra piece for the flap. If possible, these tents might be set up off stage and thrust on, in which case small platforms on castors would have to take the place of bases.

Tombs. The tomb that opens (*Titus Andronicus*, I, 1) or the tomb that can be wrenched open (*Romeo and Juliet*, V, 2) presents a problem until we remember that caves opened and cliffs were "cleft" in the Court masques, and that similar devices seem to have been part of the technique of revealing interiors in the street theatres. It seems reasonable to suppose then that flats that could be drawn apart must have been a well-known scenic device. Inner-stage curtains opening to reveal a solid rock face—painted canvas stretched on frames—which could be drawn apart by hand on either side was possibly all that was needed at the Globe, and certainly will be all that is needed in a modern amateur production.

Board Ship. There are numerous board-ship scenes, and, although no scenic properties seem to have been needed, the setting no doubt added something to the general effect. For instance, there is no doubt that *The Tempest*, I, 1, and *Pericles*, III, 1, were presented on the balcony stage. The banquet scene on Pompey's anchored galley (*Antony and Cleopatra*, II, 7) on the other hand was certainly played on the middle stage. Although it is easy to place Pericles reclining in his pavilion (*Pericles*, V, 1), on board his ship on the middle stage, the barge lying alongside to which people "descend" and in which they "put off" is another matter. Perhaps after all, it was very simple, merely necessitating a climb up or down a ladder set in the Grave.

Lists. There are references to the "lists" on the stage in *Richard II* and in *Pericles.* These are simply barriers, or palisades, surrounding the ground set apart for tilting.

UTILITY PROPERTIES

The utility properties called for in the plays are limited to household, Court, and institutional furnishings, and these fortunately are not hard to find. Originals may be seen in museums and in palaces and houses of royalty and nobility that are open to the public. If none of these is easy of access, there are fine photographs of all important pieces in the many excellent books on Elizabethan and Jacobean furnishings (see pp. 94–95).

Owing to the continued popularity of the furniture of these periods, reproductions are to be found very easily, and certainly the scholar-player property man will not have to search far for them. There are few academic buildings that do not have such reproductions that, on request, may be borrowed or hired.[1]

If the company of scholar-players could afford to purchase a few good reproductions, that would be best of all. This is not such an expensive undertaking as may at first be imagined, for, with the aid of different sets of hangings and cushions, the same pieces can be used over and over again, and, when this is done, the maximum number of articles required is surprisingly small.

If possible, all furniture should be of oak or imitation oak, and the lighter Jacobean spindle type used instead of the extremely heavy and solid Tudor style. In the case of the necessarily large pieces of furniture, castors should be attached to feet and bases to allow for quick and easy placing and removal. It will be as well not to place large articles on the inner stage if it is being used as a localized interior scene, but only when the inner-outer stage is a unit representing a hall or council chamber, etc., and the placing of furniture on both stages is deliberately employed to link the two areas. The balcony stage, since it is used solely as a localized and self-contained unit, must be uncrowded to allow the actors as much space as possible. However, one of the largest properties of all will be used on this stage—the bed, and where this is in use there must be a minimum of other furniture on the stage at the same time, and even these should be small.

In order that the furniture may be in keeping with the stage setting, we must first consider the articles in daily use in Elizabethan and Jacobean houses, palaces, and institutional buildings, and then we can proceed with more assurance to select those articles that we require for production.

Beds. There were two kinds of beds, the heavy four-poster with corniced tester hung with curtains at the sides and foot, having a high, panelled headboard; and a small bed with low, panelled head- and footboards. The former is the one called for in the plays and presents the greatest problems of acquisition, manipulation, and storage, for such a bed is difficult to buy, borrow, hire, or make, and the fact that it will be required on the balcony stage as well as on the inner and outer stages presents the difficulty of getting such a cumbersome property up and down the narrow stairways. A solution is to be found, perhaps, in having a separate frame, capable of being dis-

---

[1] This is particularly true of American colleges of the institutional-Gothic type.

mantled, which consists of the tester, four posts, and headboard. This could be set up over a simple bed and easily dismantled for transport or storage.[1] In this case a bed could be kept on each floor and the frame easily carried up and down and adjusted to either bed, as required. (See p. 73.)

Chairs. There are four types of chairs that can be used together or separately:

1. The panelled chair with a very high back and a boxed-in seat, suitable for persons of ecclesiastical or noble rank to use on formal occasions, such as Wolsey in the court scene in *Henry VIII*, II, 4; the Duke in the court scene in *The Merchant of Venice*; and the King and Queen in *Hamlet*, as they watch the play (Act III, scene 2). (See p. 73.)

2. The "turned" chair composed of a series of spindles with arms, and, often, a triangular seat. This could be used in all domestic interiors.

3. The X chair, which, although earlier in date, has been in constant use in all periods down to today. It is a particularly graceful type and can be used in court, palace, and castle scenes. (See p. 73.)

4. The "farthingale" chair. Since all the above chairs have arms, and women find them difficult to use with their "cartwheel" hipped skirts, a few chairs of this fourth type are indispensable. This chair is without arms, has a large square seat with a shoulder-high back, and is the only one of the period on which upholstery appears.

Settles, Thrones, Stools. The high-backed settle of the period (p. 73) is not indispensable but would be found very convenient for seating two or three persons close to one another for an exchange of confidences, especially if they are women with wide farthingales—Mistress Ford and Mistress Page in *The Merry Wives of Windsor*, IV, 2, for instance. Such a seat might also meet the seating requirements of Falstaff. Again, if a settle is placed in a strategic position, a person can hide behind it for the purpose of eavesdropping; with its back turned to the audience, characters can, by standing on the seat, represent the prisoners in a court of justice. If the settle is boxed in and has a hinged seat, it can serve as a hiding-place for a small person, or be employed for the storage of properties when not in use.

One kind of settle peculiar to the period has a back that can be pulled up and over the seat to form a table. If a settle of this type could be hired or borrowed or purchased, it would be a useful and economical property since it would serve two purposes.

A property that should be a permanent possession of a Shakespearean repertory theatre is a throne of state (p. 73). Copies of the coronation chair used by the kings of England seem to have been used frequently in the past,

---

[1] Such an apparently separate frame is seen in an illustration in Airne, C. W., *The Story of Tudor and Stuart Britain Told in Pictures*, p. 27.

and originally this wide and heavy property was lowered by tackle and pulley from the "huts" on to that part of the stage immediately in front of the inner-stage curtains. A modern copy made of light wood or metal can easily be "thrust out" through the inner-stage curtains. If representative curtains are hung behind it, the nationality of the monarch can be established and in this way the one throne can serve for two or more purposes. In *Henry V*, for instance, with a red curtain covered with golden lions rampant, it becomes the English throne (Act I, scene 2), and with a blue curtain covered with silver fleur-de-lis, the French throne (Act II, scene 4).

Among the essential seating properties must be included a number of joint stools, so often mentioned in the plays (see p. 73). These will serve many purposes and can be placed and removed with dispatch. The name "joint" serves to distinguish the article made by a joiner from the rough-hewn one used in farmhouses and cottages. There were many types of joint stools and all of them, or nearly all of them, are procurable in repro-duction. There are "high stools", "low stools", "box stools", and "kneeling stools"; some upholstered and some carved, some with splayed feet, some with turned or spindle legs, and some with seats that lift up to discover a shallow box beneath. It would be well to get the lightest kind for easy handling and to have at least four of one type, so that they can be placed together to form a bench in out-of-door scenes.

Chests. One or two fairly large chests, *on very short legs*, not only will be authentic period pieces for domestic interiors, but will serve for low tables or even supply sitting accommodation. Off stage they supply ex-cellent storage space for valuable properties and hangings. (See p. 73.)

Tables. For the most part tables were long, narrow, and heavy, and while there was great variety in the shape of the legs and the decoration of the friezes, the simplest will serve for all scenes where long tables are required, even including courts of justice, council rooms, and banqueting halls (see p. 73). The popular and easily obtained gate-leg table will serve for all other purposes.

Sideboards. Many uses will be found for a small two-tiered sideboard or buffet, and, though this is not absolutely necessary, it is convenient to use in place of more cumbersome furniture. For instance, though it would give "atmosphere" to have a dresser in inn rooms, kitchens, and cottage scenes, the height, width, and weight of such a property, to say nothing of all the articles that would have to be placed on its shelves, would make it extremely heavy to handle, whereas the buffet, small and light to handle, will be found to serve all purposes for which a dresser ordinarily would be used.

Cupboards. A large cupboard can always be indicated by the curtained alcoves on the inner and balcony stages, thus obviating the necessity for such

Elizabethan stage furniture. *a* Boxed-in chair. *b* Coronation chair. *c* High-backed settle. *d* Inlaid walnut bed. *e* Oak draw-table. *f* X chair. *g* Chest, linen-fold design. *h* Joint box stool. *i* Joint stool

a heavy space-filling property as the Tudor or Jacobean "Court cupboard", or "armoire".[1] The small cupboard mounted on spindle legs, or even placed on a gate-leg table, is not only a decorative but a very useful property in interior scenes.

Boxes. Long, rather narrow, flat-lidded boxes, known as "Bible boxes", should be included in utility properties, for these can be used not only as receptacles for letters, papers, and books, but also for jewels and toiletries in such scenes as the unrobing of Desdemona in *Othello*, IV, 3, the scene between Hero and Ursula when the former is being dressed for her wedding in *Much Ado about Nothing*, III, 4, and even in the Portia and Nerissa scene in *The Merchant of Venice*, I, 2, if we consider the discussion of the suitors to be taking place in Portia's "closet". (See p. 75.)

Hand Properties. Smaller furnishings, such as goblets, flagons, plates, dishes, tankards, caskets, basins, and ewers, were costly and ornate, and here again we shall need to consult illustrations of those that are known to have been in use between 1580 and 1613. Originals of these can be seen in many museums, the finest and most complete collection being in the Victoria and Albert Museum in London. Reproductions might be purchased in theatrical supply stores or hired from professional property warehouses. Failing these possible sources of supply, substitutes will have to be purchased or made that are as representative as possible. (See pp. 75 and 95.)

Hangings. Curtains before the inner and balcony stages seem to have ranged from the most costly velvets and silks, used in the private theatres, to the ones made of rough canvas painted to represent tapestry that are known to have been used in the public theatres. These latter, known as "painted cloths", often seem to have had a pictorial representation of some episode from classical myth or story. It is safe to conjecture that these were replaced during the performance by simple representations of out-of-door scenes or by pictures having a symbolic significance.[2]

Perhaps it would be safe to guess that, as a newly built playhouse, the Globe was furnished with real tapestries, and there is much evidence to prove that these were replaced by black hangings when a tragedy was to be presented. (We hear of hangings being made of black velvet in a Court performance of *Northward Hoe.*)[3] Again, there is no doubt that these curtains were of the rod-and-ring type and were always drawn by means of cords

---

[1] In spite of the order given for the removal of the "Court cupboard" in *Romeo and Juliet*, I, 5, the lines (7–8) very probably did not refer to an actual property on the stage, but were only part of the orders being shouted on and off the stage by the servants in all the haste and excitement attendant upon turning a dining-hall into a ballroom.

[2] This suggests the use of more than one set of rods and rings. These were possibly arranged one behind the other and ensured the quick and invisible changing needed for such representations as those suggested in Part I, Chap. 1.

[3] Chambers, (Sir) Edmund K., *The Elizabethan Stage*, Vol. III, p. 79.

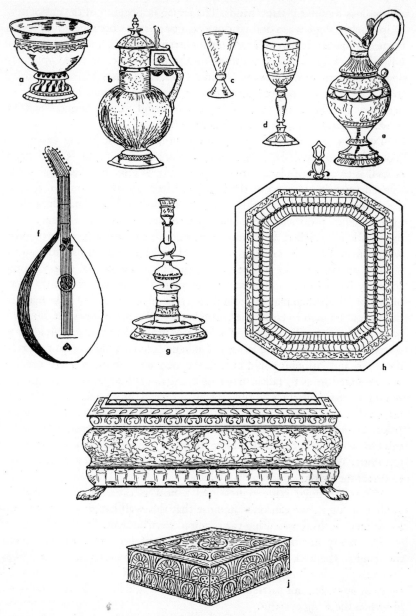

Elizabethan stage properties. *a, b* Marble bowl and stoneware jug, both mounted in silver gilt. *c* Glass. *d* Silver cup. *e* Silver ewer. *f* Lute. *g* Silver candlestick. *h* Wooden-framed mirror. *i* Italian carved chest. *j* Bible box

and pulleys by unseen stage-hands. The apparent opening of the curtains by people on the stage was a dramatic device. For instance, they were supposedly opened by pages as part of ceremonial entrance or exit, and when an actor wished to reveal or shut out a scene on the inner stage, he could appear to open or close them with his own hands. The fact that they were manipulated from backstage was of great advantage to magic revelations for it was only necessary for the actor, supposedly in command of supernatural powers, to wave a wand or hand for the curtains to fly apart.

Two sets of curtains of some heavy upholstery fabric having an appearance of tapestry will be needed for a reconstruction of the Globe stage, as well as two sets of black curtains, preferably of some rich heavy material. The side curtains (wings) of the inner and balcony stages could also be of the imitation tapestry, but this might be found too heavy and difficult to manage when properties were being placed and removed in a hurry. If the back walls are panelled, as we suppose those at the Globe to have been, light-weight material of the same brown would perhaps be the most satisfactory.

The curtains to the alcoves on both upper and lower stages should certainly be of imitation tapestry to represent the "arras" frequently mentioned in Elizabethan plays,[1] and if these were of very wide but light material they could be used to cover the entire back wall when a formal setting was needed. The Queen's closet in *Hamlet*, set on the balcony stage, could be so staged. The curtains on the left side (audience's left) could stop just short of the door, and Polonius could hide in the alcove if a division in the curtains was arranged so as to fall in front of it. Again, this tapestried background would be particularly effective when a formal inner-outer interior was required, as in the ball scenes where the dancing takes place in *Romeo and Juliet*, *Much Ado about Nothing*, and *Henry VIII*. In *The Merchant of Venice*, this tapestried background would be dignified and useful in the casket scene. On Portia's command, Nerissa would open the alcove curtains wide enough to reveal the caskets standing on a table.

When the inner stage represented a bower, cave, or grassy bank in garden or forest, we can only suppose that this wall hanging was replaced by painted cloths representing the required environment.

As already mentioned, there appear to have been rods running from the front to the back of the inner stage, upon which curtains, referred to as "traverses", were hung when the stage was divided to represent a row of shops or tents. For our particular purpose these could be of the same uniform brown as the wing curtains.

Two other sets of hangings remain to be considered—the curtains at

[1] A complete covering of walls by tapestry hung from frames projecting a few feet from the wall and known as the "arras" was a common feature of Elizabethan rooms.

the back of the bay-window stages and the one in front of the minstrels' gallery. In many cases this "gallery" seems to have been nothing more than a wide casement window, with material of some thin, but opaque, texture hung directly against the frame. In the window stages, curtains would be needed to shut off the acting space from the tiring room or storage space behind and would have to be hung as far back as possible to allow enough room for two or more actors—or musicians. These curtains, too, might be made of the same material as that used for wings in the alcove and on the balcony stages.

Floor coverings. There is no doubt that the floor of inner, balcony, and platform stages in the Elizabethan playhouse were strewn with rushes, but how long this custom was retained we do not know. Not until the production of *Henry VIII* in 1613 do we hear of matting being used as a floor covering. It may have been used before, but the fact that it is mentioned suggests that it was an innovation.

The rushes offer many problems. For instance, were they spread uniformly over the platform stage, and, if so, what happened when the traps were used? How were small properties that had to be thrown down recovered (the ring in *Twelfth Night*, for example)? Was it possible to dance on a rush-strewn floor? Even if rushes were procurable today, which is doubtful, it begins to look as though they would be more of a liability than an asset, and it would be folly to follow an unhygienic and inconvenient custom for the sake of chronological correctness. It is likely that the matter will be settled in any case by the Fire Department, for there is no doubt that a rush-strewn stage would constitute a serious fire hazard.

ACTING PROPERTIES

Apart from scenic properties, described above, there are a number of acting properties that present difficulties to the modern stage director, and it will be as well to consider these in some detail.

Carrying Chair. A number of times in the plays a carrying chair is used, and, fortunately, there is an illustration of the type of thing that this must have been in *Shakespeare's England*, Vol. I, p. 210. A glance at this will suggest the possibility of using a strong kitchen chair with two stout poles passed under the solid seat and lashed to the sides of the back rest. If these poles protrude far enough at the back and front, it will be an easy matter for two men to lift and carry the chair and its occupant.

Double Throne. Double thrones for kings and queens sitting in state need be nothing more elaborate than two boxed-in chairs (see p. 73) set on a dais backed by hangings (the inner-stage curtains).

Seating for the Senate. One other method of seating needs explanation. It occurs in *Julius Caesar*, III, 1. The stage description "Before the Capitol" points to the possibility of the first few speeches being made on the middle stage to suggest that they take place in the street. The next description, "Goes up to Senate", would be accompanied by a parting of the curtains to discover the Senate seated on scaffolds on the inner stage, and, further, a chair on a dais could be placed in front of these scaffolds to indicate that the scene has now shifted to "Inside the Capitol". This scaffold seating was common in the bear gardens, in the innyards, and along the routes of processions, and the setting up of risers and boards would not have been a difficult task. It will certainly be a possible and effective setting for the modern production.

Horrors. It is extremely unlikely that any theatrical company today, whether amateur or professional, will even consider a performance of *Titus Andronicus*. It is a poor play, and its unrelieved brutality and violence make it doubtful stuff to present to a modern audience, prone as it is, when reaching a degree of satiety—"supp'd full of horrors"—to find relief in uproarious or hysterical laughter. With this play excluded from the repertoire there will be no need to consider the means of representing severed hands, bloody stumps, slit throats, torn-out tongues, and blood pouring out copiously enough to be caught in a basin. But in the grim chronicle plays and in some of the tragedies, where Death forever stalks, swinging his scythe at all and sundry, the disposal of the dead becomes a major consideration. For general purposes, stretchers, or "litters", seem to have been used, though we must also consider the wheeled catafalque as being used in some cases. Another possibility is a tablelike stretcher with legs and carrying poles. The dead, conveyed on any of these, could have been covered by a pall when they did not have to be exposed, and have been suggested by pillows or padding—a perfectly practical procedure today. In Elizabethan productions, when the pall was suddenly thrown back and the dead exposed, as in *Richard III*, I, 2, and in *Julius Caesar*, III, 2, horrific dummies with bloody gaping wounds and mutilations were used—a procedure not advised in modern production. Further restraint in presenting the ghastly might extend to similar properties. Severed heads are, of course, action properties, but rather than follow the Elizabethan custom of using a wax representation of the supposed decapitated person, modelled from the actor's face and complete with hair of his colour and dreadful appendages, a bundle, suggesting that the head has been gathered up in a cloth, can be substituted. Only if the exposed head is an essential part of action, as in the case of the head of York on the Gates, *3 Henry VI*, II, 2, should anything more realistic be attempted.

In the case of death taking place on the fore- or middle stage bodies seem frequently to have been dragged off by the heels, a custom underscored by Hamlet's removal of the corpse of Polonius,[1] while carrying devices, such as shields, were sometimes used for the illustrious dead. It certainly expedites these removals if stretchers are used and helps to discourage irrepressible giggles on the part of the more risible section of the audience.

When death has supposedly occurred off stage and the bodies are brought on, as in the case of Regan, Goneril, and Cordelia in *King Lear*, there is no reason why the actors should not represent the corpses.

Bodies on the balcony or inner stages present no problems as the closing of the curtains at the end of scenes takes care of all removals.

Banquet. In many of the plays a banquet "appears", and, since this is a property so frequently in demand, it can be set up with table carpet, goblets, plates, and dishes more or less permanently. All small ornamental properties can be fastened down—with scotch tape—to facilitate transport.

Dagger. A suspended dagger that moved and oozed with blood was, no doubt, a prideful property in the Elizabethan production of *Macbeth*. With a literal-minded audience this could not remain a dagger of the mind, as it most certainly will today.

"Machines": Supernatural Appearances and Disappearances. In *Macbeth* there are even more complicated matters to consider. There are the appearances and disappearances of the Witches, for instance. Their first brief scene might be on the middle stage, or even on the tarras; their next two will certainly be centre, when they will arrive and depart on the large trap. In the last of these scenes, Hecate appears on the tarras where a little spirit in a cloud waits for her and, at the end of the scene, she mounts the cloud and is drawn up through the trap-door in the "heavens". This brings us to the whole question of aerial manipulation.

In the Elizabethan theatre persons and properties, such as the heavy throne of state, were "let down" and "drawn up" by the simple expedient of ropes or wires, pulleys, and hand-turned windlasses, all of which were situated in the "heavens" and "huts".[2] That the method was noisy and clumsy in the beginning there is no doubt, for not only are there scoffing allusions to it in contemporary accounts of playhouse performances, but the stage directions for all such business call for accompanying "music"

---

[1] As this takes place on the balcony stage, the removal of Polonius's body seems at first unnecessary until we remember that the hiding of the body is a deliberate "antic" gesture on the part of Hamlet and so constitutes essential plot business.

[2] It has been proved conclusively that ropes were sometimes lowered to be fastened to persons or things that had to be drawn up to the second level. This certainly makes the raising of Antony to the Monument less of a problem.

or "thunder", or both, which were, obviously, devices to drown the creaking of the machinery.

As time went on and the productions of the King's Men were more and more frequently performed at Court, improvements in aerial equipment must have been influenced by the wonderful suspended, and rising and falling, scenes that were being introduced into the Court masques. The "cloud" in *Macbeth* was certainly something more than the offspring of the medieval cloud in which God descended in the pageant; it may have been a tiny emanation of the gorgeous clouds that Inigo Jones was presenting to the wondering eyes of the Court. There was one aerial novelty that may actually have been designed for a Shakespearean play by this scenic artist himself. In *Cymbeline*, V, 4, Jove arrives on the back of an eagle, and in an extant design[1] by Inigo Jones we have this same deity arriving in the same fashion complete with thunderbolt.[2] The design was used for a Court masque (*Tempe Restored*) in 1632, but there is no reason why it should not have been originally drawn for a Court production of *Cymbeline*. This supposition is supported by a suggestion made by Allardyce Nicoll,[3] that three extant drawings of scenic settings, one by Inigo Jones, may have been made for a proposed Court production of *Cymbeline*. By the time of the first production of *The Tempest*—about 1613—flying apparatus must have advanced considerably. According to the stage directions for Ariel, a spectacle of wonder and delight must have ravished the Globe audience.[4] Designs for the improved mechanism used in the Court masques are fortunately extant, and reproductions of these are to be found in Allardyce Nicoll's *Stuart Masques and the Renaissance Stage*.

It is doubtful if any but professional stages should attempt these effects. Certainly the amateur company's budget would never stand the expense of installing modern flying apparatus. It will be up to the agility and grace of the actors and the skill of the director to replace flying entrances and exits by ingenious and unexpected "discoveries" and "disappearances".[5]

Now, to return to the Witches in *Macbeth*. The scene of the apparitions (Act IV, scene 1) is not nearly so difficult as it sounds. A low screen, representing the cauldron, can be set in front of the open Grave on the inner

[1] This design is reproduced in Nicoll, Allardyce, *Stuart Masques and the Renaissance Stage*, p. 94.
[2] We have to remember, however, as Mr. Nicoll points out (*ibid.*, p. 180), that in Italy, as early as 1589, deities were arriving on eagles, lions, and even goats.
[3] *Ibid.*, p. 150.
[4] There is, in the British Museum, a sheet of Pelham Humphrey's musical setting for "Where the bee sucks". It was composed some time in the reign of Charles II and has the following stage direction, "A Song in the Machines by Ariel's Spirits." This suggests that the "flying ballet" is far older than has been generally believed.
[5] A delightful piece of business for Puck's first entrance is suggested by Ronald Watkins in his *Moonlight at the Globe*, pp. 25-6.

stage, stage flame appearing at the sides.[1] From below, the figures will, one by one, mount a ladder that can rest against the front of the Grave, and will appear actually to rise in the midst of the cauldron. At the end of this scene, the screen-cauldron will be lowered into the Grave—a piece of business that can be masked by the Witches—and the Grave flap will be closed. The Kings will then enter through the door at the back of the inner stage, pass across, and exit between the side curtains on the left (audience's left).

Animals.[2] Animals always constitute a difficulty on the stage. If they are real, they are unpredictable and tricky properties; if imitation, a complete failure. There is no doubt that Launce's dog was real, and it is easy to suppose that Moonlight's dog was also a sad little mongrel, but was it a real bear that chased Antigonus in *The Winter's Tale*, III, 3? There is in *Titus Andronicus*, *The Tempest*, and *A Midsummer Night's Dream* a pack of hounds which, although they do not appear in the first and last of these plays, are at least heard giving tongue. Again we can imagine that the cry of hounds "off" was certainly introduced in the forest scenes of *As You Like It*. How was it done? We hear of an entire hunt being suggested off stage in a play presented before the Queen at Oxford! Were they real hounds? Well, the effect presents no problem for the modern director. Sound-effect records (see p. 293) can be used that are realistic enough to be accepted without comment by the most exacting members of the audience. As to the hounds that appear in *The Tempest*, these were undoubtedly men in antic costume.

Macbeth and Banquo are supposed to be on horseback when they first encounter the Witches, and in the chronicle plays there are many scenes in which mounted men take part. We can only guess that we have the explanation of these horses in the lines of the Chorus at the opening of *Henry V*.

> "Think when we talk of horses that you see them
> Printing their proud hoofs i' the receiving earth."

For the rest, possibly the old hooves-heard-off trick[3] and the entrance of the supposed riders with whips and spurs will have sufficed.

[1] Long streamers of red and yellow paper or silk blown into fluttering tongues by an electric fan.
[2] Two survivals of the old animal cults which passed into the mumming plays are used in *A Midsummer Night's Dream* and *The Merry Wives of Windsor*. In the first, Bottom has his head replaced by the head of an ass, and in the second a buck's head is worn by Falstaff.
[3] Two empty half shells of a coconut are grasped in the palms of the hands and brought down in rapid alternation on a slate. The property man usually hangs the slate round his neck and walks from the back of the stage to the wings clip-clopping as he comes, or goes from the wings to the back of the stage, depending on the arrival or departure of the "horses".

S.S.P.—F

Sound Effects

There are many sound effects called for in Shakespeare's plays. By far the most numerous have to do with martial music (see p. 298), but "noises of battle" would be a good second. There is one battle that consists entirely of sounds heard off. It occurs in *Antony and Cleopatra*, III, 8, and is indicated by "noise of a sea fight off". We know that for such effects cannon, fireworks, drums, clashes of metal on metal, shaking of chains, "thunder", and confused shouting were used, and these, or their substitutes, will do equally well today.

There is one property that a Shakespearean company must possess even at heavy expense, and that is a large deep-toned bell. For impressive dramatic effect this property is indispensable. Nor is there any satisfactory substitute.[1] Was there ever such an opening to a great tragedy as the twelve solemn strokes of midnight that sound before the human voices are heard on the dark battlements of Elsinore! The horror that sweeps over the castle where a king is found foully murdered is increased to terror by the clashing of the great alarm bell. The solemn striking of a clock, marking the time for some event of evil or solemnity, the reverberations of a bell heralding some dreadful apparition, the slow beating of time in the ears of the imprisoned or dying, the sweet sound of midnight to the brides and bridegrooms —that is also the signal for the spirits of earth, air, water, and fire to bless the house—all these and many others prove how important Shakespeare himself considered the great bell which hung in the tower of the Globe.

In regard to the rest of the "noises heard off", such as a murmuring, an angry, or a jubilant crowd, the sounds of hunting, of storms, or of marching men—these will give little trouble, for the modern producer has at his command sound-effect records that will give a convincing representation of any sound or noise required in the plays. A company that specializes in this type of record is Major Sound Effect Records. (See p. 293 for address.)

---

[1] Fine sound-effect records can be had for many small-bell purposes, such as striking clocks, and chimes. See pages 297–8.

Books for Reference & Reading[1]

*ADAMS, JOHN CRANFORD, *The Globe Playhouse: Its Design and Equipment*, Harvard University Press, Cambridge, Mass., 1942. Since the staging suggested in Part I of this book is based wholly on Mr. Adams's conjectural reconstruction of the Globe, his book is obviously indispensable for reference and collateral reading.

ADAMS, JOSEPH QUINCY, *A Life of William Shakespeare*, Constable and Company, Ltd., London, 1923. For a description of the Elizabethan repertory companies, see Chaps. 10–14.

——, *Shakespearean Playhouses: A History of English Theatres from the Beginnings to the Restoration*, Houghton Mifflin Company, Boston, 1917.

AIRNE, C. W., *The Story of Tudor and Stuart Britain Told in Pictures*, Sankey, Hudson & Co., Manchester, England, n.d.

*ALBRIGHT, VICTOR E., *The Shakesperian Stage*, Columbia University Press, New York, 1909.

BAKER, GEORGE PIERCE, *The Development of Shakespeare as a Dramatist*, The Macmillan Company, New York, 1907.

BALDWIN, THOMAS WHITFIELD, *The Organization and Personnel of the Shakespearean Company*, Princeton University Press, Princeton, 1927.

BASKERVILLE, CHARLES READ, "The Custom of Sitting on the Stage," *Modern Philology*, VIII, No. 4, April, 1911.

BESANT, (Sir) WALTER, *London*, Chatto & Windus, London, 1900.

——, *London in the Time of the Tudors*, Adam & Charles Black, London, 1904.

——, *South London*, Frederick A. Stokes Company, Philadelphia, c. 1898.

BRADLEY, A. C., *Shakespearean Tragedy: Lectures on Hamlet, Othello, King Lear, Macbeth*, The Macmillan Company, New York, 1937. Distinguished dramatic appreciations of the four great tragedies. Those in charge of lighting would do well to read of Shakespeare's use of "darkness" in *Macbeth*, pp. 333–335.

BROPHY, JOHN, *Gentleman of Stratford*, Harper & Brothers, New York, 1940. A delightful novel woven round Will Shakespeare and four women who, possibly, influenced his life. Based on a great deal of known fact, this book high-lights much of the life of the London Shakespeare knew. For an excellent description of a conjectural Globe theatre, see pp. 84–85.

CAMPBELL, LILY B., *Scenes and Machines on the English Stage during the Renaissance, a Classical Revival*, University Press, Cambridge, England, 1923. Important. For classical influence on the scenery and properties of the Court, university, and public theatres, see Chaps. 7 and 9.

*CHAMBERS, (Sir) EDMUND K., *The Elizabethan Stage*, 4 vols., Oxford University Press, New York, 1923. The four volumes of this great work, together with the two volumes of Sir Edmund's *William Shakespeare*, are generally recognized as the

---

[1] An asterisk (*) indicates books that are especially recommended for their practical value to the producer and scholar-player.

most complete source of authentic data on all that pertains to Shakespeare's life and work.

CHAMBERS, (Sir) EDMUND K., *The Mediaeval Stage*, 2 vols., Oxford University Press, New York, 1903.

——, *Shakespearean Gleanings*, Oxford University Press, New York, 1944. For timing of Shakespearean plays, see pp. 36–41.

——, *William Shakespeare: A Study of Facts and Problems*, 2 vols., Oxford University Press, New York, 1930.

CHENEY, SHELDON, *The Theatre: Three Thousand Years of Drama, Acting and Stagecraft*, Longmans, Green & Co., Inc., New York, 1929.

CHILD, HAROLD, "The Elizabethan Theatre," *Cambridge History of English Literature*, Vol. VI, Chap. 10, The Macmillan Company, New York, 1933.

*CHUTE, MARCHETTE, *Shakespeare of London*, E. P. Dutton & Co., Inc., New York, 1949. This account of the years Shakespeare spent in London brings before our eyes a vital and colourful picture drawn from authentic sources.

DEKKER, THOMAS, *The Gull's Hornbook*, edited by R. B. McKERROW, Chatto & Windus, London, 1907. (Also published by John W. Luce and Company, Boston, 1907.) A contemporary account, both witty and satirical, of the fops of Shakespeare's time. See especially Chap. 6, "How a Gallant Should Behave Himself in the Playhouse". (This chapter may also be found in CHAMBERS, (Sir) EDMUND K., *The Elizabethan Stage*, Vol. IV, Appendix H, pp. 365–369.)

EBERLEIN, HAROLD DONALDSON, and ABBOT McCLURE, *The Practical Book of Period Furniture*, J. B. Lippincott Company, Philadelphia, 1914.

Elizabethan England, edited by FRANKLIN B. WILLIAMS, Museum Extension Publications, Museum of Fine Arts, Boston, c. 1939.

FENN, FREDERICK, and B. WYLIE, *Old English Furniture*, Charles Scribner's Sons, New York, 1913.

FOLGER SHAKESPEARE LIBRARY, *Folger Shakespeare Library Prints*, Folger Shakespeare Library, Washington, D.C. See especially the two series, "The Shakespearian Theatre" and "Shakespeare's London".

FOSTER, JOSEPH, "Folger: Biggest Little Library in the World", *The National Geographic Magazine*, September, 1951, pp. 411–444, National Geographic Society, Washington, D.C.

GARSIDE, JOSHUA T., *Old English Furniture, a View of Its Characteristics from Tudor Times to the Regency*, Charles Scribner's Sons, New York, 1924.

GAYLEY, CHARLES MILLS, *The Classic Myths in English Literature and in Art*, Ginn & Company, Boston, 1911. This, or any other good mythology, is useful for information on designs in Elizabethan tapestry.

GILMAN, ROGER, *Great Styles of Interior Architecture with Their Decoration and Furniture*, Harper & Brothers, New York, 1924.

GOTCH, J. ALFRED, "Architecture", *Shakespeare's England*, Vol. II, Chap. 17, Oxford University Press, New York, 1932.

——, *Inigo Jones*, Methuen & Co., Ltd., London, 1928.

HAIGH, A. E., *The Attic Theatre*, Oxford University Press, New York, 1907.

*HARBAGE, ALFRED, *Shakespeare's Audience*, Columbia University Press, New York,

1941. A masterly analysis of the audience for whom Shakespeare wrote most of his plays.

HARRISON, G. B., *Introducing Shakespeare*, Penguin Books, Inc., New York, 1939.

HARRISON, WILLIAM, *Harrison's Description of England in Shakespere's Youth, Being the Second and Third Books of His Description of Britaine and England*, edited from the first two editions of Holinshed's *Chronicle*, 1577, 1587, by FREDERICK J. FURNIVALL, published in three parts for The New Shakspere Society by N. Trübner & Co., London, 1877, 1878, 1881.

HAZLITT, WILLIAM CAREW, editor, *A Selection of Old English Plays*, originally published by ROBERT DODSLEY (compiler) in the year 1774, 15 vols., 4th ed., 1874–1876. Vol. XV contains JAMES WRIGHT's *Historia Histrionica* (q.v.).

*HENSLOWE, PHILIP, *Diary*, edited by WALTER WILSON GREG, 2 vols., A. H. Bullen, London, 1904, 1908. Vol. I, Text; Vol. II, Commentary. This diary, by one of Shakespeare's contemporaries, is a mine of information relating to the costumes and properties of the Elizabethan stage.

*HODGES, C. WALTER, *Shakespeare and the Players*, Coward-McCann, Inc., New York, 1948. Although written for young people, the scholar-player of any age will find delight and interest in this little book.

——, "Unworthy Scaffolds", *Shakespeare Survey*, edited by ALLARDYCE NICOLL, Vol. III, pp. 83–94, University Press, Cambridge, England, 1950 .

HOTSON, LESLIE J., *The Commonwealth and Restoration Stage*, Harvard University Press, Cambridge, Mass., 1928.

HUNTER, GEORGE LELAND, *The Practical Book of Tapestries*, J. B. Lippincott Company, Philadelphia, 1925. For pictorial subjects in English tapestry, see Chap. 16.

JONES, INIGO, *Designs by Inigo Jones for Masques and Plays at Court*, printed for the Walpole and Malone Societies, University Press, Oxford, 1924. These designs reveal the high standard of theatrical art at Court that may have influenced the productions of Shakespeare's final plays.

KERNODLE, GEORGE R., *From Art to Theatre: Form and Convention in the Renaissance*, University of Chicago Press, Chicago, 1944.

——, "The Medieval Pageant Wagons of Louvain", *The Theatre Annual*, 1943, The Theatre Library Association, New York.

KNIGHT, G. WILSON, *Principles of Shakespearean Production, with Especial Reference to the Tragedies*, Faber & Faber, Ltd., London, 1936.

*LAWRENCE, WILLIAM J., *The Elizabethan Playhouse and Other Studies*, Shakespeare Head Press, Stratford-on-Avon, 1912.

*——, *Old Theatre Days and Ways*, George G. Harrap & Co., Ltd., London, 1935.

*——, *Pre-Restoration Stage Studies*, Harvard University Press, Cambridge, Mass., 1927.

*——, *Shakespeare's Workshop*, Houghton Mifflin Company, Boston, 1928.

*——, *Those Nut-cracking Elizabethans: Studies of the Early Theatre and Drama*, The Argonaut Press, London, 1935.

MACQUOID, PERCY, "The Home", *Shakespeare's England*, Vol. II, Chap. 20, Oxford University Press, New York, 1932.

——, and RALPH EDWARDS, *The Dictionary of English Furniture, from the Middle Ages to the Late Georgian Period,* 3 vols., Charles Scribner's Sons, New York, 1924–1927. These splendid books, though too expensive for the average purchaser, can be found in large libraries. They should be consulted by all who are looking for the most magnificent examples of authentic Elizabethan furniture and furnishings.

*MASEFIELD, JOHN, *A Macbeth Production,* The Macmillan Company, New York, 1946. Most colourful and imaginative suggestions for a presentation of *Macbeth.*

MUSEUM OF FINE ARTS, BOSTON, *English Decorative Arts.* Sheets of photographs of Museum exhibits. (See also *Elizabethan England.*)

NEILSON, WILLIAM ALLAN, and ASHLEY H. THORNDIKE, *The Facts about Shakespeare,* rev. ed., The Macmillan Company, New York, 1933.

NICOLL, ALLARDYCE, *British Drama: An Historical Survey from the Beginnings to the Present Time,* 3rd rev. ed., George G. Harrap & Co., Ltd., London, 1932.

*——, *The Development of the Theatre: A Study of Theatrical Art from the Beginnings to the Present Day,* Harcourt, Brace and Company, Inc., New York, 1937.

——, *Stuart Masques and the Renaissance Stage,* George G. Harrap & Co., Ltd., London, 1937.

——, *World Drama, from Aeschylus to Anouilh,* George G. Harrap & Co., Ltd., London, 1949.

NORRIS, EDWIN, editor and translator, *The Ancient Cornish Drama,* 2 vols., University Press, Oxford, 1859.

QUENNELL, MARJORIE, and C. H. B. QUENNELL, *A History of Everyday Things in England,* 1066–1799, B. T. Batsford, Ltd., London, 1918.

QUILLER-COUCH, (Sir) ARTHUR, *Shakespeare's Workmanship,* T. Fisher Unwin, Ltd., London, 1927.

REMINGTON, PRESTON, *English Domestic Needlework,* The Metropolitan Museum of Art, New York, 1945.

RHODES, R. COMPTON, *The Stagery of Shakespeare,* Cornish Bros., Birmingham, England, 1922.

ROBIE, VIRGINIA HUNTINGTON, *Historic Styles in Furniture,* Houghton Mifflin Company, Boston, 1916.

ROSENFELD, SYBIL, *Strolling Players and Drama in the Provinces,* 1660–1765, The University Press, Cambridge, England, 1939.

ROWSE, A. L., *The England of Elizabeth: The Structure of Society,* The Macmillan Company, New York, 1951. The first two chapters of the prologue of this book should be read by all who are interested in the magnificent achievement of the Elizabethans in all fields of human endeavour and progress. Mr. Rowse introduces us to one of the most remarkable periods in the history of man with the profundity of the scholar and the wit and warmth of a man of the world.

Shakespeare Quarterly, The Shakespeare Association of America, Inc., 322 East 57th Street, New York.

Shakespeare Survey, edited by ALLARDYCE NICOLL, issued annually since 1948, University Press, Cambridge, England.

**Shakespeare's England: An Account of the Life and Manners of His Age,* 2 vols., Oxford University Press, New York, 1932.

SHELLEY, HENRY C., *Inns and Taverns of Old London*, L. C. Page & Company, Inc., Boston, 1909.

SIMPSON, PERCY, and C. F. BELL, editors, *Designs by Inigo Jones for Masques and Plays at Court, a Descriptive Catalogue of Drawings for Scenery and Costumes Mainly in the Collection of His Grace the Duke of Devonshire*, University Press, Oxford, 1924.

★SMITH, DONALD, *Old Furniture and Woodwork*, B. T. Batsford, London, 1947.

SPEAIGHT, ROBERT, *Drama since 1939*, Longmans, Green & Co., Inc., New York, 1947.

SPRAGUE, ARTHUR COLBY, *Shakespeare and the Actors: The Stage Business in His Plays* (1660–1905), Harvard University Press, Cambridge, Mass., 1944.

★——, *Shakespeare and the Audience: A Study in the Technique of Exposition*, Harvard University Press, Cambridge, Mass., 1935. In this book the actor of Shakespeare's plays will find a great deal that will guide and control his interpretation and presentation.

THORNDIKE, ASHLEY H., *Shakespeare's Theater*, The Macmillan Company, New York, 1938.

VANEZKY, ALICE, *Pageantry on the Shakespearian Stage*, Twayne Publishers, New York, 1951.

VICTORIA AND ALBERT MUSEUM, *Elizabethan Embroidery* (Pamphlet 5). Obtainable at the Victoria and Albert Museum, South Kensington, London, and at The British Library of Information, Rockefeller Plaza, New York.

——, *Tudor Domestic Silver* (Pamphlet 6). See note above.

★WATKINS, RONALD, *Moonlight at the Globe: An Essay in Shakespeare Production Based on Performance of A Midsummer Night's Dream at Harrow School*, Michael Joseph, Ltd., London, 1946.

★——, *On Producing Shakespeare*, Michael Joseph, Ltd., London, 1950.

★WHANSLAW, H. W., *The Bankside Stage-book*, Wells Gardner, Darton & Co., Ltd., London, 1924. Detailed description of how to make a model Tudor playhouse, properties, and character figures in miniature. Valuable also for life-size production.

WILSON, J. DOVER, compiler, *Life in Shakespeare's England: A Book of Elizabethan Prose*, Penguin Books, Inc., New York, 1949.

WRIGHT, JAMES, *Historia Histrionica: An Historical Account of the English Stage, Shewing the Ancient Use, Improvement, and Perfection of Dramatic Representations in This Nation, in a Dialogue of Plays and Players*, reprinted in *A Selection of Old English Plays*, originally published by ROBERT DODSLEY (compiler) in the year 1774, 15 vols., 4th ed., 1874–1876. See Vol. XV, pp. 399–431.

Sources for Illustrations

GREEK THEATRE

CHENEY, SHELDON, *The Theatre*, p. 54a: Theatre of Dionysus, Athens. P. 54b: Theatre at Epidaurus. Pp. 60, 62: Reconstructions by Fiechter.

NICOLL, ALLARDYCE, *The Development of the Theatre*, frontispiece: Theatre of Dionysus, Athens. P. 23: Theatre at Epidaurus.

——, *World Drama*, p. 33: Theatre at Epidaurus.

ROMAN THEATRE

CHENEY, SHELDON, *The Theatre*, pp. 63, 89, 163*a*: Theatre at Aspendos. P. 98: Stage of theatre at Orange (reconstruction). P. 163*b*: Theatre at Ephesus.

NICOLL, ALLARDYCE, *The Development of the Theatre*, pp. 52–55 (Figs. 42–47): Theatres at Aspendos and Orange. (Note roof over stage in Fig. 44.)

——, *World Drama*, p. 113: Theatre at Orange. P. 128: Theatre at Taormina.

CORNISH "ROUND" AT PERRANZABULO

ALBRIGHT, VICTOR E., *The Shakesperian Stage*, p. 18: Ground plan and cross section. This round is thought by some scholars to be of Roman origin, by others to be British remains later used by the Romans.

MEDIEVAL STAGING OF RELIGIOUS DRAMA

Church Setting of Liturgical Plays

ALBRIGHT, VICTOR E., *The Shakesperian Stage*, p. 12: Resurrection play, 12th century (conjectural). P. 13: Plan of Donaueschingen Passion-play stage, 16th century.

CHAMBERS (Sir) EDMUND K., *The Mediaeval Stage*, Vol. II, p. 83: Conjectural setting. P. 84: Plan for Donaueschingen Passion-play stage, 16th century.

NICOLL, ALLARDYCE, *The Development of the Theatre*, pp. 65, 67: Reproductions of the two illustrations from Chambers above.

Stationary Staging outside the Church

ALBRIGHT, VICTOR E., *The Shakesperian Stage*, p. 16: author's conjectural plan of the stage of *Mary Magdalene*, 15th century.

CHENEY, SHELDON, *The Theatre*, p. 162: Valenciennes Passion Play of 1547 in progress (recent reconstruction based on a contemporary sketch).

Pageants

AIRNE, C. W., *The Story of Tudor and Stuart Britain Told in Pictures*, p. 17: A mystery at Coventry.

CHENEY, SHELDON, *The Theatre*, p. 166: A play in progress.

WHANSLAW, H. B., *The Bankside Stage-book*, p. 9: A "station" or "scaffold" in a mystery play.

STAGES USED BY STROLLING PLAYERS

BAKER, GEORGE PIERCE, *The Development of Shakespeare as a Dramatist*, p. 190: A trestle stage.

CHENEY, SHELDON, *The Theatre*, p. 234: A board-and-barrel stage.

NICOLL, ALLARDYCE, *The Development of the Theatre*, p. 73: A platform stage.

Shakespeare Survey, Vol. III, p. 87: Mountebank stage at a fair (note the unusual height of the trestles).

STREET-THEATRE, OR *Tableaux-vivants*, STAGING

The British Drama League Magazine, Summer number, 1951, "Drama Festival of Britain, 1951", p. 38: A play in progress on a stage built on a motor truck.

KERNODLE, GEORGE R., *From Art to Theatre*, p. 79: *Tableau vivant* over an arch. P. 170: Street theatre for a play of the *Judgment of Soloman*, Louvain, 1594 (see trestle stage and curtain backing for a throne).

Shakespeare Survey, Vol. III, Plate V: 17th-century triumphal car, which gives a good idea of a setting of a street theatre. Plate VI: A typical street-theatre stage.

UNIVERSITY STAGING

CHENEY, SHELDON, *The Theatre*, p. 185: Scenes from comedies of Terence on a platform stage.

KERNODLE, GEORGE R., *From Art to Theatre*, p. 161 (Fig. 48): Two arcade façades (illustrations for an edition of Terence, Lyons, 1493).

NICOLL, ALLARDYCE, *The Development of the Theatre*, p. 84: Settings for two plays by Terence, 1493.

INNYARD STAGING

ADAMS, JOSEPH QUINCY, *Shakespearean Playhouses*, p. 4: White Hart Inn, Southwark (with ground plan).

BAKER, GEORGE PIERCE, *The Development of Shakespeare as a Dramatist*, p. 200: Play in progress.

BESANT, (Sir) WALTER, *London*, p. 235: Bull and Mouth Inn, St. Martin's-le-Grand.

——, *South London*, pp. 137 (notice how the galleries jut forward), 239, 261, 268, 321: Old innyards.

HODGES, C. WALTER, *Shakespeare and the Players*, p. 15: Play in progress.

LAWRENCE, WILLIAM J., *Pre-Restoration Stage Studies*, frontispiece: New Inn, Gloucester (including ground plan).

SHELLEY, HENRY C., *Inns and Taverns of Old London*, p. 76: Yard of Belle Sauvage Inn, London (known to have been used by the players in Shakespeare's time).

SPEAIGHT, ROBERT, *Drama since 1939*, p. 10: A performance of *The Merchant of Venice* at the George Inn, Southwark, in wartime England.

BEARBAITING RINGS

ADAMS, JOSEPH QUINCY, *Shakespearean Playhouses*, p. 120a: Bankside, 1554–1558. P. 120b: Bankside, 1580. P. 330: Faithorne's Map of London, 1658.

BAKER, GEORGE PIERCE, *The Development of Shakespeare as a Dramatist*, p. 18: London showing Bankside, 1588 (coloured). P. 174: Visscher's View of London, 1616.

BESANT, (Sir) WALTER, *South London*, p. 213: Bear garden.

GREAT HALLS

Elizabethan England, Plate 19: Middle Temple Hall (note the two doors and gallery).

HARRISON, G. B., *Introducing Shakespeare*, p. 97: Middle Temple Hall.

QUENNELL, MARJORIE, and C. H. B. QUENNELL, *A History of Everyday Things in England*, Vol. II, p. 27: The old hall, Berkhamsted School. P. 54: Elizabethan hall. *Shakespeare's England*, Vol. II, p. 66: Middle Temple Hall.

ELIZABETHAN THEATRES

Contemporary Pictures—Exteriors

ADAMS, JOHN CRANFORD, *The Globe Playhouse*, frontispiece: Globe, about 1612 (Visscher's *View*, 1616). P. 18a: Rose and bear garden (Keere's *View*, 1593). P. 18b: Rose, first Globe, and bear garden, as in 1603 (Delarem). P. 203: Rose, about 1593 (Hondius's *View*, 1611). P. 387: Rose, about 1593 (Baker's *Chronicle*, 1643).

ADAMS, JOSEPH QUINCY, *A Life of William Shakespeare*, p. 120: Rose, as in 1589–1599 (Speed's *Atlas*, 1611). P. 266: Swan, about 1612 (Visscher's *View*, 1616). P. 280: First Globe (Visscher). P. 406: Site of Blackfriars, marked on Ogilby and Morgan's *Map of London*, 1677.

——, *Shakespearean Playhouses*, p. 147a: Rose and bear garden (Norden's *Map of London*, 1593). P. 147b: Same (Baker's *Chronicle*, 1643). P. 149: Rose and bear garden, as in 1589–1599 (Speed's *Atlas*, 1611). P. 246: Rose, first Globe, and bear garden, 1603 (Delarem). P. 253: First Globe (Visscher's *View*, 1616). P. 256: Bankside playhouses, about 1612 (Merian's *View*, 1638). P. 260: Second Globe (Hollar's *View*, 1647). P. 326: Hope, or second bear garden (Hollar).

BAKER, GEORGE PIERCE, *The Development of Shakespeare as a Dramatist*, frontispiece: London in 1610, showing the first Globe (Hondius's *View*, 1611). P. 165a: Rose (Hollar's *View*, 1647). P. 165b: Swan, about 1612 (Visscher's *View*, 1616). P. 175a: Second Globe (Visscher). P. 175b: Hope and bear garden (Visscher).

CHENEY, SHELDON, *The Theatre*, p. 275: Bankside (Visscher's *View*, 1616).

FOLGER, SHAKESPEARE LIBRARY PRINTS, *The Shakespearian Theatre*.

Shakespeare Survey, Vol. I, Plate X: Bankside showing three playhouses (Delarem). Plate XIII: Second Globe and bear garden (Hollar's *View*, 1647). Very fine enlarged reproduction. Vol. II, Plate XII: Second Globe and bear garden (Hollar).

THORNDIKE, ASHLEY H., *Shakespeare's Theater*, frontispiece: Swan, Hope, and Globe (Visscher's *View*, 1616). P. 33: London (Hondius's *View*, 1611).

WILSON, J. DOVER, *Life in Shakespeare's England*, between pp. 192 and 193: Globe and bear garden (Hollar's *View*, 1647).

Contemporary Pictures—Interiors

ADAMS, JOHN CRANFORD, *The Globe Playhouse*, p. 42: Vignette from title page of *Roxana*, 1632 (play in progress). P. 114: Vignette from title page of *Messallina*, 1640 (front stage, curtains closed). P. 162: Frontispiece of *The Wits*, 1642 (Performance in progress). P. 306: Swan, based on De Witt's "observations", 1596.

ADAMS, JOSEPH QUINCY, *A Life of William Shakespeare*, p. 268: Swan (De Witt, 1596).

BAKER, GEORGE PIERCE, *The Development of Shakespeare as a Dramatist*, p. 210: Swan (De Witt, 1596). P. 230: Stage of the Red Bull Theatre (?). (See quoted comment under Lawrence, William J., on the facing page.)

CHAMBERS, (Sir) EDMUND K., *The Elizabethan Stage*, Vol. II, p. 521: Swan (De Witt, 1596).

CHENEY, SHELDON, *The Theatre*, p. 271: Swan (De Witt, 1596). P. 284*a*: Vignette from title page of *Roxana*, 1632 (play in progress). P. 284*b*: Vignette from *Messallina*, 1640 (front stage, curtains closed).

FOLGER SHAKESPEARE LIBRARY PRINTS, *The Shakespearian Theatre*.

HARRISON, G. B., *Introducing Shakespeare*, p. 92: Swan (De Witt, 1596).

LAWRENCE, WILLIAM J., *The Elizabethan Playhouse*, p. 18: Frontispiece to *The Wits*, "usually misdescribed as the Red Bull Theatre".

NICOLL, ALLARDYCE, *The Development of the Theatre*, p. 121: Swan (De Witt, 1596). P. 123*a*: Vignette from the title page of *Roxana*, 1632 (play in progress). P. 123*b*: Vignette from *Messallina*, 1640. P. 125: Reconstruction drawn by S. B. Marston.

Shakespeare's Survey, Vol. I, Plate III: Swan (De Witt, 1596).

Shakespeare's England, Vol. II, p. 286: Title page of *Roxana* (see stage in middle panel at bottom). P. 299: Swan (De Witt, 1596).

THORNDIKE, ASHLEY H., *Shakespeare's Theater*, p. 51: Swan (De Witt, 1596).

Conjectural Reconstructions

ADAMS, JOSEPH QUINCY, *A Life of William Shakespeare*, p. 284: Globe, cross section. P. 286: Globe, interior.

AIRNE, C. W., *The Story of Tudor and Stuart Britain Told in Pictures*, p. 17: Globe, play in progress.

ALBRIGHT, VICTOR E., *The Shakesperian Stage*, frontispiece: A typical Shakespearean stage—perspective view. Plate 8: Ground plans of the same. Plate 11: Set for *Timon of Athens*, V,3—inner scene. Plate 12: Set for *Timon of Athens*, V,4—outer scene. (All these conjectural reconstructions are by the author.)

BAKER, GEORGE PIERCE, *The Development of Shakespeare as a Dramatist*, p. 180: Globe. P. 220: Cross section. P. 240: Stage used by Elizabethan Stage Society. Pp. 250, 260: Harvard University Elizabethan stage. P. 280: An "Elizabethan" stage, showing use of a painted cloth in upper stage.

BESANT, (Sir) WALTER, *South London*, p. 209: Globe (note three gables, bell, and flag tower).

CHAMBERS, (Sir) EDMUND K., *The Elizabethan Stage*, Vol. III, p. 84: A square theatre (proportions of the Fortune). P. 85: An octagonal theatre (e.g. the Globe, size of the Fortune).

——, *Shakespearean Gleanings*, p. 98: Globe.

CHENEY, SHELDON, *The Theatre*, p. 268: Fortune.

HARRISON, G. B., *Introducing Shakespeare*, p. 100: A reconstruction by Walter H. Godfrey.

HODGES, C. WALTER, *Shakespeare and the Players*, frontispiece: A delightful coloured print of the Theatre and the Curtain. Pp. 36, 63: Globe. Pp. 69–85: Many scenes of a play in progress at the Globe.

KERNODLE, GEORGE R., *From Art to Theatre*, p. 152: "Reconstruction of a composite façade with the basic pattern of the Elizabethan stage. Every detail of decoration here is known to have been used on either a theatre or a tableau façade in England or Flanders."

LAWRENCE, WILLIAM J., *Old Theatre Days and Ways*, p. 68: Photograph of a model of the first Globe designed by W. Noel Hills.

——, *Those Nut-cracking Elizabethans*, frontispiece: A typical Elizabethan public theatre.

The National Geographic Magazine, September, 1951, p. 416: John Cranford Adams's model of the Globe. P. 417: Elizabethan stage at the Folger Shakespeare Library.

NICOLL, ALLARDYCE, *The Development of the Theatre*, p. 125: A reconstruction of an Elizabethan theatre drawn by S. B. Marston.

QUENNELL, MARJORIE, and C. H. B. QUENNELL, *A History of Everyday Things in England*, Vol. II, p. 71: An Elizabethan playhouse (play in progress).

Shakespeare Quarterly, January, 1950, frontispiece: Scenes from typical Oregon Shakespeare Festival presentations illustrating use of the Elizabethan stage. P. 7: Line drawing of the same stage.

——, January, 1951, frontispiece: Photograph of the John Cranford Adams model of the Globe stage. P. 8: Sign and main entrance of the above. P. 9: "Heavens" and upper stage of the above. P. 13: Artist's sketch of the Globe.

Shakespeare Survey, Vol. I, Plate XVI: The Elizabethan stage at the Folger Shakespeare Library. Vol. II, Plates I–X: twenty-four photographs of modern settings showing adaptations of the Shakespearean stage. Vol. III, p. 86: Basic platform stage. P. 89: Burbage's theatre. (The tiring-house booth of the street theatre has here been built up to correspond with the galleries, but the "heavens" canopy has not yet been added.) P. 91: Reconstruction of the Fortune stage.

Shakespeare's England, Vol. II, 306: Fortune, as reconstructed by Walter H. Godfrey.

THORNDIKE, ASHLEY H., *Shakespeare's Theater*, p. 75: Fortune, ground plan. P. 88: Albright's ground plans. P. 96: Fortune, as reconstructed by Walter H. Godfrey.

WATKINS, RONALD, *Moonlight at the Globe*. Many delightful drawings by Maurice Percival of the Globe and of the adaptations of these to the Harrow stage.

——, *On Producing Shakespeare*. More delightful drawings by Maurice Percival.

WHANSLAW, H. W., *The Bankside Stage-book*, frontispiece: Fortune. P. 67: Ground plan of the Fortune. P. 132: Another view of the Fortune.

WILSON, J. DOVER, *Life in Shakespeare's England*, p. 161: An Elizabethan stage (from Albright).

DETAILS OF STAGE CONSTRUCTION

Balcony Railings

Shakespeare's England, Vol. II, pp. 306, 341 (notice wide interstices to allow for fullest possible visibility).

Bay Windows

ADAMS, JOSEPH QUINCY, *A Life of William Shakespeare*, p. 18: Shakespeare's birthplace (notice the bay window at the extreme right).

BESANT, (Sir) WALTER, *South London*, pp. 254, 255: Old houses with the type of bay window probably used in the Elizabethan theatre.

HOTSON, LESLIE J., *The Commonwealth and Restoration Stages*, p. 10: Puritan attack on Cavaliers, 1641 (shows two types of fitting in one window—top ones fixed and lower ones opening casementwise).

Curtains

HARRISON, WILLIAM, *Description of England* (Furnivall edition), frontispiece of Part II, The Third Book: Cheapside in 1638, showing street decorations in honour of the visit of Marie de Medicis. All the shops are hung with curtains described as "blue cloth" (p. 2*). This description, however, would seem to be inaccurate for the hangings have many different designs, suggesting that "painted clothes" were used. These curtains, of the rod-and-ring type, and the three-storied houses with a "juttey forward" give an idea of the probable appearance of the tiring house.

HOTSON, LESLIE J., *The Commonwealth and Restoration Stages*, p. 30: A Cavalier cartoon, 1649 (shows hand of stagehand drawing curtain).

Shakespeare's England, Vol. II, p. 186: George Gascoigne presenting his book to the Queen (shows the means of suspending the arras, or wall hangings; also a hand lowering a "property").

WILSON, J. DOVER, *Life in Shakespeare's England*, p. 192: George Gascoigne presenting his book to the Queen (see note above).

Doors to Stage—Survival to the Present Time

CHENEY, SHELDON, *The Theatre*, pp. 393, 397, 399, 415, 418, 419: Various stages from the 18th century on, showing doors.

LAWRENCE, WILLIAM J., *The Elizabethan Playhouse* (limited edition), pp. 169, 177, 184, 189: Various stages showing doors.

Gated Stairway

Shakespeare's England, Vol. II, p. 72: Stairway at Hatfield House.

"Juttey Forward"

AIRNE, C. W., *The Story of Tudor and Stuart Britain Told in Pictures*, p. 19: Harvard House, Stratford, etc.

BESANT, (Sir) WALTER, *London*, pp. 217, 221: Old inns.

——, *South London*, pp. 159, 249: Old houses.

Shakespeare's England, Vol. II, p. 4: Grammar school, Stratford.

Scenic Walls

ALBRIGHT, VICTOR E., *The Shakesperian Stage*, Plate 12: Conjectural use of scenic walls in *Timon of Athens*.

Traps

HOTSON, LESLIE J., *The Commonwealth and Restoration Stages*, p. 10: Cartoon, a Puritan attack on the Cavaliers (shows hinged trap cover with steps leading down, as used in the "grave").

LAWRENCE, WILLIAM J., *Pre-Restoration Studies*, p. 169: A stage trap being manipulated (from E. M. Laumann's *La Machinerie au Théâtre*, Paris, 1897).

ROSENFELD, SYBIL, *Strolling Players and Drama in the Provinces*, frontispiece: Witches in *Macbeth* rising on a trap.

SPRAGUE, ARTHUR COLBY, *Shakespeare and the Actors*, p. 142: Cruikshank illustration, dated 1844, showing the Ghost in *Hamlet* descending his trap.

LIGHTING

NICOLL, ALLARDYCE, *Stuart Masques and the Renaissance Stage*, p. 134: A 16th-century glass lamp.

WHANSLAW, H. W., *The Bankside Stage-book*, pp. 141–150: Drawings of every kind or lighting used in Shakespeare's day, with directions for making them and adapting them to electricity.

PROPERTIES

Scenic Properties

NICOLL, ALLARDYCE, *Stuart Masques and the Renaissance Stage*, p. 68: A scenic cave. Pp. 66, 76, 77, 106, 107, 124: Clouds and cloud machines. Pp. 94, 180: Aerial machines. Pp. 128, 129, 132: Aerial chariots.

Furniture

Elizabethan England, Plates 20, 21: Panelled rooms with furniture. Plate 22: Bed and joint stool. Plate 23: Table and Court cupboard.

MUSEUM OF FINE ARTS, BOSTON, *English Decorative Arts*—sheets of photographs showing clavicord, virginal, cupboards, panelled Tudor rooms, and other exhibits in the Museum.

Shakespeare's England, Vol. II, p. 124: Buffet. P. 132: Panel-backed chair. P. 148: Dining table.

WHANSLAW, H. W., *The Bankside Stage-book*, p. 202: Bed. P. 204: Stool, table, and chest.

Further illustrations of furniture will be found in the following books, for which full bibliographical data are given on pages 83–87: AIRNE, C. W., *The Story of Tudor and Stuart Britain Told in Pictures*; FENN, FREDERICK, and B. WYLIE, *Old English Furniture*; GARSIDE, JOSHUA T., *Old English Furniture*; MACQUOID, PERCY, and RALPH EDWARDS, *The Dictionary of English Furniture*; QUENNELL, MARJORIE, and C. H. B. QUENNELL, *A History of Everyday Things in England*; ROBIE, VIRGINIA HUNTINGTON, *Historic Styles in Furniture*.

Musical Instruments and Other Small Properties

Elizabethan England, Plate 24: Tableware, including saltcellar, spoon, knife and covered cup. Plate 32: Embroidered table cover.

LAWRENCE, WILLIAM J., *Those Nut-cracking Elizabethans,* p. 127: Title page to Greene's *Friar Bacon and Friar Bungay,* 1630 (shows pipe and tabor, scenic giant head, and stool, chair, and table).

The National Geographic Magazine, September, 1951, p. 424: Lute (1598) at the Folger Shakespeare Library, Washington, D.C.

VICTORIA AND ALBERT MUSEUM, *Elizabethan Embroidery* (Pamphlet 5): Photographs of domestic upholstery and drapery, as well as of costume.

——, *Tudor Domestic Silver* (Pamphlet 6): Photographs of tableware, ewers, basins, jugs, etc.

WHANSLAW, H. W., *The Bankside Stage-book,* p. 192: Rapiers and daggers. P. 199: Bottles and jugs. P. 211: Virginal. P. 213: Viols. P. 214: Rebec, lute, psaltery. P. 216: Recorder, shawm, hornpipe, cornet. P. 229: Pipe and tabor.

Part Two

Actors & Acting

I

Actors & the Acting Companies of Elizabethan London

It was the happiness of the Actors of those times to have such Poets as these to instruct them and write for them; and no less those Poets, to have such docile and excellent Actors to act their plays as Field and Burbage.

Richard Flecknoe, *Short Discourses of the English Stage* (1664)

As far as actors are concerned they, as I noticed in England, are daily instructed as it were in a school, so that even the most eminent actors have to allow themselves to be instructed by the dramatists, which arrangement gives life and ornament to a well-written play, so that *it is no wonder that the English players* (I speak of the skilled ones) *surpass and have the advantage of others.*

Johannes Rhenanus, preface to his adaptation of Tomkis's *Lingua, or the Combat of the Tongue and the Five Senses* (1613)

THE GLOBE begins to emerge from the twilight of the past into the clear light of a summer day. Within the "wooden O", a boisterous crowd fills the air with shouts, cries, laughter, and snatches of song. In the yard, there are abuse and blows as the groundlings fight for front-line places round the stage. In the galleries, the gorgeously gowned matrons of the City settle their farthingales, straighten their head tires, and fold their ringed hands in their velvet laps. Their merchant husbands gather the ends of their fur-bordered gowns between their knees and lean their slashed and braided arms on the balcony rail. Lean apprentices cast speculative glances at solitary women who, unidentifiable behind their masks, sit amid the splendour of velvet, satin, rare lace, and cobweb lawn in silence—withdrawn, discreet. A courtesan or lady of the Court? Who can say? On the stage, exquisite young lords lounge and display their magnificence with languid grace.

The sun is high. A golden light pours into the playhouse, and a glow reflected back from the walls brims up and overflows at the thatch-edged lip of the cup.

Behind the walls of the tiring house, hired men fidget in their finery; the property master checks the "platte" with the line of furniture and properties waiting in the order of their use; the prompter licks a preparatory thumb.

The noise in the yard dies down, all heads are thrown back, all eyes watch the man who has appeared on the platform high overhead. In the silence the snapping of the house flag on the pole above the tower can be heard, and the calls of the watermen from the river sounding thin and plaintive. The man raises a trumpet and sends three clear, full, prolonged notes into the summer air! Below on the stage, one of the side doors has opened. There is a stir as the crowd suddenly leans forward, there is the faint sighing sound of indrawn breath; expectancy has drawn attention as taut as a bow-string. Glowing with colour, glistening with sheen of silk, sparkling with gold and silver, the velvet and brocade of their garments sweeping the rushes with a rich susurrus, the actors enter—the men and boys for whom Shakespeare wrote his plays.

Let us look at them. Do they represent any one type or class? Do they reflect a common heritage? Where do they come from? Who are they?

These actors, like their predecessors, contemporaries, and successors, reflect no common heritage, conform to no one social class, come from no one type of environment, but, in a strange way, illustrate the vicissitudes of all players down through the centuries. At this time in the City of London there were, singly and in groups, representatives of every type of actor known to history. There were, for instance, itinerant men who, singly or in small groups, had arrived from the countryside where, as minstrels, "tumbling boys", strolling players, and animal leaders, they had offered their various forms of entertainment on village greens, fairgrounds, and in and about market places. Such men were the descendants of the professional actors and entertainers of the Roman theatres, who, finding their occupation gone with the decline of the Empire, wandered over the countries of Europe in search of a livelihood. As time went on, some of their descendants found noble and royal patrons, and they turn up as jesters and "interlude plaiers" attached to the households of nobility and the courts of kings. In the castles of noblemen they performed at the festivals of Christmas, New Year, Twelfth Night, Easter, and Whitsuntide, and on the occasions of family celebrations, such as birthdays, christenings, and weddings, but at other times in the year they were free to perform when and where they pleased. A certain security resulted from the "rewards" given by their patron, and his uniform and badge, which they wore, assured them of a certain amount of respect from the heads of other noble houses or from civic authorities in the towns where they might apply to show their skill.

As far back as the reign of Richard III, we hear of four "interlude plaiers" being attached to the household of the King, and by the reign of Henry VIII the number had increased to eight, a number subsequently retained by Edward VI, Mary, and Elizabeth. The members of these royal groups were also allowed to perform outside the Court, but when in residence they often augmented the fitful bounty of their sovereigns by working as servants in the royal household.[1]

The ecclesiastical actors of the early Church drama were represented by the bands of boy choristers who, under royal patronage, became the famous Children of Paul's and Children of the Chapel Royal. These latter, as we know, became serious rivals to the professional adult companies.

Great-grandchildren of the medieval guild actors, who must be considered as folk, or amateur, performers, still appeared in folk plays and mummings in Shakespeare's day, and, although the annual cycles of mysteries had fallen into disuse, there is an account of one being performed as late as the reign of James I. In London (and, indeed, in almost all cities and large towns in England) various types of civic shows, which had been a feature of medieval spectacles, still flourished. They consisted of stationary pageants, triumphal arches, and street theatres with figures, real or painted, representing virtues, the Muses, and the like, which were drawn up along the route taken by some royal or noble visitor to the city.[2] Although these amateur performances were spectacular rather than verbal, they served to keep alive interest and participation in theatrical art, while the elaborate painted scenery designed and built by clever artists and craftsmen, which was of an especially high order, made a direct contribution to the decorative designs of the first professional theatres.

Here, then, were three types of actors reflecting the classical and the medieval stage traditions—both ecclesiastical and secular. To them we must now add the amateurs of the more privileged groups of society and so fill out a picture of stage-struck England which was contemporary with, and,

---

[1] The last glimpse of Elizabeth's "interlude plaiers" that history reveals is as touring entertainers at Stratford-on-Avon, 1568–1569.
[2] There is one survival of this to be seen today in the Lord Mayor's Show.

perhaps, in no small degree responsible for, the high standard of professional acting.

The study of classical drama in the universities and schools led to the presentation of the plays of Terence, Seneca, Plautus, and Aristophanes, and "masters" and their scholars began to write plays in the classical manner for performance in institutions of learning, in spite of Puritan opposition. In grammar school a boy at an early age might start acting classical plays in Latin and Greek and continue until leaving school. At college, in emulation of his instructors and fellow scholars, he might try his hand at playwriting and, in all, receive, besides this practice and experience in the actual composition of plays, a pretty comprehensive grounding of dramaturgy as a whole. The results of this early and continuous training are exemplified by the University Wits, inpecunious young B.A.s who, starting as amateurs, became the early Elizabethan professional playwrights and men of the London theatres. Their scholarly training and their drastic criticism of the contemporary stage helped to raise the whole standard of plays and players. From their ranks came such men as Lodge, Peele, Nash, Greene, and Marlowe, who brought to Elizabethan drama their learning and wit, their sparkling talent, and, in the case of Marlowe, fiery genius.

The students at the Inns of Court, who belonged, for the most part, to the families of the nobility and to those of the affluent gentry class, were ardent amateur actors, and there are many tributes attesting to their excellence. But by far the most illustrious group of amateurs was to be found at the Court. Starting with the enthusiasm of Elizabeth and James I for all forms of dramatic entertainment, the Court gradually became the patron and employer of artists, poets, musicians, costume and scenic designers and skilled craftsmen of many kinds for the production of magnificent masques. Performing in these lavish spectacles were lords and ladies of the Court, and, later, in the reign of James, members of the royal household. Although this type of entertainment did not call for great acting skill, yet it did require that the performers sing, dance, move with grace and purpose, and, on occasion, speak verse intelligibly.

The picture is now complete, and we realize that, in all walks of life, from the lowest to the highest, men and women were attending theatrical performances of one kind or another in schools, universities, Inns of Court, town halls, market places, halls of the nobility, the yards of inns, and the playhouses. In all walks of life, there was participation in various types of dramatic performance. There was not a group in the heterogeneous audience of Shakespeare's theatre that did not contain some members who had had acting experience—the "stinkards" in the yards, in folk plays and mummings;

the burghers in the galleries, in street theatres and civic pageantry; the fops and lordlings on the sides of the stage and in the gentlemen's rooms, in plays at the universities, at the Inns of Court, in private performances in the houses of the nobility, and in the masques at Court. It is even safe to say that the greater part of the Globe audience had some knowledge or experience of acting and dramatic presentation and that they looked upon plays and spectacles from the actor's, as well as from the audience's, point of view.

On the stage itself, the companies of the public playhouses were composed basically of men whose forebears had been, for generations, professional entertainers. Some of them had been "tumbling boys", some, itinerant "jig-makers", and some came from groups of interlude players under noble patronage, but with them were also talented amateurs and, later, young actors who had been trained in the fine tradition of the Children of Paul's and the Children of the Chapel Royal, and who had spent their childhood in and about the Court. It is to one such heterogeneous group of players that we shall turn, in the next chapter, for information relative to the acting of Shakespeare's plays.

The skill and popularity of these acting companies grew steadily,[1] and patrons not only presented their "servants" in performances before the Queen on the occasion of her visits to their castles and manors, but brought them to London to perform at Court. It became a mark of distinction for a noble to lend his patronage to a group of players, and there is no doubt that competition among the companies must have been keen.

In 1583, we find Sir Francis Walsingham, at the Queen's high-handed request, taking twelve of the best actors from these companies to form a group known as "the Queen's Men". Following the usual custom, they received liveries and badges but were a little more fortunate than their fellows inasmuch as they also received a regular, though small, stipend from the royal exchequer. However, after the death of Tarleton, the popular and talented clown of the group, they do not seem to have been able to compete with the companies who now owned and operated their own playhouses. On this account they were forced to go into the provinces to find places for their performances. They were called to Court less and less frequently, the Queen commanding the services of the companies of the public playhouses in their stead. Finally they did not return to London at all, and the few members left alive lost, at the time of the Queen's death in 1603, their right to royal name and stipend.

The company of which Shakespeare became a member and in which he remained for the rest of his professional life may be said to have started in 1564 under the patronage of Lord Hunsdon. By 1581 there was a change

[1] There were twenty-four such companies in England during Shakespeare's lifetime.

of personnel and a reorganization of the company, and in that same year
their patron, who was now deputy Lord Chamberlain, brought them to
Court to play before the Queen. In 1585, when their patron became Lord
Chamberlain, we find them under the title of "the Lord Chamberlain's
Men" in conjunction with another company under the patronage of Lord
Admiral Howard. It is possible that both companies lost members to the
Queen's Men and that such merging was advantageous to both. However,
this arrangement does not seem to have lasted long. The last time we hear
of their performing together is in 1586, when on January 6 they appeared
before the Queen. After the terrible ravages of the plague in 1594, a new
company emerged and from this time on they seem to have settled in
London, with the exception of brief periods in 1596, 1597, and 1601, when
we hear of them in the provinces.[1] At first they played in summer at the
Theatre and the Curtain, both houses possibly belonging to their manager,
James Burbage, and in winter at the innyards of the City.

We first hear of Shakespeare as an actor-playwright in 1592, and as a
member of the Chamberlain's Men in 1594. In 1599, the company moved
to their new playhouse, the Globe. The two theatres known as the "first"
and "second" Globe respectively were the homes of the company for the
rest of Shakespeare's life and long after. Not until 1642, when all the theatres
were closed by order of the Puritans, did the company cease to occupy the
Globe as summer quarters. After the death of Elizabeth in 1603, the famous
company came under the patronage of James I, and from that time on were
known as "the King's Men". In 1609, the private theatre at Blackfriars
became their winter home.

When we consider the restrictions that the repertory-company system
imposed on the Elizabethan playwright, our appreciation of Shakespeare's
work takes on an added degree of wonder and respect, for it becomes
evident that narrowing necessity had no power to restrict or inhibit his
genius, and that this ability to reconcile practical demands with creative
imagination made him the popular and successful man of the theatre that his
contemporaries approved and applauded.

Let us look at the preliminary considerations in regard to the actors
that had to be faced before the playwright of that day could give form to the
play. First he had to take into account the particular ability of his principal
actors, together with the age and physical appearance of each one; and then
he had to consider the number of actors, apprentices, and "hired men"
available for the cast.

[1] In 1596, their patron died, and for a time the company was known as the "servantes
of the late Lord Chamberlayne and now servantes of Lord Hunsdon". This Lord Hunsdon,
son and heir of their patron, became Chamberlain himself in 1596, and after this the
company reverted to their old title of "the Lord Chamberlain's Men".

An investigation of these considerations in the light of what is known about the actors and acting in the Elizabethan playhouses will be of inestimable value to the scholar-player, for from it he will get not only ideas of the physical types and chief characteristics of the leading parts in Shakespeare's plays, but some hint of the delivery of his lines that Shakespeare himself expected.

II

The Actors in Shakespeare's Company

POLONIUS: "The best actors in the world, either for tragedy, comedy, history, pastoral, pastoral-comical, historical-pastoral, tragical-historical, tragical-comical-historical-pastoral, scene individual, or poem unlimited; Seneca cannot be too heavy, nor Plautus too light. For the law of writ and the liberty, these are the only men."

Hamlet, II, 2

THE ELIZABETHAN playwright was frequently influenced and restricted by considerations that are almost unknown to the playwright of today. For instance, many of them wrote for one company only and were compelled to write plays adapted to the personnel of that company; it was, in fact, type-casting in reverse. The leading parts were fashioned to fit the leading actors (who were often not only permanent members but actually shareholders in the company) and the young boy apprentices, who played the women's parts as long as their youth lasted.

When John Heminges and Henry Condell (two actors of Shakespeare's company) published the First Folio of the plays in 1623, they included a list of all the leading actors who had appeared in the plays up to that time.[1] This list included the sharers and the apprentices—many of the latter became sharers during and after Shakespeare's attachment to the company—and

[1] Since many of these names will appear in the pages that follow, it may be of interest to have at hand the list as it appeared in the First Folio: "The Names of the Principall Actors in all these Playes—William Shakespeare, Richard Burbadge, John Hemmings, Augustine Phillips, William Kempt, Thomas Poope, George Bryan, Henry Condell, William Slye, Richard Cowly, John Lowine, Samuell Crosse, Alexander Cooke, Samuel Gilburne, Robert Armin, William Ostler, Nathan Field, John Vnderwood, Nicholas Tooley, William Ecclestone, Joseph Taylor, Robert Benfield, Robert Gough, Richard Robinson, John Shancke, John Rice" (from Chambers, (Sir) Edmund K., *William Shakespeare*, Vol. II, p. 77).

represents both permanent and temporary actors associated with the production of the plays for a period of approximately twenty-three years. Although little is known of their personal lives, with the exception of the outstandingly famous, yet it is possible to deduce their types and special "lines" from the casts of certain plays that are extant, and this in turn enables us to see at a glance how the personnel of the acting company determined to a great extent the types of plays. For instance, between 1590 and 1594 the company was predominantly light, having Will Kempe and Thomas Pope, both low comedians; John Heminges and Augustine Phillips, character comedians; and George Bryan, who was a "straight" though not strong actor—and we find Shakespeare writing *The Comedy of Errors*, *The Two Gentlemen of Verona*, and *Love's Labour's Lost*. When young Richard Burbage joined the company in 1594, Condell, high-comedy actor, and William Sly, character actor, had just graduated from apprenticeship. As a result, the balance of comedy and tragedy was easier to maintain—and from this time until 1597 Shakespeare wrote *Richard III*, *Romeo and Juliet*, *Richard II*, *King John*, and *The Merchant of Venice*. In 1597, Bryan, a serious actor, was replaced by Richard Cowley, a comedian, and the balance tipped toward comedy—and the next two years saw *Henry V*, *The Taming of the Shrew*, *The Merry Wives of Windsor*, *Much Ado about Nothing*, and *As You Like It*. In 1599, Will Kempe, the famous slapstick comedian, left the company, and his place was taken soon after by Robert Armin, a quieter and far more subtle comedian—and from this time on the clowns in the plays alter noticeably, Feste in *Twelfth Night* being the first of this new type. There seems to have been little or no alteration in the company for the next three years, which saw the production of *All's Well That Ends Well*, *Measure for Measure*, *Troilus and Cressida*, and *Julius Caesar*. But in 1603 the comedian Pope died and was replaced by Lowin, a "villain" type, and the *major* humorous actor was succeeded by a graduating apprentice, an inexperienced *minor* actor of the same type. At the same time Nicholas Tooley and Alexander Cooke graduated from apprenticeship, the former a comedian but one who specialized in major comico-villains and gulls. The company was now heavily loaded on the tragedy side, and from 1603 to 1608 Shakespeare wrote *Hamlet*, *Othello*, *King Lear*, *Macbeth*, *Antony and Cleopatra*, *Coriolanus*, and *Timon of Athens*. In 1608, the company began to alter radically. William Sly and Lawrence Fletcher died and Shakespeare wished to retire, or perhaps had already done so. With the Blackfriars private theatre for their winter home, a more ambitious year's programme could be planned, and this called for an extension of personnel. Breaking their strict rule, which hitherto had allowed only their own graduating apprentices to fill sharers' vacancies, the company took in young actors from the disintegrating company of the Children of the Queen's Revels; of these we know that William Ostler and John Underwood were two, and that they were later joined by the famous Nat Field. The plays Shakespeare wrote for this new company, which included skilful actors trained in the exquisite and sophisticated style of the Children's companies, were *Cymbeline*, *The Winter's Tale*, and *The Tempest*.

Shakespeare may have thought, as did Stanislavski, that a repertory company should consist of a group of players so matched in excellence that they could share equal honours in popular esteem. But already, in Shakespeare's time, the "star" system had started, and, with a few exceptions, has been taken for granted by playwright, actor, and audience ever since. Which came first—the playwright who built a play round a central figure, or the actor whose ability and physique suggested a role of major importance? It all started with Marlowe, of course, who first wrote "one-man" plays, but could he have dared to trust a single man with the responsibility of Tamerlane, for instance, or Doctor Faustus if there had not been to hand an actor of such gigantic stature and tremendous voice as Edward Alleyn?

With such a system introduced to and accepted by the public, it was inevitable that Shakespeare should write plays in terms of a "leading man", and that, as time went on and the actor who always played the star parts became increasingly competent and popular, that central figure should become more and more the core of his tragedies. But this would not have happened, perhaps, had there not been, besides Alleyn, another star rising in the Elizabethan firmament in the person of Richard Burbage, the talented young son of James Burbage, and had not this actor joined Shakespeare's company in 1594. A brief outline of the life of Richard Burbage will give us some idea of the actor for whom Shakespeare wrote leading parts for over seventeen years.

Richard Burbage was born about 1573, and, like all professionals of his time, must have begun to act when he was ten years old. We do not know, but there can be little doubt, that he started his career under the tutelage of his father, and he must have played in the companies that came under his father's control at the Theatre and at the second playhouse, possibly built by his father, the Curtain. But his experience does not seem to have been limited to these companies, for in 1592 we hear of his playing in the provinces with Edward Alleyn in the Lord Strange's company, and in 1593, when Alleyn returned to London, he is said to have taken Alleyn's place in the provinces as leading man.

In 1594, when, after the terrible plague year, the newly reorganized Lord Chamberlain's Men emerged, Richard Burbage was their leading actor, and, as such, a sharer. He continued to hold this position up to within a few weeks of his death in 1619.

From 1594 to 1602, Shakespeare wrote youthful leads for him. In fact, Burbage's actual age is sometimes mentioned as that of the character he was playing: in 1596, Prince Hal (*Henry IV, Parts I* and *II*) is said to be twenty-two; in 1599, as Henry V, he is twenty-five; and as Hamlet, in 1603, he is thirty. After this Shakespeare's leading characters become more and more mature to fit Richard's increasing years,[1] and in the part of Antony (*Antony and Cleopatra*) he is said to be going grey. Shakespeare's last period of writing includes leading men of advanced years, until finally, in 1613, we find Burbage playing Wolsey in *Henry VIII*. But it is not age alone that is accounted for in the parts, but also changes in physical appearance.[2] Take his figure, for example: Prince Hal is "thin"; Hamlet is "fat and scant of breath"; Antony, Coriolanus, and Posthumus are all weighty, even portly, men. Further, the Nurse in *Romeo and Juliet* tells us that he was handsome and graceful; Rosalind, that his hair was chestnut brown. We do not know the colour of his eyes, but, since they were not blue (Rosalind again), they might have been brown. As a young man he either could not or did not grow a beard, that indispensable sign of manhood in Elizabethan times, and allusions are made to this lack in the characters of Prince Hal, Orlando, and Claudio (*Much Ado about Nothing*). That Burbage later grew a beard is evident from the self-portrait painted in middle life and now hanging in The College of God's Gift at Dulwich in South London.

An actor of renown, a painter, a citizen of repute, a man of property, the acquaintance of the lordly and the great, Richard Burbage is far from being one of the "Comon Players", "Roges, Vacaboondes, and Sturdy Beggers" of the statute of 1572.[3]

The lives and fortunes of all the professional actors of the London theatres were now taking a turn for the better, and by the end of the century we find that most of the leading men of the companies were of substance and repute. Not until the nineteenth century, when actors began to attain the honour of knighthood, did they stand so high in public favour and esteem. This is particularly true of Shakespeare's company, as a brief record of the lives of the sharers will show.

John Heminges was born sometime during 1556 or 1557, and he is believed to have been about thirty-one when he joined the company in

---

[1] One exception to this is the part of King Lear, a far older man than Richard Burbage was in 1605.

[2] For personal allusions to the actors in Shakespeare's plays, see Baldwin, T. N., *The Organization and Personnel of the Shakespearean Company*, Appendix VI, pp. 394–514, and Appendix VIII, pp. 441–4.

[3] For the document, see Chambers, (Sir) Edmund K., *The Elizabethan Stage*, Vol. IV, pp. 269–71.

1588. Like all Elizabethans he was versatile, and it is difficult to say whether he was better as actor or as business manager. Certainly the sound finance of the company was due to his shrewdness and honesty, and as Shakespeare's business adviser and well-loved colleague he was remembered in his will. Heminges and his close friend and fellow actor Henry Condell were church-wardens to St. Mary Aldermanbury, Cripplegate, and, with Condell, Heminges was joint editor of the first collected edition of Shakespeare's plays, published in 1623. He was closely associated with all public and private activities of the company. In 1599, he is, together with Richard and Cuthbert Burbage, Phillips, Pope, and Kempe, a member of the syndicate formed for the purpose of building the Globe, and later one of the seven sharers who took over the Blackfriars lease; he, together with Richard Burbage, was joint executor of the will of their fellow actor Augustine Phillips. In 1600, he is one of the members mentioned in the Royal Patent. A fine citizen, a kindly father, a beloved and honoured friend, he attracted the respect and admiration of all classes of men, both for himself and for the company of which he was an outstanding member. As an actor he was, by reason of his age and particular ability, the interpreter of the old men in Shakespeare's plays, and we see old gentlemen of either humorous or whimsical or hot-tempered or irascible turn of mind appearing in almost every play. Here are a few of the parts he undoubtedly played: Boyet in *Love's Labour's Lost*, Aegeon in *The Comedy of Errors*, Duke of Milan in *The Two Gentlemen of Verona*, Hastings in *Richard III*, Egeus in *A Midsummer Night's Dream*, Capulet in *Romeo and Juliet*, Leonato in *Much Ado about Nothing*, Exeter in *Henry V*, Duke Senior in *As You Like It*, Polonius in *Hamlet*, Brabantio in *Othello*, Kent in *King Lear*, and Gonzalo in *The Tempest*.

One of the most famous members of Shakespeare's company, indeed sharing honour as a box-office draw with Richard Burbage, was the low-comedy clown Will Kempe. Born sometime in 1554 or 1555, we first hear of him in 1583, when he was attached as a "jesting player" to the Earl of Leicester's "boys". This group was touring the Low Countries in 1585 and 1586. In the reorganization of Lord Strange's Men in 1593, his name appears on a licence granted to the company at that time. In 1594, he heads the list of players in Shakespeare's company, a placing which may point to his popularity, or may merely indicate his seniority.

Kempe is essentially of the strolling-player type, and his comings and goings between England and the Continent had by 1589 earned for him an international reputation. He seems never to have stayed long with any one group, and during his five years' attachment to the Chamberlain's Men it has been suggested that he was away on one of his foreign tours during 1595 and 1596. The reason for this belief is the fact that his type of part drops out of Shakespeare's plays at that time. But this is scarcely conclusive evidence since it must be remembered that Kempe was an extemporary wit and may have made up his own parts, as the low comedians did in the melodrama of the nineteenth and early twentieth centuries. That he did this is further substantiated by the fact that we know he played Peter in *Romeo and Juliet*, and the part, as it comes down to us, is too small to have been played by anyone as important as Kempe unless he padded it—which is what he undoubtedly did. Will Kempe's name is joined with those of the four other sharers in the syndicate that built the Globe, but a year later (1599) he sold his share, and there is every reason to believe that he did not return to the company. In the spring of 1600, he staged his famous publicity stunt of dancing from London to Norwich, starting on the 11th of February and arriving on the 11th of March. Kempe's account of this feat was entered in the Stationers' Register on April 22, 1600, as "Kemp's morris to Nor-wiche". Soon after this he went to Italy and Germany but returned to England in September of 1601. The last we hear of him is as making a loan from Henslowe, the manager of the Admiral's Men, and of being attached to Worcester's Men during the winter of 1602–1603. We do not hear of him again except that he is mentioned as dead in *An Apology for Actors* by Thomas Heywood (*c.* 1612). Apart from Kempe's account of his dance to Norwich, which he called "Kemp's Nine Daies Wonder, Performed in a Daunce from London to Norwich", he wrote scripts for his low-comedy turns. These turns, known as "jigs", were the indispensable tailpieces of Elizabethan drama up until the turn of the century. Printed with a play called *A Knack to Know a Knave*, in 1594, is "Kemp's Applauded Merriments of the Men of Goteham in Receiving the King of Goteham".

Kempe was the zany type of clown and very versatile. His greatest success in Shakespeare's plays was doubtless Dogberry in *Much Ado about Nothing*. But, popular though he was, his independence and vanity must have made him a doubtful blessing to any group of actors. It is thought by some that Shakespeare made him satirize himself as Bottom in *A Midsummer Night's Dream* and that all the railing against the clowns contained in Hamlet's advice to the players refers to Kempe's unfair and vulgar tricks. Apart from Peter and Dogberry, parts he is known to have played, Shakespeare must have had him in mind when he created Launce in *The Two Gentlemen of Verona*, Bottom in *A Midsummer Night's Dream*, Launcelot Gobbo in *The Merchant of Venice*, Shallow in *Henry IV*, and Grumio in *The Taming of the Shrew*.

One feature that Elizabethan clowns seem to have had in common is smallness of stature. We know that Tarleton was tiny, as was his "adopted son", Armin. Kempe is referred to as thin, bearded, and short, and this is all we know of his physical appearance. There is one contemporary woodcut of him, but it is doubtful whether this can be considered as an actual portrait.

When Will Kempe left the company, his place as chief comedian was taken, as has been said, by Robert Armin, and from the time when this alteration took place to the time of the writing of his last play Shakespeare replaced the knockabout, low-comedian type with one that is a direct result of Robert Armin's peculiar ability.

We do not know when Armin was born, but, if we are to believe Tarleton in his *Tarleton's Jest*, he was a boy serving his apprenticeship to a goldsmith in the City of London in 1581.

This bright little cockney wag caught the great clown's fancy, and Tarleton went so far as to say that he considered him as his adopted son and prophesied that the boy would succeed him as a comedian. However, it is as an author that he first earned a reputation, with a preface to *A Brief Resolution of the Right Religion* in 1590, and *Foole upon Foole, or Six Sorts of Sottes* in 1600. The latter must have been popular for we find that an enlarged edition, under the title of *A Nest of Ninnies*, was published in 1608. This work, which is really a collection of essays on psychologically abnormal characters, is particularly interesting to us, for it marks the strange pre-occupation of Armin with all manifestations of real or assumed insanity.

In 1609, when a play by him entitled *Two Maids of Moreclacke* was revived in a performance given by the Children of the King's Revels, in the preface of the edition published that year Armin regrets that he cannot "*again*" play John for them. This character is one of his "ninnies", "John of the Hospitall", and the fact that he had at some time played the part shows that he used his study of abnormal mentality to supply himself with parts suitable to his own peculiar type of acting. Armin saw the "innocent", or idiot, as a figure of fun, as did most of his contemporaries, and, as such, legitimate material for the purpose of entertainment.

With the advent into Shakespeare's company of this subtle and complex man, this skilled musician and sweet singer, there appears Feste in *Twelfth Night*—Feste, the sly professional jester attached to the household of the Countess Olivia, who incites others to folly, makes shrewd observations with the licence permitted to the feeble-minded, and sings his way into the favour of all, extracting gratuities as he goes. According to Feste's description of himself, he is neither tall nor thin, which leads us to imagine Armin as a little fat man with a sweet voice, a nimble wit, and an unusual ability to play every kind of fool.[1] After Feste in 1600, there follow in rapid succession Touchstone in *As You Like It* and the Clown in *All's Well That Ends Well*.

---

[1] The woodcut on the title page of *Two Maids of Moreclacke* may be a portrait of Armin. This is reprinted in the Shakespeare Society's *Fools and Jesters* (1842).

In 1603, there is First Gravedigger in *Hamlet*, followed closely by Evans in *The Merry Wives of Windsor* and Pompey in *Measure for Measure*. Later come the Clown in *Othello*, the Fool in *Lear* (a part greatly to Armin's taste, no doubt), the Porter in *Macbeth*, the fool in *Timon of Athens*, the Clown in *Antony and Cleopatra*, Boult in *Pericles*, First Citizen in *Coriolanus*, the Clown in *The Winter's Tale*, and Trinculo in *The Tempest*.[1]

Robert Armin's name appears in a list of the company's actors in 1610, but not in one of 1611, and we must conclude that he dropped out or died sometime within that year.

A glance at predominant types that appear in the plays will give us more than a hint of the characteristics of the rest of the leading actors of Shakespeare's company.

There is the middle-aged swashbuckler who belongs in the category of "high comedians". Whether he is playing the cowardly braggart or the ranting villain, his physical attributes are the same: he is a tall, heavy man with a stentorian voice. Such a man was Thomas Pope, who probably joined the company in 1594 and who died sometime between 1603 and 1604. He doubtless played Armado in *Love's Labour's Lost*, Parolles in *All's Well That Ends Well*, Aaron in *Titus Andronicus*, Fluellen in *Henry V*, Falstaff in *Henry VI, Parts I and II*, and in *The Merry Wives of Windsor*, Petruchio in *The Taming of the Shrew*, Sir Toby Belch in *Twelfth Night*, and, since it was undoubtedly played as a high-comedy part, Shylock in *The Merchant of Venice*.

There is the handsome and dashing near-villain who is, in the early plays, the fickle or unprincipled lover. Suffolk in *Henry VI*, Proteus in *The Two Gentlemen of Verona*, Berowne in *Love's Labour's Lost*, and Antipholus of Ephesus in *The Comedy of Errors* are all examples of the type. Later, similar characteristics are found in the moody, gay, or aggressive noblemen, such as Bolingbroke in *Richard II*, Don John in *Much Ado about Nothing*, Duke Frederick in *As You Like It*, Gratiano in *The Merchant of Venice*, and Bertram in *All's Well That Ends Well*. Augustine Phillips, who was in youth "complete in feature", is believed to be the prototype of these dashing unprincipled young men. That he later became lanky and cadaverous may account for his playing the "lean and hungry" Cassius and may also have determined the sour pomposity of Malvolio in *Twelfth Night*. It has been suggested that Claudio in *Hamlet* is a study of Phillips in the last years of his life.[2]

And so they pass before our eyes as we read the plays: William Sly,

---

[1] If Armin played Trinculo, it must be assumed that *The Tempest* was first performed before 1611.

[2] Baldwin, Thomas Whitfield, *The Organization and Personnel of the Shakespearean Company*, Appendix VI, pp. 407-8.

the fiery young swordsman who undoubtedly played Hotspur in *Henry IV*, Tybalt in *Romeo and Juliet*, and Laertes in *Hamlet*; Richard Cowley, thin-faced and forlorn, playing jilted lovers, always with the laugh against him in such parts as William in *As You Like It*, Sir Andrew Aguecheek in *Twelfth Night*, and Roderigo in *Othello*; Henry Condell of regal and dignified mien playing sympathetic second juvenile leads, such as Paris in *Romeo and Juliet*, and, later, Antonio in *The Merchant of Venice*, Malcolm in *Macbeth*, and Edgar in *King Lear*; George Bryan, the fine elocutionist for whom splendid and impressive speeches were written, such as the dying speech of John of Gaunt in *Richard II*, the soliloquy of Friar Laurence in *Romeo and Juliet*, and all the splendour and ringing grandeur of the speech of kings, potentates, and ecclesiastical dignitaries.

Glancing over the names of the actors given in the First Folio of Shakespeare's plays, we find that here is represented every type of professional actor known to the period. From the city streets, noblemen's houses, and apprentices' garrets, from country schools and village cottages, from the very hedgerows, men of various talents and diverse experience drifted together and gave service and loyalty, some for as long as twenty-five years. Here is the group of "fellowes", many of whom, to a certain degree, helped to shape the characters of the greatest actor-playwright of all times.

Numbers and Classification

Most amateur directors, when considering a Shakespearean play for production, will view the long lists of the casts with dismay, but a glance at the organization and numbers of the Elizabethan repertory company shows him a way of presenting these imposing numbers of characters without running into difficulties, financial or otherwise. It will also give him practical hints that may apply to the organizing and selection of his own group.

Shakespeare's company, at the time of his death, consisted of twelve leading actors, and this seems to have been the usual number in the successful London companies. Of these twelve, six or seven might be "sharers", that is, outstanding and popular artists who were in receipt of all entrance money at the door (the extra payments for seats, "rooms", and stools on the stage being collected by the "house-holder" or by the builder of the theatre and his backers, who, in turn, paid rent to the owner of the land on which the playhouse stood). When we consider that the entrance fee was only a penny for old plays and two pence for new, and that the sharers had to pay the stagehands, hired men, wig-and-costume "masters", prompter, and, possibly, musicians, and bear the heavy expense of costuming the plays, it is surprising to find how many of them died comparatively wealthy men. But we have to consider that at the turn of the century the sharers demanded and got half the takings of the galleries; that sometimes, as in the case of the group of sharers of which Shakespeare was one, they were actually joint owners of the playhouses in which they performed—in this case, the Globe and the Blackfriars theatres; that they received considerable additions to their incomes from the special performances they gave at Court, in the Inns of Court, and in noblemen's houses; and finally that the value of money at that time was nearly twenty-five times higher than it is today. These facts certainly help to explain those fortunes in money and lands seen in the wills of the actors, and it becomes easy to understand that their "shares", on their deaths, were important enough to be willed either to members of their families, or to the company to be divided among the other sharers.

In the case of Shakespeare's company, their sound finance and lack of litigation, so common in that day, was due to the fact that Heminges not only was their excellent man of business, but was himself a sharer. It is no wonder that this sound and prosperous company kept its organization intact for forty-eight years and ceased to function only when all the theatres were closed in 1642.

Supporting the sharers and contributing to the *continuous* excellence of the acting were the apprentices. Starting at the age of ten, these boys may have paid a premium, as all trade apprentices did, but even if they did not, it must have been seven years at least before they received a salary. In the meantime, each one seems to have been attached to a sharer, with whom he lodged and boarded. He was trained by the experienced actor to play the women's parts and also, it has been suggested, the actor's own particular type of part, in order that the boy on attaining manhood might take his master's place on the latter's retirement or death. Of the boys themselves we know little, but that little is significant and enables us to form opinions that have direct bearing on their place and worth in the company. We have to keep in mind, in judging their ability, that here again Shakespeare had to fit his characters to his cast, and when we think of the heroines he created we begin to get a glimpse of the astonishing talent of these youngsters.

In the early chronicle plays, women have but small place, an occurrence which can be partly explained by the type of these plays, which call for the clash of arms in battle and the clash of factions in intrigue and have little concern with "the soft phrase of peace". Moreover, when these plays were written it is doubtful whether there had been time to allow for the years of careful training that was later to prove so beneficial to young actors. So we find that the few chief women characters in the casts of these early plays are, for the most part, women of middle or advanced age, and such parts were always played by men. The few young women, children, and pages that would be played by boys are all minor roles, and well within the scope of children of ten or twelve serving their apprenticeships and "walking on" to get experience. Later, when time had allowed for the requisite training of these boys, we find, in the comedies especially, that women are of first importance, and that in some of these plays the leading lady—Rosalind in *As You Like It* and Portia in *The Merchant of Venice*, for instance—has a part the lines of which far outnumber those of any other role in the play. In the tragedies and Roman plays, which are essentially one-man plays, the women, though subordinate, are of vital importance and call for the most profound art in character delineation and emotional power.

It seems from the few facts we possess that the apprentices were six in number working in pairs. Two would be newcomers of ten years of age or thereabouts, who, at this early stage, would be learning fundamentals, walking on, and sustaining small parts. The next two would be the twelve-to-fourteen age group and would be playing important secondary parts. The last pair, of, say, fifteen to eighteen years, would be leading ladies as long as their voices and physical appearances allowed. After this they would graduate to the adult status and play secondary young men, with the possibility of becoming sharers just ahead. As this third pair left the boys' group, a new pair would be taken on at the ten-year-old level, the second pair would attain the distinction of leading ladies, and so on.

It would seem from the casts that these pairs usually consisted of a beautiful "serious" boy—preferably blond and grey-eyed—yoked with a "comedy" boy of the small brunet type. We can see them as Silvia and Julia (*The Two Gentlemen of Verona*), the Princess of France and Rosaline (*Love's Labour's Lost*), Helena and Hermia (*A Midsummer Night's Dream*), Portia and Nerissa (*The Merchant of Venice*), Bianca and Katharine (*The Taming of the Shrew*), Rosalind and Celia (*As You Like It*), Hero and Beatrice (*Much Ado about Nothing*), Olivia and Viola (*Twelfth Night*), and Cleopatra and Octavia (*Antony and Cleopatra*).

We know a few of these young actors. Robert Gough—or Goffe or Gouch—was a Welsh boy[1] who joined the company under the tutelage of Augustine Phillips. He seems to have been a consistently good actor, playing Juliet at fourteen and Portia near the end of his apprenticeship. William Ecclestone was the small dark boy who must have been his running-mate and played the lively second leads. Sometimes, as Katharine in *The Taming of the Shrew* and as Beatrice in *Much Ado about Nothing*, he evidently played the first lead. We get a hint of the vital high-spirited performance he must have given when we find that after graduation he did not play romantic

---

[1] He undoubtedly sang the Welsh song as Lady Mortimer in *1 Henry IV*, III, 1.

heroes but rollicking singing soldier parts. Samuel Gilburne is another golden-haired, grey-eyed heroine with, as possible partner, the black-haired, black-eyed Jack Wilson, the latter specializing in serious singing heroines—a possible Ophelia and Desdemona. Of John Edmans we know nothing beyond the fact that he was probably the brilliant boy who played Cleopatra, and that in 1617 he left the company to join the provincial company of Queen Anne.

As in the case of the men, the actual physical appearance of the boy actor is often described in the play in which he appears. A boy named James Sands, playing Octavia in *Antony and Cleopatra*, is described by the Messenger as having brown hair, a low forehead, a round face, and "dwarfish" stature, and as speaking with a low voice. Duke Orsino describes the delicate femininity of the disguised Viola (*Twelfth Night*); Rosalind describes the black-eyed Phoebe, and Phoebe gives an ecstatic account of Rosalind (*As You Like It*).

All these hints are obvious guides to the characterization and physical appearance, i.e., make-up, of the heroines. But there is still another point that has to be taken into account, a point made most strongly by such authorities as Sir Walter Raleigh[1] and W. Robertson Davies;[2] and this must be given serious consideration by the modern actress playing a Shakespearean heroine. Since the parts of the heroines were written for boys, Shakespeare was particularly careful to avoid over-emphasis on sex in these parts. Furthermore, such restraint would help to avoid detrimental criticism from the Puritan element in London. So the heroines were acted simply and directly without individual mannerisms or self-conscious display.[3] Always keeping in mind the boy actor, *for whom the part was written*, the young actress of today should allow only so much of her own femininity to emerge as her artistic integrity allows, and in the scenes where she is disguised as a boy, as she is in many of the comedies, should subdue even that little. Uncontrolled emotion must be guarded against with unceasing vigilance, and always she should think of herself as an exquisitely tuned instrument sounding with simplicity and fidelity the loveliest poetry in the English language. The young actress who can do this should go far to refute Sir Walter Raleigh's statement that

with the disappearance of the boy players the poetic drama died in England, and it has had no second life.[4]

[1] Raleigh, (Sir) Walter, *Shakespeare*, p. 120.
[2] Davies, W. Robertson, *Shakespeare's Boy Actors*, pp. 195–200.
[3] It is interesting to notice how little embracing occurs in the love scenes. The kiss in the opening scene between Antony and Cleopatra and those given by Othello to the sleeping Desdemona are two of the rare exceptions.
[4] Raleigh, (Sir) Walter, *loc. cit.*

These two permanent groups, sharers and apprentices, who played all the important parts, formed the heart of the company, but they were, in turn, dependent on the "hired men", those minor actors who were paid a small weekly wage by the actors and hired as they were required. The extraordinary skill and versatility of the humble "extras" will be apparent when we consider that it was for these men that Shakespeare created so many complete small-part characters. This, if nothing else, should convince us of their ability. There is a possibility that the high repute of Shakespeare's company was in part due to the fact that many of its hired men at the Globe and Blackfriars had been members and even sharers of companies that had failed, owing to keen competition and the limited audience in the London of that day.

The various known facts begin to fall into place and the whole picture of the day-by-day life of the company to emerge. We also begin to understand how, with actors of skill and experience to play leads, with boys trained to the highest standard of excellence to play the women, and with men of ability and, possibly, of expert training to play small parts, Shakespeare could write for his company such plays as *Hamlet*, *Macbeth*, *Othello*, and *King Lear*, secure in the conviction of the ability of his actors to perform them.

DOUBLING

To return to the numbers of actors available for the casts. So far we know that there were twelve adults and six boys in the majority of the London companies. And at this point we reconcile those huge casts with this comparatively small number of players by the realization that doubling, one of the oldest expedients of the classical theatres, was still an accepted fact in the English theatre. In the Greek theatre there were only two, or at most three, actors, but these few, with the aid of masks and, doubtless, different-coloured garments, played all the parts in the drama. The interlude players of medieval times, although seldom more than four in number, thought nothing of presenting short sketches with large casts; one, *The Tyde Tarrieth for No Man*, has a cast of eighteen! The strolling-player groups of Shakespeare's own time seem to have consisted of four men and a boy, a number borne out by a reference in *Sir Thomas Moore*.[1] "The king", the "adventurous knight", "the lover", "the humorous man", "the clown", and "the lady" in the group that Hamlet describes before the players appear

---

[1] A play of unknown authorship in which Shakespeare is believed to have had a hand. In line 931, More says to a player, "How manie are ye?" and the player responds, "Ffoure men and a boy, Sir." (See *The Book of Sir Thomas More*, *The Malone Society Reprints*, Oxford University Press, New York, 1911, p. 32.)

suggest five players. But in the performance of "The Mousetrap", as far as it goes, only four characters are presented, and, since it should have been easy for Prologue and Lucianus to double, there might have been only three members in the actual performance.

It will be asked how this doubling could be carried out sufficiently well to be convincing. First as regards the actors: the multiple-disguise man—who survives today in the "quick-change" artist of the Music Halls—must have been a specialist in his own line, and his popularity is confirmed by the fact that Henslowe's company, the Admiral's Men, presented a whole group of plays during Shakespeare's lifetime which featured multiple disguise. In one play, *Look about You*, one character plays seven different parts, many of which appear two or three times during the course of the play. Multiple-disguise work must have been an indispensable part of the hired man's equipment for obtaining work in an Elizabethan repertory company.

To consider the technique of doubling from the playwright's point of view, he had to keep in mind that there could be no meeting of the different characters played by one man, and the considerate playwright would try to finish with one part before presenting the doubling actor with another. William J. Lawrence has pointed out the following facts in the construction of *Hamlet* that illustrate these points:[1]

Act I. Three minor characters begin and end (Francisco, Bernardo, and Marcellus).

Act II. Seven new characters appear (Reynaldo, Rosencrantz, Guildenstern, and four Players (three?)). Three characters disappear (Voltimand, Cornelius, and Reynaldo).

Act III. No new character is introduced. Six old ones disappear at the end of the act (four Players, Polonius, and the Ghost).

Act IV. Five new characters and two new minor parts appear (Fortinbras, Captain, Gentleman, two Danes, minor Servant, and Sailor). Three old ones are withdrawn (Rosencrantz, Guildenstern, and Ophelia).

Act V. Seven new characters are introduced (two Gravediggers, two Priests, Osric, Lord, and Ambassador), and "supers" as mourners.

Only five characters remain throughout the play (Hamlet, Horatio, Laertes, Claudius, and Gertrude).

A careful study of the plays of Shakespeare from this particular point of view will enable the amateur producer to decide on the number of parts that can be doubled, and, if he decides to use this expedient, he will be giving some of his scholar-players the incomparable experience of developing ability to play "character" parts. This will widen their experience and,

---

[1] Lawrence, William J., *Pre-Restoration Stage Studies*, Chap. 3, "The Practice of Doubling and Its Influence on Early Dramaturgy".

if the producer is willing, give them a chance to do a bit of creative interpretation on their own.

We know that the London companies presented as many as forty plays a season, a good half of which were new, so that a leading actor must have played at least thirty parts a season, and when we consider the number of plays performed each week—we know of one instance where Henslowe's company played a different play *every day* for eleven days—the arduousness of the life becomes apparent. Rehearsing all the morning, playing in the afternoon, and memorizing new parts at night would be the daily round of the Elizabethan repertory actor. It is safe to guess that Shakespeare, who carried the added burden of writing and revising plays, would see to it that the parts he wrote for himself were short and that these characters appeared infrequently. This is borne out by the belief that he played Adam in *As You Like It* and the Ghost in *Hamlet*. If the life of the leading members of the cast was strenuous, those of the humble hired men seem almost superhuman, for in their case they had, added to the usual repertory routine, the task of doubling, playing as many as four parts at least in every play.

ACTING IN THE INNYARDS AND PUBLIC PLAYHOUSES

Judging by the crude tragedies of blood of the early sixteenth century, we can conclude that nothing was expected of the actor but mouthing and rant, while the slapstick comedies called for little more than gross clowning.

In 1587, however, the rise of great poetic drama brought the need for men who could speak with power and dignity, and this challenge was taken up with such spirit that the actor became a recognized artist who brought distinction to a now acknowledged profession. The one-man plays of Marlowe, as has been said, saw the beginning of the star system, and it is Marlowe himself who proclaims the change in plays and acting for which he himself was so largely responsible. In the introduction to *Tamerlane* he says:

> "From jigging veins of rhyming mother wits
> And such conceits as clowning keeps in pay,
> We'll lead you to the stately tent of war
> Where you shall hear the Scythian Tamerlane
> Threat'ning the world with high astounding terms."

The years 1587 to 1590, a period of "high astounding terms", are full of tragedies and historical plays which call for little more than vigorous declamation.

By 1590 actors began to appear who were bred to the profession in the metropolitan playhouses. The long, careful training which had previously been the exclusive privilege of the Children of Paul's and the Children of the Chapel Royal was now available to the professional apprentices, attached to secure companies which owned their own playhouses. These competent youngsters began to meet the varied demands made by the brilliant comedies and tragi-comedies that were written for them. The clowns still had their place and the jig[1] still followed the play, but the standard of acting was of a high order on the whole.

Shakespeare's period of great tragedy begins in 1600, and inability of the actors to rise to its demands at first may have been the cause of Hamlet's advice to the players. There is no doubt that Shakespeare felt the need for reform in the actor's art and that he was responsible to a great extent for bringing it about. In fact we can consider that the results of his teaching and advice led to the beginning of modern acting with its emphasis on identification of the actor with the character and the apparent spontaneity of expression of that character in speech, voice, and action.

We are safe, therefore, in considering 1603 to 1613 as one of the periods of great acting on the English stage. After this, there seems to have been a slow decline in acting and in the acknowledged reputation of the actors until the closing of the theatres in 1642.

TRAINING OF ELIZABETHAN ACTORS

It will be well for us now to consider the type of training that the young apprentices received who had the advantage of being connected with the permanent companies of the public playhouses. First and foremost, the boy of ten received instruction and drill in enunciation and voice production, followed by training in music, dancing, and general deportment. He would, for instance, learn to manage his feminine attire with grace and charm. During the years of his initial training he would be constantly in the environment of professional performances and in contact with professional actors, and, as the years went by, he would be participating in the company's productions to a gradually increasing extent. He would not only watch, but himself receive instruction from, the famous playwrights of the day. In many cases these playwrights were, or had been, actors themselves, and, when we consider that, in the case of Shakespeare and Jonson, they created parts for their fellow actors, it becomes evident that they were not only the best but the inevitable directors of their own plays.

[1] The jig was outlawed at the General Session of the Peace for Middlesex, October 1, 1612. According to the Order, the jig was attracting the scum of the City and causing "tumults and outrages wherebye His Majesties peace is often broke." (Chambers, Sir Edmund K., *The Elizabethan Stage*, Vol. IV, p. 340.)

There is no doubt that Shakespeare was an excellent director, demanding a very high standard of acting from his fellow players. The need for reform in interpretation he realized fully, and did not hesitate to mock the actors who strove to please no more than that section of the public who demanded little—and that little, crude and obvious. In *Troilus and Cressida*, I, 3, lines 153–156, we have a comment on the exaggerated stride and stamping used by some actors; in *Antony and Cleopatra*, V, 2, lines 218–219, the problem of the boys' broken voices; in *Richard III*, III, 5, lines 5–9, the external acting that remained as part of the formal and traditional ranting of the old miracle plays and the insincerity of stage tricks; and in *A Midsummer Night's Dream*, I, 2; III, 1; and IV, 1, all the makeshifts and petty jealousies of the tiring house, the selfishness and stupidity of comedians, the pomposity and ignorance of leading men.

But not only do we have Shakespeare's criticisms of current acting. In *Hamlet*, we are in possession of a most intimate account of what he must often have said to the actors at rehearsals, and the advice he gave is so valuable to all actors, at all times, that sincere scholar-players will give it the closest attention. It will be remembered that, quite suddenly, Hamlet, the Prince of Denmark, steps right out of character in order to take coals to Newcastle in the shape of a lesson in acting to the actors who visit Elsinore, and shows at the same time that he is conversant, to a professional degree, with the dramatic coach's demands, despairs, and aspirations. The play stops suddenly at this point, and Shakespeare, not Hamlet, steps forward to say, in the hearing of the audience, that which there was such need to say that he could no longer refrain from a public declaration.

"Speak the speech, I pray you, [he says] as I pronounced it to you, trippingly on the tongue."

That "trippingly" means fluently, which in turn means swiftly and intelligibly. It is a well-established fact that the average time for the presentation of an Elizabethan play was not longer than two and a half hours, and this may have included one intermission, but not the jig at the end. This could mean that the average rate of speech would be about twenty lines a minute. The modern actor will find that speed and intelligibility of speech, especially when the lines contain unusual words and unusual combinations of speech sounds, require continual practice, and it is here that he should start his technical training and continue his most consistent effort.

'But if you mouth it, as many of your players do, [he continues] I had as lief the town crier spoke my lines.'

Here we catch a glimpse of the exaggerated elocution that was common in Shakespeare's day. The stentorian voice and ridiculous formation of speech sounds which still characterize the "calling" of the town crier, wherever that almost obsolete figure appears, were, up to recent times, employed by the old stock-company Shakespearean actor, whose mouthing and ranting of the part of Hamlet have given us that deadly epithet "ham", that is, to act with sound and fury signifying nothing.

"Nor do not saw the air too much with your hand, thus; but use all gently: for in the very torrent, tempest, and—as I may say—whirlwind of passion, you must acquire and beget a temperance that may give it smoothness."

Here we not only get a warning against wild, meaningless gesture, but learn the value of that secret of all great acting, controlled emotion. "Smoothness" is a beautiful word with which to describe the seeming effortlessness that results from temperate and intelligent use of emotional energy.

"O! it offends me to the soul to hear a robustious periwig-pated fellow tear a passion to tatters, to very rags, to split the ears of the groundlings, who for the most part are capable of nothing but inexplicable dumb shows and noise: I would have such a fellow whipped for o'er-doing Termagant; it out-herods Herod: pray you, avoid it."

Here is a description of the type of acting that Shakespeare abhorred, and it is interesting that he exemplifies it by reference to the amateur acting of the old miracle plays. He must have seen a good deal of rustic and provincial acting in and around Stratford and Warwick in his youth and have remembered the effect it had on him when he came to write the scene of the yokels acting the "Nine Worthies" in *Love's Labour's Lost*, and the "hard-handed" men of Athens playing the "lamentable comedy of Pyramus and Thisby" in *A Midsummer Night's Dream*. His gibe at the groundlings is bitter, but their failure to appreciate anything but obvious gesture and rant is nothing to his contempt for the actor who plays down to them.

"Be not too tame neither, but let your own discretion be your tutor: suit the action to the word, the word to the action; with this special observance that you o'erstep not the modesty of nature; for anything so overdone is from the purpose of playing, whose end, both at the first and now, was and is, to hold, as 'twere, the mirror up to nature; to show virtue her own feature, scorn her own image, and the very age and body of the time his form and pressure."

Vapid and devitalized acting, on the other hand, is equally bad, and Shakespeare suggests that the only safe guide to the degree of intensity with which a part is played is the actor's own intelligent judgment, which will not reduce but control emotional energy. All bodily movement should be used in such a way as to augment and enhance the vocal expression of logical and emotional meaning, but here again the effect produced should be one as spontaneous and effortless as artless nature shows. The actor, remembering the unchanging purpose of acting, which is to reflect life, should strive to reproduce not only the emotions of the character he is portraying, but also the contemporary manners of the period in which the play is supposedly taking place.

"Now, this overdone, or come tardy off, though it make the unskilful laugh, cannot but make the judicious grieve; the censure of which one must in your allowance o'erweigh a whole theatre of others."

While over- or under-acting may raise a laugh from the crowd, it will be a matter for regret to the discerning few—the few whose judgment must be the final criterion for the sincere and honest actor.

"O! there be players that I have seen play, and heard others praise, and that highly, not to speak it profanely, that neither having the accent of Christians nor the gait of Christian, pagan, nor man, have so strutted and bellowed that I have thought some of nature's journeymen had made men and not made them well, they imitated humanity so abominably."

Hamlet, or rather Shakespeare, had often heard lavish praise from the undiscerning for artificial and insincere actors whose performances were so wooden that, far from imitating living men, they suggested effigies made by unskilled carpenters who had bungled the job.

". . . And let those that play your clowns speak no more than is set down for them; for there be of them that will themselves laugh, to set on some quantity of barren spectators to laugh too, though in the meantime some necessary question of the play be then to be considered; that's villainous, and shows a most pitiful ambition in the fool that uses it."

In the last remark we hear the director-playwright's voice sounding a warning to his fellow director-playwrights to curb the licence of the clowns on the contemporary stage, first by cancelling the custom of letting them ad-lib their parts and making them keep to a definite text; secondly, by not allowing them to steal serious scenes by diverting the attention of the audience to their mockery of the scene. The anger implicit in these final condemnations suggests personal experience, and it has been suggested (see p. 111) that the lines were levelled at Will Kempe.

In brief, Shakespeare demanded of the actor of his day:

1. Speedy and intelligible speech
2. Controlled and directed emotional energy
3. Naturalness of deportment and gesture
4. Identity of the actor, as far as possible, with the character being portrayed, including a lively awareness of his environment and times
5. Utter disregard for easily won laurels, and serious regard for the comments of the judicious critic

These demands still hold good for all actors in all times and in all places.

Contemporary actors who meet these demands to a remarkable degree are Sir John Gielgud, Sir Laurence Olivier,[1] and Sir Ralph Richardson (see illustrations between pp. 128–129).

---

[1] It is interesting to note that Sir Laurence started his acting career at fifteen by playing, as did the boys in Shakespeare's company, a female role—Katharine in *The Taming of the Shrew* at Stratford-on-Avon.

III

Shakespearean Acting on a Reconstructed Elizabethan Stage

BOTTOM: "Get your apparel together, good strings to your beards, new ribbons to your pumps. . . . Every man look o'er his parts for the short and the long is, our play is preferred."

A Midsummer Night's Dream, IV, 2

IF WE take it for granted that the scholar-player will be performing in a theatre that approximates the Elizabethan playhouse, it follows that he will have to adjust his acting to this particular type of stage and auditorium, and here words of advice and warning may perhaps save him some disconcerting experiences.

We are, happily, in possession of evidence showing how a modern actor feels when he first performs on an Elizabethan stage, and it will be encouraging to consider this before the more technical aspects of the experience.

Some years ago [writes Professor George Pierce Baker] when Ben Jonson's *Silent Woman* was revived at Harvard University, the professional actors, when they first saw the wide expanse of undecorated stage and the eager pittites sitting close up to the very edge of it, almost refused to carry on their work. They said: "These people are too close; we have nothing to set our imaginations afire. All this will chill us inevitably into tameness." But at the end of the first act, to which they had been forced, they came off tingling with enthusiasm and delight because, as one of them said: "Why, I have never known anything like this. There are no footlights to get over, there is no proscenium arch to frame us in. As quick as I do anything the audience comes back at me with a response. Those old fellows certainly knew the right conditions for the actor."[1]

[1] Baker, George Pierce, *The Development of Shakespeare as a Dramatist*, p. 308.

126

In regard to the technique of exposition in the Elizabethan theatre there were certain severe handicaps under which both actor and playwright laboured, and these presented problems that are not entirely absent from the theatre of today. The audience, comprising as it did so many different social and intellectual levels, made conflicting demands of both author and actor, and most of those demands had to be met in the typical five acts if the play was to be a popular success. This meant that the playwright must present variety and contrast in plot and types of characters, and that the actors must have a continuous lively awareness of this variety and contrast in their presentation. Not only must the actors underscore all lines that helped the audience to disentangle and follow the complexity of plot, but they must have the power to direct audience reaction from tragedy to comedy, from subjective pity to active condemnation, from fustian prose to the most exquisite poetry, all this and more in a comparatively short space of time. There could be nothing fumbling and vague about this interpretation; it would have to be definite, swift, and skilful in its economy of stroke, a poster technique that made the picture instantly intelligible to every level of comprehension.

The fact that there was no programme to aid identification of character, of time, of place, meant that there must be signposts in the script itself to guide the listening audience, and that the actor must underscore such indications by isolating them by pause and reinforcing them by emphasis. For instance, the lines describing or naming a character, or both, just before his entrance must be of clarion clearness and of arresting pitch and power. Lines indicating time of day or season of year, if contributory to plot, must be spoken with more significance than descriptive passages that had no expository duties. Places which could not be suggested, as they can today, by realistic (?) scenery must either be described in anticipation in a preceding scene, or be described on the—supposed—spot, and, again, the actor must speak these lines with arresting clarity and force. Here we might mention one bit of symbolic technique that had remained from the church and pageant performances, that of suggesting a "journey" by a symbolic walking around the stage. This business is sometimes used at the end of *Romeo and Juliet*, I, 4 (see footnote 1, p. 36).

An audience as unruly and boisterous as the one for whom Shakespeare wrote his plays would be hard to hold unless the actors played with vigorous certitude. The fact of their being on and around three sides of the stage meant that there must be a certain amount of integration of actor and audience by way of glance and gesture, especially in such direct address as indicated in "Prologue", "Chorus", and some types of soliloquy, and the fact that such an audience looked for and, apparently, enjoyed long rhetorical passages, whether comprehended or not, tended to foster the technique of declamation. It has even been suggested by Sir Arthur Quiller-Couch[1] that, in order to point up such passages, the actor would advance to the very front of the stage and direct the speech—whether a soliloquy or part of a dialogue —full at the audience, and, upon its conclusion, bow in acknowledgment of the applause and return back into the play.

We can see that this stage, auditorium, and audience allowed for no subtlety of suggestion, no delicacy of understatement, no introspective muttering, but that all acting must be bold, vital, and compelling. When we remember that Shakespeare knew that the lines he was writing would be delivered in this fashion, we can understand how this fact must have influenced the writing of, for instance, the early chronicle plays destined for production in the innyards and public theatres. However, plays performed at Court, at the Inns of Court, and later in the private theatre at Blackfriars could be acted with more subtlety of suggestion since, with a more sophisticated audience, more intelligent comprehension could be expected, and playwright and player alike must have welcomed this far greater challenge to their creative genius. But these performances were few and far between, and the company was not playing regularly at Blackfriars until the last phase of Shakespeare's career. We must conclude that he, with the help of his talented company, slowly but surely educated his public-theatre audience to a pitch where they were at least acquiescent to, if not receptive of, the magic of exquisite poetry, the most profound philosophy, the most stirring and complex emotions.

Summary of Shakespearean Acting Techniques for Use on the Modern Stage

TIME: Brisk and lively in comedy. Natural urgency of impassioned speech in tragedy.

VOICE: Full, clear, and resonant; wide range of intonation and easy modulation from one key to another.

SPEECH: Clean-cut formation and musical tone of vowels, and accurate, distinct, and firm articulation of consonants. While at no time must intelligibility be sacrificed to speed, yet a fine pace is desirable, and verbal fluency must be practised until it is effortless and smooth.

EMOTION: In comedy, this ranges from the spirited firing of verbal squibs to boisterous physical knockabout, and in every case comedy must hold the tone of high good humour and must keep within the actor's own

---

[1] Quiller-Couch, (Sir) Arthur, *Shakespeare's Workmanship*, pp. 63–64.

Sir Ralph Richardson as Falstaff

John Vickers

Sir Ralph Richardson as Petruchio

Vandamm, New York

John Gielgud as King Lear

John Gielgud as Hamlet

Sir Laurence Olivier as Hotspur

John Vickers

Sir Laurence Olivier as Justice
Shallow

John Vickers

capacity to feel the delight and fun he expresses. In tragedy, the range runs from the subjective inertia of melancholy, sickness and imminent death to the violence of denunciatory hatred, agonized remorse, abandonment to grief or fear. In both comedy and tragedy there must be, on the part of the actor, full and perfect comprehension of the logical and emotional meaning of the words he speaks and an acute awareness of their significant implications. With guiding and controlling intelligence in the saddle, expression can be given plenty of rein, but the actor must remember that the unpardonable sin in acting is that of expressing more emotion than he feels. The acquisition of that "temperance that may give . . . smoothness" is the first objective, and it follows that there will be unceasing work to gain it, but, in spite of this, there must always be a freshness of speech and manner in delivery that suggests complete spontaneity. Fortunately there is little chance of Shakespeare's lines going stale through constant repetition, for the more the intelligent actor goes over his part the more he will realize the wonders of its inner meaning.

MOVEMENT: There is a practical matter to be considered here: how far will costume hinder deportment and gesture? Usually this is discovered only at the dress rehearsal, and last-minute adjustments of business are fatal to that sense of security that gives firmness of attack on the first night. For this reason the actual costume, or a facsimile, should be worn at rehearsals from the time the blocking of the play starts.[1] In Shakespearean acting, speech is more rapid, voice more resolute, and emotion more firm than in the acting of modern plays, so movement—which is not an isolated indicator but an integrated element of emotional manifestation—is more definite, free, and significant than in almost any other type of acting. The form and pressure of the time is one of intense *vitality*—controlled and directed, but unmistakably there.

EXPOSITION: Interpretation of a work of genius is a grave responsibility, and the actor who realizes this spares no pains to "put across" the playwright's intentions in regard to verbal meaning, characterization, and plot. He will find that, even with such definite signposts as programmes with the list of characters, the sequence of scenes, the stated locality, and, perhaps, a synopsis of plot, there will still be a part of the audience in a state of dazed befuddlement. He will find as many levels of comprehension and receptivity as Richard Burbage did at the Globe, and he will realize that meaning cannot be made too clear if it is to reach the lowest intelligence group that may comprise the greater part of his audience. His (the actor's) duty then is to reinforce interpretation by every device known in exposition. *Emphasis* of

---

[1] The ruff and the farthingale, in particular, may require weeks of practice before they can be worn with ease and grace.

plot lines, of distinguishing names of persons and places, and for collecting a scattered order of words must be strong. *Pauses* should be used before an emphatic or important statement to point attention to what is to come and, after a speech of tremendous import, to give time for this to be grasped. *Varying tempo* must be used to express the tightening or slackening of emotional tensity, and all these elements must be reinforced by bodily movement, including skilful miming. The actor must do his best to aid comprehension of (1) unusual or obsolete words and grammar and (2) packed condensation of meaning implied in images. The best way for the actor to set about this is to consult glossaries and Variorum editions of the plays; then, having made thought and form clear to himself, to translate these into his own colloquial speech, and with this in mind to speak his part. It is quite remarkable how easy it becomes for the audience to grasp, or guess, the meaning when this is done. The language no longer seems archaic and stiff to those unused to Elizabethan drama, but vital and meaningful, and the actor gives the impression of a person of Shakespeare's own time speaking the habitual prose of castle, street, market-place, or tavern, and the greatest poetry of the whole rich life that wrapt him round.[1] The plays which to some may have been no more than dusty museum pieces will then take on life, and the timeless worth of these works of genius will be revealed to them in the light of their own comprehension.

---

[1] For special suggestions for the speaking of blank verse, see Webster, Margaret, *Shakespeare without Tears*, pp. 78–84, and de Banke, Cécile, *The Art of Choral Speaking*, Baker's Plays, Boston, 1937, pp. 117–122.

Books for Reference & Reading

BACKGROUND OF THE ACTORS:

THEIR LIVES, TRAINING, AND ART

ADAMS, JOSEPH QUINCY, *A Life of William Shakespeare*, Houghton Mifflin Company, Boston, 1923. See Chap. 7, "The Rise of Professionalism in the Drama", and Chap. 10, "With the Lord Chamberlain's Company".

BALDWIN, THOMAS WHITFIELD, *The Organization and Personnel of the Shakespearean Company*, Princeton University Press, Princeton, 1927. Valuable for reference to all that pertains to law, customs, finance, personnel, and division of labour in the Elizabethan repertory company.

BRADBROOK, MURIEL CLARA, *Elizabethan Stage Conditions: A Study of Their Place in the Interpretation of Shakespeare's Plays*, Cambridge University Press, New York, 1932. See Chap. 6, "The Question of Characterization", and Chap. 7, "Shakespeare and the Profession".

CHAMBERS, (Sir) EDMUND K., *The Elizabethan Stage*, Oxford University Press, New York, 1923. See Vol. I, Chap. 10, "The Actor's Quality"; Vol. II, Chap. 12, "The Boy Companies"; Chap. 13, "The Adult Companies"; Chap. 15, "Actors" (biographical details of Elizabethan actors).

——, *William Shakespeare: A Study of Facts and Problems*, 2 vols., Oxford University Press, New York, 1930. Indispensable for reference.

DAVIES, WILLIAM ROBERTSON, *Shakespeare's Boy Actors*, J. M. Dent & Sons, Ltd., London, 1939.

HART, A., "The Time Allotted for Representation of Elizabethan and Jacobean Plays", R.E.S. VIII, October, 1932. Mentioned by John Cranford Adams in *The Globe Playhouse*, p. 190, Harvard University Press, Cambridge, Mass., 1942.

HILLEBRAND, HAROLD NEWCOMB, *The Child Actors: A Chapter in Elizabethan Stage History*, University of Illinois Press, Urbana, 1926.

HODGES, C. WALTER, *Shakespeare and the Players*, Coward-McCann, Inc., New York, 1948. Excellent illustrations of actors performing *Richard III* on a reconstructed Elizabethan stage.

JOSEPH, B. L., *Elizabethan Acting*, Oxford University Press, New York, 1951.

LAWRENCE, WILLIAM J., *Old Theatre Days and Ways*, George G. Harrap & Co., Ltd., London, 1935. See Chap. 4, "Old-time Rehearsing", and Chap. 5, "Elizabethan Acrobats".

——, *Pre-Restoration Stage Studies*, Harvard University Press, Cambridge, Mass., 1927. See Chap. 3, "The Practice of Doubling and Its Influence on Early Dramaturgy", and Chap. 12, "The Rise and Progress of the Complex-disguise Play".

——, *Shakespeare's Workshop*, Houghton Mifflin, Boston, 1928. See pages 12–13 for an account of how Elizabethan dramatists wrote the parts for the actor members of the company.

131

LAWRENCE, WILLIAM J., *Speeding Up Shakespeare*, Argonaut Press, London, 1937. See Chap. 1, "On the Underrated Genius of Dick Tarleton". A glimpse of the comedian who set the pattern for clowns. Fine reprint of portrait.

——, *Those Nut-cracking Elizabethans: Studies of the Early Theatre and Drama*, Argonaut Press, London, 1935. See the chapter on "Shakespeare's Supers".

MOTTER, T. H. VAIL, *The School Drama in England*, Longmans, Green & Co., Inc., New York, 1929.

RALEIGH, (Sir) WALTER, *Shakespeare*, English Men of Letters Series, Macmillan & Co., Ltd., London, 1928. See page 120 for an opinion of the superiority of the Elizabethan boy actors over the modern actresses in Shakespeare's female roles.

SIMPSON, PERCY, "Actors and Acting", *Shakespeare's England*, Vol. II, Chap. 24, Oxford University Press, New York, 1932. Reproductions of portraits of leading actors of the time.

SISSON, C. J., "The Theatres and Companies", *A Companion to Shakespeare Studies*, edited by HARLEY GRANVILLE-BARKER and G. B. HARRISON, The Macmillan Company, New York, 1934.

SPRAGUE, ARTHUR COLBY, *Shakespeare and the Audience: A Study in the Technique of Exposition*, Harvard University Press, Cambridge, Mass., 1935. Most important for aiding the actors to realize Shakespeare's techniques of exposition.

STOPES, (Mrs.) C. C., *Burbage and Shakespeare's Stage*, A. Moring, Ltd., The De la More Press, London, 1913.

THORNDIKE, ASHLEY H., *Shakespeare's Theater*, The Macmillan Company, New York, 1938. See Chap. 13, "Actors and Acting", and reproductions of portraits of famous Elizabethan actors.

WALLACE, CHARLES WILLIAM, *The Evolution of the English Drama up to Shakespeare, with a History of the First Blackfriars Theatre*, G. Reimer, Berlin, 1912. For a history of the Children's companies.

WILSON, JOHN DOVER, compiler, *Shakespeare's England: A Book of Elizabethan Prose*, Penguin Books, Inc., New York, 1949. See Book VII, Chap. 4, "The Actor and His Craft".

MODERN INTERPRETATION OF SHAKESPEARE'S PLAYS[1]

ANDERSON, RUTH LEILA, *Elizabethan Psychology and Shakespeare's Plays*, University of Iowa Humanistic Studies, III, No. 4, University of Iowa Press, Iowa City, 1927. A guide for the student's investigation of apparent discrepancies and inconsistencies in character behaviour.

ARNOLD, MORRIS LEROY, *Soliloquies of Shakespeare: A Study in Technic*, Columbia University Press, New York, 1911.

[1] A further guide to interpretation by the amateur actor is to be found in the fine recordings of speeches and scenes made by the most distinguished actors of the last thirty years. The rapidity with which these recordings are being made and issued makes it impossible to give an up-to-date list here. The following, however, are suggested: Sir John Gielgud, in The Shakespeare Series (The Linguaphone Institute, London); Maurice Evans in *Richard II* (Columbia); Paul Robeson in *Othello* (Columbia); and Sir Laurence Olivier in *Henry V* (Victor).

BAKER, GEORGE PIERCE, *The Development of Shakespeare as a Dramatist*, The Macmillan Company, New York, 1907. See especially Chap. 8, "Late Experimentation".

BETHELL, S. L., *Shakespeare and the Popular Dramatic Tradition*, Duke University Press, Durham, 1944. See Chaps. 4 and 5 on the treatment of character.

BRADBROOK, MURIEL CLARA, *Elizabethan Stage Conditions: A Study of Their Place in the Interpretation of Shakespeare's Plays*, University Press, Cambridge, England, 1932. See Chap. 6, "The Question of Characterization".

BRADLEY, A. C., *Shakespearean Tragedy: Lectures on Hamlet, Othello, King Lear, Macbeth*, The Macmillan Company, New York, 1937.

BUCKNILL, JOHN CHARLES, *The Mad Folk of Shakespeare: Psychological Essays*, Macmillan & Co., Ltd., London, 1867. Studies of Macbeth, Hamlet, Ophelia, King Lear, Timon of Athens, Constance, Jaques, Malvolio, and Christopher Sly.

CAMPBELL, LILY B., *Shakespeare's Tragic Heroes: Slaves of Passion*, University Press, Cambridge, England, 1930.

CLARKE, CHARLES COWDEN, *Shakespeare Characters, Chiefly Those Subordinate*, Smith, Elder & Co., London, 1863.

COLERIDGE, SAMUEL TAYLOR, *Essays and Lectures on Shakespeare and Some Other Old Poets and Dramatists*, Everyman edition, E. P. Dutton & Co, New York, n.d.

DOWDEN, EDWARD, *Transcripts and Studies*, K. Paul, Trench, Trübner and Co., Ltd., London, 1896. See the essay on "Female Characters".

DRAPER, JOHN W. *The Hamlet of Shakespeare's Audience*, Duke University Press, Durham, 1938. Useful and informative.

——, *The Twelfth Night of Shakespeare's Audience*, Stanford University Press, Stanford University, Calif., 1950. Of value to both producer and actor.

FAUCIT, HELENA LADY MARTIN, *Some of Shakespeare's Female Characters, by One Who Has Impersonated Them*, William Blackwood & Sons, Ltd., Edinburgh, 1891.

GERWIG, GEORGE WILLIAM, *Shakespeare's Ideals of Womanhood*, The Roycroft Shops, East Aurora, N.Y., 1929.

GILDER, ROSAMUND, *John Gielgud's Hamlet: A Record of a Performance*, Oxford University Press, New York, 1937.

GODDARD, HAROLD C., *The Meaning of Shakespeare*, University of Chicago Press, Chicago, 1951. Though we may not agree with some of the author's conclusions, this book can be of help to the scholar-player since the psychological evaluation of character, the analysis of motivation, and the minute study of every aspect of the plays are expressed with a rare blend of passion and sensitivity.

GORDON, GEORGE, *Shakespearean Comedy and Other Studies*, Oxford University Press, New York, 1944. See Chap. 7, "Shakespeare's Women", and Chap. 8, "Shakespeare's Clowns".

GRANVILLE-BARKER, HARLEY, *Prefaces to Shakespeare*, Series I, II, and III, Sidgwick & Jackson, Ltd., London, 1927, 1930, 1937. Series I: *Love's Labour's Lost, Julius Caesar*, and *King Lear*; Series II: *Romeo and Juliet, The Merchant of Venice, Antony and Cleopatra*, and *Cymbeline*; Series III: *Hamlet*. Analysis of each play and the main problems of its staging in Elizabethan and in modern times.

HAZLITT, WILLIAM, *Characters of Shakespeare's Plays*, World's Classics, Oxford University Press, New York, 1924.

HUDSON, HENRY NORMAN, *Shakespeare: His Life, Art, and Characters*, 2 vols., 4th ed., Ginn & Company, Boston, 1872, 1875. See the section on characters.

KEMBLE, FRANCES ANNE, *Notes upon Some of Shakespeare's Plays*, R. Bentley & Son, London, 1882. Discussions of *Macbeth, Henry VIII, The Tempest*, and *Romeo and Juliet* from the point of view of the actress approaching the interpretation of her part. Masterly analysis of Lady Macbeth—useful even if one does not agree with the conclusions.

KITTREDGE, GEORGE LYMAN, *Shakspere: An Address Delivered on April 23, 1916, in Sanders Theatre at the Request of the President and Fellows of Harvard College*, Harvard University Press, Cambridge, Mass., 1916. Includes a discussion of the degree to which the actor identifies himself with the character that he portrays.

KNIGHT, GEORGE WILSON, *The Crown of Life: Essays in Interpretation of Shakespeare's Final Plays*, Methuen & Co., Ltd., London, 1948. Discussions of *Pericles, The Winter's Tale, Cymbeline, The Tempest*, and *Henry VIII*.

——, *The Imperial Theme: Further Interpretations of Shakespeare's Tragedies including the Roman Plays*, Oxford University Press, New York, 1931.

——, *Principles of Shakespearian Production, with Special Reference to the Tragedies*, The Macmillan Company, New York, 1937. See Chap. 3, "Some Actual Productions", accounts of performances produced at Hart House Theatre for the Toronto Shakespeare Society by Professor Knight.

——, *The Shakespearian Tempest*, Oxford University Press, New York, 1932.

KREIDER, PAUL V., *Repetition in Shakespeare's Plays*, Princeton University Press (for the University of Cincinnati), Princeton, 1941. Remarkable analysis of the villains in Chaps. 2–7.

LAWRENCE, WILLIAM J., *Old Theatre Days and Ways*, George C. Harrap & Co., Ltd., London, 1935. See Chap. 4, "Old-time Rehearsing", and Chap. 12, "The Black-a-vised Stage Villain".

——, *Pre-Restoration Stage Studies*, Harvard University Press, Cambridge, Mass., 1927. See Chap. 5, "*Hamlet* as Shakespeare Staged It".

——, *Shakespeare's Workshop*, Houghton Mifflin Company, Boston, 1927. See Chap. 3, "Shakespeare's Lost Characters", and Chap. 8, "The Ghost in *Hamlet*".

LAWRENCE, WILLIAM WITHERLE, *Shakespeare's Problem Comedies*, The Macmillan Company, New York, 1931. Fine analysis of these difficult plays: *All's Well That Ends Well, Measure for Measure, Troilus and Cressida*, with comments on certain aspects of *Cymbeline*.

LEE, (Sir) SIDNEY, *Shakespeare and the Modern Stage*, Charles Scribner's Sons, New York, 1906. See especially Part I, Chaps. 1–3.

LEWIS, CHARLTON M., *The Genesis of Hamlet*, Henry Holt and Company, Inc., New York, 1907.

MACCALLUM, M. W., *Shakespeare's Roman Plays and Their Background*, Macmillan & Co., Ltd., London, 1910. Valuable for the production of *Julius Caesar, Antony and Cleopatra*, and *Coriolanus*.

MACKENZIE, AGNES MURE, *Women in Shakespeare's Plays*, Doubleday & Company, Inc., New York, 1924.

MASEFIELD, JOHN, *A Macbeth Production*, The Macmillan Company, New York, 1946.

MATHESON, BELLE SEDDON, *The Invented Personages of Shakespeare's Plays*, University of Pennsylvania Press, Philadelphia, 1932.

MOULTON, RICHARD G., *Shakespeare as a Dramatic Artist*, Oxford University Press, New York, 1893.

PALMER, JOHH LESLIE, *Comic Characters of Shakespeare*, Macmillan & Co., Ltd., London, 1946. Deals with the characters of Berowne, Touchstone, Shylock, Bottom, and Beatrice and Benedick.

——, *Political Characters of Shakespeare*, Macmillan & Co., Ltd., London, 1945. Discussions of Marcus Brutus, Richard of Gloucester, Richard of Bordeaux, Henry of Monmouth, and Caius Marcius Coriolanus.

QUILLER-COUCH, (Sir) ARTHUR, *Shakespeare's Workmanship*, T. Fisher Unwin, London, 1927. Chapters on *Macbeth, A Midsummer Night's Dream, The Merchant of Venice, As You Like It*, the story of Falstaff, *Hamlet, Pericles, King Henry VIII, Cymbeline, The Winter's Tale*, and *The Tempest*.

SARGEAUNT, W. D., *Macbeth: A New Interpretation of Shakespeare's Play*, Heath Cranton, Ltd., London, 1937. Line-by-line interpretation.

SCHÜCKING, LEVIN L., *Character Problems in Shakespeare's Plays*, Henry Holt and Company, Inc., New York, 1922.

Shakespeare Criticism: A Selection, introduction by D. Nichol Smith, World's Classics, Oxford University Press, New York, 1926. See particularly Dr. Johnson's "Preface to Shakespeare (1765)", on pages 89–142.

SPENCER, HAZELTON, *The Art and Life of William Shakespeare*, Harcourt Brace and Company, Inc., New York, 1940. Fine portraits of Richard Burbage, William Sly, John Lowin, John Fletcher, Ben Jonson, Thomas Betterton, James Quin as Falstaff, Edmund Kean as Richard III, Ellen Terry as Portia, John Philip Kemble as Hamlet, Edwin Booth as Hamlet, and David Garrick as King Lear.

SPRAGUE, ARTHUR COLBY, *Shakespeare and the Actors: The Stage Business in His Plays (1660–1905)*, Harvard University Press, Cambridge, Mass., 1944. A study of the interpretations of leading parts by famous actors.

——, *Shakespeare and the Audience: A Study in the Technique of Exposition*, Harvard University Press, Cambridge, Mass., 1935. Very important.

STAUFFER, DONALD A., *Shakespeare's World of Images: The Development of His Moral Ideas*, W. W. Norton & Company, New York, 1949. A fine aid to the actor's interpretation of characters. Especially revealing analysis of *Measure for Measure*.

STILL, COLIN, *Shakespeare's Mystery Play: A Study of "The Tempest"*, Cecil Palmer, London, 1921.

STOLL, ELMER EDGAR, *Art and Artifice in Shakespeare: A Study in Dramatic Contrast and Illusion*, University Press, Cambridge, England, 1938.

——, *Shakespeare Studies, Historical and Comparative in Method*, The Macmillan Company, New York, 1927. See particularly Chap. 5, "The Ghosts"; Chap. 6 "Shylock"; Chap. 7, "The Criminals"; and Chap. 8, "Falstaff".

——, *Shakespeare's Young Lovers*, Toronto University Alexander Lectures in English, 1935, Oxford University Press, New York, 1937. Lecture I, *Romeo and Juliet*; Lecture II, *The Maidens of Shakespeare's Prime—Portia*, Beatrice, Rosalind, Viola; Lecture III, *The Maidens in the Dramatic Romances—Imogen*, Perdita, Miranda.

THORNDIKE, ASHLEY H., *Shakespeare's Theater*, The Macmillan Company, New York, 1938. See pages 397–403 for outstanding characteristics of Elizabethan acting.

TILLYARD, E. M. W., *Shakespeare's History Plays*, The Macmillan Company, New York, 1946.

——, *Shakespeare's Last Plays*, Chatto & Windus, London, 1938. Discussions o *Cymbeline, The Winter's Tale,* and *The Tempest.*

WARDE, FREDERICK, *The Fools of Shakespeare*, McBride, Nast and Company, New York, 1913. The analysis deals with Touchstone, Trinculo, Feste, Launcelot Gobbo, the Citizen in *Julius Caesar*, the Clown in *Antony and Cleopatra*, the Gravediggers in *Hamlet*, Launce and Speed in *The Two Gentlemen of Verona*, and the Fool in *King Lear.*

WATKINS, RONALD, *Moonlight at the Globe: An Essay in Shakespeare Production Based on Performance of "A Midsummer Night's Dream" at Harrow School*, Michael Joseph, Ltd., London, 1946. Many useful suggestions will be found in this delightful account of a performance that was directed by the author. Beautifully illustrated with pen drawings by Maurice Percival.

WEBSTER, MARGARET, *Shakespeare without Tears*, introduction by John Mason Brown, McGraw-Hill Book Company, Inc., New York, 1942.

WELLES, ORSON, and ROGER HILL, editors, *Everybody's Shakespeare*, three plays edited for reading and arranged for staging (*Julius Caesar, The Merchant of Venice, Twelfth Night*), The Todd Press, Woodstock, Ill., 1934. Delightful sketches which are extremely helpful in suggesting characterization and business.

WELSFORD, ENID, *The Fool: His Social and Literary History*, Faber & Faber, Ltd., London, 1936.

WILSON, JOHN DOVER, *The Fortunes of Falstaff*, The Macmillan Company, New York, 1944.

——, *What Happens in Hamlet*, The Macmillan Company, New York, 1935. Excellent for expository business.

YATES, FRANCIS A., *A Study of Love's Labour's Lost*, University Press, Cambridge, England, 1936.

Part Three

Costume

I

Costume in Elizabethan England

CARLO BUFFONE: "To be an accomplished gentleman . . . 'twere good you turn'd four or five hundred acres of your best land into two or three trunks of apparel."

Ben Jonson, *Every Man out of His Humour*, I, 1

AT NO time in the social history of England do we find such all-pervading magnificence and extravagance of costume as in the period that coincides with the rise and decline of Elizabethan drama.

At Court, the importance attached to sartorial display led courtiers to sell their lands and manors to meet the expenses of outdressing their rivals, and among the nobility in general the amount spent on clothes was out of proportion to all other personal and household expenditure. In the City, the new-rich merchant class followed the example set by their social superiors, and Jaques—in *As You Like It*, II, 7—could say that

> "the city woman bears
> The cost of princes on unworthy shoulders,"

and

> ". . . such a one as she such is her neighbour."

Among the less affluent, this passion for display often led to privation and debt. In 1592 the Duke of Würtemberg, in a letter describing English customs, said:

139

"Many a one does not hesitate to wear velvet in the streets, which is common with them, whilst at home they have not a piece of dry bread."

It was even found necessary to pass laws in order to prohibit the wearing of costly clothes by those who could not afford them, but these laws were more frequently ignored than obeyed.

For the first time we begin to hear of the obligation to "follow the fashion", and, as the facilities for travel increased, of the importation of foreign fashions. This last resulted in polyglot costumes in which the fashions of Spain, France, Italy, and Germany were inextricably mixed.

Not everyone was caught in this tide of folly. Indeed it is from the censure of the sober-minded and the ridicule of the witty that we are able to deduce the outstanding characteristics of the costume of the period. Again and again we hear of inappropriate and pretentious magnificence of attire, of haphazard mixing of foreign importations, and of the absurd and exacting dictates of flying fashions.

TRADITIONAL SPLENDOUR OF STAGE CLOTHES

What effect did this royal, courtly and civic display of costly clothes have on the costuming of the contemporary drama? Did the actors vie with the magnificence of the audience in the matter of clothes? Did they attempt to keep abreast of the fashion? Did they reflect the idiosyncrasies of mixed importations? Above all, how did they meet the expense of clothing the members of their companies—however simply—in as many as forty plays a season?

In answering these questions it is necessary to consider first the long tradition of colourful splendour associated with the costuming of the drama. There were the magnificent ecclesiastical vestments used in early liturgical drama; the reflection of this magnificence, in appearance at least, in the costuming of the miracles and mysteries; and the rich splendour of costumes worn by professional entertainers attached to royal and noble houses. (See a description of the costumes worn by Queen Elizabeth's woman Fool, p. 176.)

This tradition had sprung from the need for spectacle to offset the lack of scenery and the need to invest the performers, especially the local amateurs, with dignity, beauty, and otherworldness on the one hand, and with arresting eccentricity, terror, or horror on the other. More worldly considerations had also contributed to the tradition for it became a matter of pride in early times for kings and nobles to dress their entertainers in costly and striking clothing. Here, then, is the answer to the first question. Through long association, the actors were expected to appear in rich and beautiful costumes. Their improved social status had also made it obligatory to attempt, at least, to vie with the splendour of clothing seen on the nobles and young men of fashion *seated on the stage* and on the wealthy merchants and their wives thronging the galleries. The competition must have been a cruel burden, for it was customary for the entire audience to wear its best to the playhouse and, in the case of those seated on the stage, to make it a parade ground for the latest fashion.

In regard to reflecting the rapidly changing fashions and continental importations on the Elizabethan stage, it seems that the actors circumvented this by dressing one character, now and then, in a parody of some transient grotesquerie, and the playwright supported the idea by writing witty or contemptuous comments on these current follies. We hear of Tarleton, the famous clown of Queen Elizabeth's company of players, wearing slops so huge that they could have held a "bushel of wheate". In *The Merchant of Venice*, I, 2, Portia says of the young baron of England:

"How oddly he is suited! I think he bought his doublet in Italy, his round hose in France, his bonnet in Germany. . . ."

In *Much Ado about Nothing*, III, 2, Don Pedro says of Benedick:

"There is no appearance of fancy in him, unless it be a fancy that he hath to strange disguises; as, to be a Dutchman today, a Frenchman tomorrow, or in the shape of two countries at once, as a German from the waist downward, all slops, and a Spaniard from the hip upward, no doublet."

The exaggerated fashions of the lords and foplings were doubtless reflected in Monsieur le Beau in *As You Like It* and in Osric in *Hamlet*, and also in Hotspur's contempt for the lord who was perfumed like a milliner and talked like a waiting-gentlewoman (*2 Henry IV*, I, 3).

Taking into account the stage's reputation for sumptuous costuming and the necessity for the actor to compete with the fine clothes of his audience, we do not wonder that the wardrobe was by far the heaviest item of expenditure in Elizabethan stage production. Nevertheless, it is with something of a shock that we learn, from Henslowe's diary, of a cloak costing more than the play in which it appeared, and of a single garment swallowing up more than a week's takings at the playhouse door. It is true that certain traditional and official garments, such as robes of state, ecclesiastical vestments, and military and civic uniforms, could be used over and over again without causing comment. Contemporary civilian clothes, however, would have to be altered or renovated[1] if they were to be used in more than one or two plays, since their reappearance would be noticed by an audience that was, for the most part, composed of the same playgoers for every new performance.

COST OF COSTUMES

The disproportionate outlay for costumes was, as has been said, borne by the actors, and our curiosity is at once roused as to how they were able to meet this responsibility. Fortunately we are in possession of a good many facts that throw light on the problem and reveal that there were many ways in which this liability was met. We know, for instance, that noblemen often willed their clothes to their servants, and that these servants, being compelled to wear family livery or the general livery of servitors (see p. 148), sold them to the actors. Needy courtiers themselves, moreover, sold their finery to the players. Nor was this use of second-hand clothing confined to the public theatres. We know that such garments were worn by the Children of the Chapel Royal. One handsome fourteen-year-old boy who played the leading lady in a performance of *Palamon and Arcite, Part II*, before the Queen received, as a reward, eight angels and the robes of the recently deceased Queen Mary *that he had worn in the play*. Other articles of Queen Mary's wardrobe were lent to scholars at Oxford University for a play that they presented to Queen Elizabeth. Another source of supply was the Revels Office, which not only costumed the actors when they appeared at Court, but quite frequently gave them these beautiful garments in place of a fee. Furthermore, the men employed in the Revels Office were allowed to augment their salaries by selling to the actors Court-masque costumes when they were deemed no longer fit for courtly wear. It is safe to consider also the possibility of the actors hiring Court-masque costumes when they were not in use. This would be especially true of Shakespeare's company after 1603, when as King's Men they were nominally members of the staff of the Royal Household.

Here then were some of the ways in which the actors were able to procure at small cost the basic garments of extravagant beauty that would otherwise have been beyond their means to purchase.

The second-hand clothing, together with the robes and uniforms already mentioned, was no doubt owned jointly and held in common usage by the sharers. New garments were purchased by them when they could afford them, and, since some of the leading actors owned their own wardrobes, these clothes were, no doubt, made for them at their own individual

[1] No wonder Henslowe had two tailors in constant employment.

cost. Indeed, it is possible that the second-hand clothes were worn chiefly by the hired men, a possibility supported by the bitter complaints of contemporary writers against the wearing of costly satins and velvets by these humble hirelings.

For the less illustrious companies there were other sources of supply. They could, for instance, hire costumes from theatre owners and managers; there were the wardrobes of defunct companies that could be bought by their more fortunate rivals; and there were the outmoded or too-familiar garments belonging to the London companies that could be purchased by small companies touring the provinces.

By way of purchasing second-hand clothes, by hire, by gifts, by communal and individual purchasing of new garments, and by the alteration and renovation of old ones, the London actors managed to uphold their reputation for fine costuming and even to compete with the magnificent clothes worn by their audiences at Court, in noblemen's houses, and in the public theatres.

It is possible that there has been no time in the history of the English stage when contemporary costuming was more beautiful, more colourful, more effective. But what of historical costume used in classical and chronicle plays? What of national costume in plays set in France, Italy, or Greece? What of symbolic and imaginative costume used in masques, plays, and supernatural episodes within the plays? Here it is to be feared that there were poor, and even ludicrous, makeshifts, but a study of the costuming of the period will not be complete without a glance at these less happy representations.

HISTORICAL COSTUME

Fortunately, through the information obtainable from Henslowe's diary and a study of the numerous portraits of the period, the modern producer has little difficulty in finding, down to the last detail, descriptions of the clothes that appeared on the stages of Elizabethan and Jacobean London. It is usually with amazement that we learn that Julius Caesar, Antony and Cleopatra, and Coriolanus appeared in doublet, hose, farthingale, ruffs, etc., that Tamerlane wore a "cotte of coper lace" and "breeches of crymson velvet", and "Harey the fifte" was decked in a "dublet and vellvet gowne".

But we must not think that attempts to introduce historical costume were not made. In a drawing of a scene from *Titus Andronicus* made in 1594,[1]

---

[1] This drawing was made by Henry Peacham, a schoolmaster who was also an epigrammist and pamphleteer. For a guide to reproductions of this drawing, see Chambers entry on p. 198 and *Shakespeare Survey* entry on p. 200.

we learn that a Moor—for it is Aaron who is depicted—was, to Elizabethans, a Negro, and this in turn explains Othello's "black" appearance. But the thing that most engages our attention in the drawing is the strange blend of historical and contemporary costume. For instance, Tamora wears the flowing garment and pointed crown of a medieval saint rather than that of a pagan queen. Titus wears a very fair attempt at classical costume, but behind him stand two soldiers in doublets and venetians, one wearing the feathered casque and upper-body armour of medieval times, while the other has an Elizabethan hat and, strangest of all, a curved Eastern scimitar. One of Tamora's sons seems to be in fairly authentic classical costume but the other has padded sleeves to his tunic. Aaron has a tunic with a shirt-top, long full sleeves, and a skirt of piccadills resembling armour, and sandals worn over half-hose, or netherstocks.

In the play *The First Part of Richard II or Thomas of Woodstock*, attention is constantly drawn to the medieval shoes worn by the king and his courtiers, the long pointed toes of which were chained to the knees.[1] In no less than five scenes references are made to these shoes, and we are left with the impression that an innovation is being featured. But this seems to be an isolated example of attempted historical accuracy for elsewhere in the same play references are made to the following Elizabethan items: French hose, Italian cloaks, Spanish hats, plumed hats, russet slops, a "big-bellied" doublet, and a lady's riding mask.

We wonder that actors, who at some time must have seen attempted accuracy in classical and medieval costume in the amateur performances at the universities and Inns of Court,[2] could be content with these inaccurate and inconsistent representations. It may, of course, be part of the unconscious absence of realism that pervaded all Elizabethan drama; it may have been thought sufficient to give one or two indicators and leave the rest to the audience's imagination; it may have been a matter of expediency, economy, or dramatic tradition.[3] However, the close contact of Shakespeare's company with the Court after 1603 must have greatly influenced their costuming. For, as we have seen already, they were able to hire or buy the actual garments worn in the masques, and were even given the beautiful clothes supplied by the Revels Office for their performances at Court.

[1] The author is indebted to Dr. G. B. Harrison for drawing her attention to this point.
[2] In 1594, the Master of Trinity wrote to ask the Lord Chancellor for the loan of historical robes housed in the Tower of London. The "auncient princely attire" appropriate for persons of "greatest estate" was needed for a tragedy that was to be "sett forth" at the College.
[3] This lighthearted inconsequence in the matter of costume was most cleverly pointed up by Margaret Webster's touring company in *The Taming of the Shrew*. Themselves strolling players, representing a band of strolling players in the play, there was a double excuse for the glorious hodgepodge of garments that they paraded with such dash and chucklesome enjoyment.

It is safe to say, therefore, that the later plays, *The Winter's Tale*, *Cymbeline*, and *The Tempest*, showed less inconsistency in costuming and conformed, in general, to the designs supplied for the Court masques by Inigo Jones.

NATIONAL COSTUME

Apart from items of costume borrowed from other countries that were part of fashionable English attire, there seems to have been some attempt in the theatres to depict national costume, in part at least. In Henslowe's diary we hear of the purchasing of material for the making of "Mores cotte" and "Turckes hedes" (turbans?); the Duke of Morocco refers to his scimitar, and Shylock to his "Jewish gaberdine". But the accepted idea of Eastern costume doubtless came from the Crusaders, by way of the Herods of the miracle plays, and that of Turkish knights and Moors, from the accounts of travellers, by way of folk and mumming plays. By 1585 these were doubtless all traditional garments that may or may not have had anything to do with the contemporary national garments of the countries they supposedly represented. In regard to contemporary comedy there was, it is certain, no attempt made to reflect foreign fashions in the costuming.

SYMBOLIC AND IMAGINATIVE COSTUME

Up to the turn of the sixteenth century symbolic and imaginative costume in the drama was largely traditional. It derived from the costuming used in the miracle and morality plays, which, in turn, had reflected its ecclesiastical origin by being obvious copies of figures seen in stained-glass windows, in statuary on altars and tombs, and in murals and illuminated manuscripts. The spiked crown (seen in the *Titus Andronicus* picture) that doubtless served for years to depict the queens of heaven, earth, and faery alike can be seen in an ancient rood-screen painting of an archangel in a church at Barton Turf in Norfolk, England.[1] Prudence, Temperance, Virginity, Continence, and Marriage, who appeared as *tableaux vivants* in the street theatres, can be found in the stained-glass windows of Canterbury Cathedral.

Devils and spirits of evil derived from horrific representations of the Last Judgment depicted in murals and illuminated manuscripts. The same old devil—tail, scales, cloven hoofs, horns and all—is to be seen in the frontispiece of an early edition of Marlowe's *Doctor Faustus* and on the title page of the masque, *The World Tost at Tennis* as acted by the Prince's Men

---

[1] For a photograph of this painting, see Borenius, Tancred, and Tristram, E. W., *English Medieval Painting*, p. 77.

S.S.P—K

in 1620. Ghosts are said to be "sheeted", and we must suppose the Ghost in *Hamlet* in full armour to be an exception to this general practice.

Clowns, as has been already mentioned, were sometimes dressed in exaggerated current fashion or as country yokels, while jesters, or fools, seem to have long retained the parti-coloured red and yellow of the medieval fool to symbolize the divided mind. However, we know that Will Summers, the famous fool of Henry VIII's Court, wore green and white, the colours of the royal livery.

II

Details of Elizabethan Costume

Petruchio: "O mercy, God! what masquing stuff is here?
What's this? a sleeve? 'tis like a demi-cannon:
What! up and down, carv'd like an apple tart?
Here's snip and nip and cut and slish and slash,
Like to a censer in a barber's shop.
Why, what, i' devil's name, tailor, call'st thou this?"

The Taming of the Shrew, IV, 3

THE COSTUME designer, facing the task of dressing a Shakespearean play, will first need to know what is chronologically correct, after which he can make adaptations that will give consideration to what is comfortable enough to be worn with ease and grace by the modern actor.

Fabrics & Colours

It will be well to start by considering what fabrics are known to have been used in the period, and for this a table of names of the better-known cotton, woollen, and silk materials, together with suggestions for their equivalents and for substitutes procurable today, will be found on pp. 149–152.

With this information in hand, the costumer can proceed to the question of colour, and here he will be delighted to find the range of hues as wide as could be wished or imagined. The dyeing of fabrics had been practised in England since the twelfth century, and in Elizabethan times had reached an advanced stage of experimentation, with the result that many beautiful coloured fabrics were available for every kind of use. The names of colours, which were as fanciful then as now, will require a word or two of

147

explanation, and, since the colour of garment played an important part in class distinction, attention will also have to be paid to the type of people who could or could not wear this or that colour. For instance, servants were limited to dark blue or tawny-coloured liveries or garments, and the costuming of a nobleman in these colours would be not only incorrect but ridiculous. Again, the introduction of green sleeves into the costume of a lady of quality would be a very doubtful procedure since these were the customary wear of the courtesan.

The symbolism of colour is a further point that might be taken into account since so much attention was given to it by all classes, and since it was applied with fine dramatic effect in the Court masques and in playhouse productions. Colour symbolism seems to have evolved as part of religious ritual from the very earliest times, and Greek tragedy, itself performed as part of religious festival, gives us—in the plays of Aeschylus, for instance— the use of colour symbolism as an effective dramatic device. The early Christian Church adopted colour symbolism from pagan ritual, both in vestments and in ecclesiastical furnishings (altar cloths, lectern covers, etc.), and these, in turn, were used in liturgical drama. When the Church drama became secular, the traditional use of symbolic colours was carried over, by way of mysteries, moralities, and miracle plays, to dramatic costuming in Tudor times.

So it comes about that the colour of an actor's costume might be chosen for more than visual effect; it might symbolize the wearer's emotional mood or allegiance. The languishing and lovelorn in willow green, the mighty and powerful in blood-red, the deranged in parti-colour were all part of dramatic device, and when it came to opposing factions—Yorkists and Lancastrians, Montagues and Capulets, English and French—the use of two distinctly different colours in the costumes of retainers and soldiers must have been highly effective and, from the audience's point of view, useful for the purpose of distinguishing the members of each faction. In recent times this usefulness was most startlingly brought to our notice in Richard Whorf's production of *Richard III*, where the difficulty of identifying the personnel of the opposing factions was completely surmounted by the simple device of dressing all the people on one side in black and white and those on the other in scarlet.[1]

On pp. 153–156, tables will be found to serve as a quick and simple guide to these various aspects of colour. Following these tables, a list of

---

[1] This dramatically effective device came about through necessity. Wishing to present *Richard III* during his service in occupied Germany, Mr. Whorf found that his only source of costume supplies consisted of the thousand of yards of red, black, and white used formerly in the Nazi rallies, and the result was so successful that he reproduced the colour scheme in his professional American production.

Fabrics

Eliza-bethan name	Description	Use	Modern facsimile or substitute
		COTTON	
Buckram	A coarse cotton cloth	Jerkins, hose, shirts, hangings, linings for garments, covering for French farthingale. A starched kind was used for stiffening	Indian head (U.S.[1]) Casement cloth (G.B.[2]) Buckram for stiffening
Fustian	Imitation velours or broadcloth	Used in place of woollen broadcloth by poor classes	Flannelette
		LINEN	
Cambric	As used today	Shirts, ruffs, bands, cuffs, handkerchiefs	Nainsook Cambric
Canvas	Heavy, natural-coloured, coarsely woven cotton	Household linen, shirts, workmen's aprons, stage costumes and properties. Jerkins of this were painted to represent mail in stage productions	Muslin (U.S.) Unbleached calico (G.B.)
Holland	As today, an oatmeal-coloured linen	Shirts	Holland Crash—when woven of coarse linen thread and cotton (G.B.)
Lawn	As used today	Sleeves, ruffs, foreparts, gowns, handkerchiefs, neckwear; frequently trimmed with metal and, later, linen lace	Handkerchief lawn (U.S.) Bishop's lawn (G.B.)
		WOOL	
Broad-cloth	As seen today	Worn by servants and pensioners	Broadcloth, velours (many inexpensive substitutes)
Buffin	The same as modern serge	Garments worn by middle classes and tradespeople	Serge

[1] U.S. means United States.
[2] G.B. means Great Britain.

Fabrics (continued)

Eliza-bethan name	Description	Use	Modern facsimile or substitute
Caddis	Coarse, heavy flannel	Garments of the very poor. In strips, for garters and girdles	Flannel, flannelette
Chamlet	Fine, soft material woven of kid's hair and wool or camel's hair and wool	Very expensive and worn exclusively by noblemen	Many substitutes made from angora wool, rabbit's hair, and wool, and, for heavier wear, camel's hair and wool
Crewel	Woollen yarn	Used for knitting netherstocks; for fringes, garters, braid, and lace	Knitting and tapestry yarns
Linsey-woolsey	Cloth made of linen thread and wool	Used by poor and middle classes for garments and drapery for beds	Flannelette Rayon with an imitation wool finish
Mockado	Cotton-backed, imitation velvet	Gowns, farthingale covers, kirtles, stomachers, breeches, jackets. Sometimes guarded with real velvet, or embroidered with gold, or trimmed with gold and silver braid and lace	Velveteen
Motley	Variegated woollen cloth	Vestments, and garments of persons of wealth	Our bright and light-coloured plaids and tweeds seem to be the only equivalent
Rash	Twilled woollen fabric	All articles of outside clothing	Gaberdine[1]
Rug	A very heavy serge or frieze	Made into heavy robes and worn for warmth by astrologers and night watchmen, and as nightgowns for nobility	Felt or drugget

[1] Our modern name for this fabric may derive from the Elizabethan garment of the name that was frequently made of rash.

Fabrics (continued)

Eliza-bethan name	Description	Use	Modern facsimile or substitute
Scarlet	Very fine woollen broadcloth. A less expensive kind was called "stammel". (See chart of Colours)	The red kind was dyed in the wool, was very expensive, and used by the royal family, their household servants and retainers, and by civic officials	Very fine velours

SILK

Eliza-bethan name	Description	Use	Modern facsimile or substitute
Baudkin, or bodkin	Cloth of silver or gold with a woven silk pattern	Used for female garments by Court and nobility, and as displayed lining in men's sleeves, doublets, hose, and cloaks	Theatrical fabric manufacturers have a great variety of beautiful substitutes for this
Cypress (smoky lawn?)	Fine, transparent material woven in black and in white	White for partlets, foresleeves and neckwear; black for mourning headwear and scarves, also to veil stomachers	Silk or rayon chiffon
Damask	Heavy silk material, woven with similar or contrasting colours in intricate designs. It was extremely expensive	Robes, kirtles, and cloaks worn by royalty, nobility, and the very wealthy	There are many heavy damasked fabrics sold for upholstery and curtains that are very beautiful and not too expensive when we take into account their extreme width
Grosgrain	Heavy corded silk	All parts of attire, both male and female	Poplin
Plush	As today, a very heavy, long-piled silk velvet	Garments worn by the wealthy	There are many inexpensive substitutes made of rayon that are used in upholstery and for imitation fur coats
Sarcenet	A soft, light material	Drapery, hats, doublets, shirts, and linings	Crêpe de Chine and rayon substitutes

Fabrics (continued)

Eliza-bethan name	Description	Use	Modern facsimile or substitute
Satin	Same as real-silk satin today	Worn by all classes except the peasantry	Many inexpensive substitutes
Tabine	Moire, or watered silk, sometimes woven with gold or silver threads	All outside garments of noble and wealthy classes, and sometimes even for petticoats	Rayon watered silk
Taffeta	Same as taffeta (U.S.), or glacé silk (G.B.). There were many kinds, such as "tufted" and "changeable"	Used for all outer garments and for women's petticoats	Taffeta and changeable taffeta (U.S.); glacé silk and shot silk (G.B.) Many rayon substitutes. It is economical to buy the very wide heavy kind used for draperies
Tissue	Metal and silk, semi-transparent material. The warp might be purple, blue, rose, or white silk, and the metal weft threads of gold or silver	Used for state occasions and signified wealth and luxury. Seems to have been used wherever silk would be used in very ornate and formal clothing, and for hangings for state banquets, weddings, coronations, etc. Its use in the Court masques was inevitable	Many substitutes for this can be found in theatrical fabric shops, and in upholstery and dry-goods departments of large stores
Velvet	Same as real silk-backed velvet today. There seem to have been variegated kinds for we hear of "black speckled with white", of one colour "figured" with another. When it was embroidered with floral designs, it was said to be "branched"	Copes, robes, kirtles, gowns, panes, and cloaks	Velvet, velveteen, and many rayon substitutes

Colours

Elizabethan name	Description	Symbolism	Use
		REDS AND PINKS	
Carnation	Deep, dark red	Love; cheerful living; when combined with white, desire	This colour can be seen in doublets, kirtles, and cloaks in contemporary portraits
Catherine pear	Russet red	Betrayal	Descriptive of the colours of beards
Flame colour	Vivid reddish orange	Associated with gallantry in love	Worn by lovers
Horseflesh	The red-brown of a bay horse	Gallantry	Very popular for all articles of clothing
Judas red	Auburn, or bright rust red	Treachery	Descriptive of the colour of hair and beards
Maiden's blush	Bright rose	Gallantry	Worn frequently by the Queen and much affected by gallants
Murrey	Mulberry; purplish red	Steadfastness in love	Very popular with all classes and used frequently on the stage and for Court masques
Peach flower	Deep coral pink	Lost courage; diminished riches	Very popular with all classes; used frequently on the stage
Scarlet	Vivid yellow-red	Nobility, pomp	See chart of Fabrics, p. 151
Stammel	A bluer red than scarlet; the colour seen in cochineal and red ink	Pomp, festivity	For formal occasions
		PURPLE	
	Same as today		Robes of state and royal drapery
		BLUE	
Azure	Lapis-lazuli blue	Honour; wisdom; when combined with green, excess of joy	Used in all articles of clothing

Colours (continued)

Eliza-bethan name	Description	Symbolism	Use
Blew, or blue	Navy blue	Servitude	A bourgeois colour, used chiefly by servants, apprentices, pensioners, orphans, beadles of hospitals, and wardens of prisons. A survival can be seen in the uniform of the bluecoat boys of Christ's Hospital
Watchet	Aquamarine or pale turquoise	Deceptive love	Worn by the Queen and courtiers, but also by courtesans

GREEN

Goose-turd	Yellowish green		A colour of starch used for bands, ruffs, and cuffs
Popinjay	Blue-green, peacock blue (G.B.)		Used by courtesans, especially for sleeves
Sea green	Bright turquoise		Worn by all classes. Its popularity was ridiculed in the drama in spite of the fact that the Queen wore it. There seems to have been a changeable taffeta that shone green and blue as the light caught warp or weft and this perhaps originated the name
Willow	Sombre grey-green	Lost love; forsaken	Often used in combination with bright colours

YELLOW

Orange-tawny	Lively dark orange	Pride	Popular in all articles of clothing; descriptive of beards

Colours (continued)

Eliza-bethan name	Description	Symbolism	Use
Primrose	Delicate pale green-yellow	Youth, young love	Often used with silver for exquisite male and female attire
Straw[1]	Bright yellow	Abundance	Mentioned as a colour for beards and stockings; worn in combination with scarlet by Court jesters
Tawney	Yellowish tan	Sadness	Used with black for mourning. Like dark blue, it was the colour of servitude, and used for servants' liveries, but, unlike dark blue, it was also worn by all other classes
Whey	A thin bluish cream		Described as "old man's beard"; a colour sometimes used in lining material

BROWN

Eliza-bethan name	Description	Symbolism	Use
Abraham	Dark chocolate brown		Descriptive of the colour of dark-brown beards
Maiden-hair	Bright tan		Favourite colour for stage costume, especially for women's garments
Russet	Dusky reddish brown	Steadfastness	Homespun woollen garments were dyed this colour; hence its association with rustic clothing. However, it was a colour that was also used in dyeing some of the most expensive fabrics

[1] Yellow is always associated with Hymen and seems to have been used in wedding attire, especially by rustic bridegrooms. It was symbolic of both love and jealousy. To suggest their love for the Queen, courtiers wore yellow stockings, and Shakespeare must have been satirizing this in Twelfth Night when Malvolio appears before his mistress in them. A jealous husband was signified by the wearing of yellow in some part of his attire. A combination of black and yellow symbolized constancy and sadness.

Colours (continued)

Eliza-bethan name	Description	Symbolism	Use
		GREY	
Ash	Soft dove grey		Velvet was frequently dyed this colour. It made a beautiful background for bright-coloured embroidery and trimming
Rat's colour	Dull, dark grey		Associated with the garments of the poor and destitute

ELIZABETHAN COLOUR COMBINATIONS USED BY COURT AND NOBILITY

White, gold, silver, red, and green (Queen Elizabeth)
Black, white, gold, pale yellow, rose, and grey
Purple, gold, white, apricot
Orange, fawn, white, gold
Black, gold, crimson
Silver, white, crimson
White, silver, peach colour
Silver, white, gold, violet
Russet, gold, silver, orange
White, silver, primrose
Maiden's blush, gold, silver
Orange and silver
Black, purple, crimson, white (Mary, Queen of Scots)
Peacock blue, white, black, gold
White, silver, brown, and pale buff
Claret red, white, gold
Crimson, green, gold, black
White, straw, gold
Coral pink, silver, grey
Emerald, black, white, silver
Claret red, white, silver
Yellow, claret, gold and silver
Black, dark tan, light tan, white, silver

COMBINATIONS OF FABRICS

Satin, velvet, taffeta, and lawn
Cloth of gold or silver, velvet, and cambric
Grosgrain, satin, lace, lawn

colour combinations taken from Elizabethan portraits and from diaries and household accounts of the time provides some idea of the beauty and complexity of colour schemes affected by both men and women of the period, and may be of value to the modern producer when he comes to consider costumes and draperies in a Shakespearean production. Fabric combinations also are listed.

With fabrics purchased in colours appropriate and effective for the characters who will wear them, attention may now be turned to the basic articles of attire of both men and women. On pp. 157–190, these garments are discussed separately and in detail, both for the sake of the seamstress and in order to assure the correct effect of the costuming as a whole.

Finally we come to trimmings, and since these embellishments do a great deal to emphasize outstanding characteristics of Elizabethan costume, they are described in detail on pp. 190–193. These descriptions should, if possible, be supplemented by a study of portraits of the period (or reproductions of them), in order to get an even clearer idea of the endless variation that taste and ingenuity supplied to these adornments.

In conclusion, the person responsible for the costumes of a Shakespearean play will want to purchase what is appropriate, effective, and durable. In order that he may do this and yet remain within the bounds of his budget, suggestions have been added, on pp. 194–197, that will enable him to keep the number of garments to a minimum without impairing the visual effectiveness of the production.

Women's Costume

Smock

This garment seems to have served alike for shirt and nightgown and was similar to the shirt worn by men. It was a straight garment with shoulder seams, the back half being a few inches longer than the front. Being about thirty or forty inches long, it reached to a little below the knee. A slit from the neckline to the middle of the chest allowed for its being pulled over the head. The edges of this slit, the collar, and the cuffs of the long full sleeve were embroidered in coloured silks or trimmed with "black-work", cutwork, "square-work", or lace of gold, silver, or linen thread. The collar of the smock was either soft, turned down, and invisible above the dress, or was starched or wired so that it stood erect above the collarless bodice, or was inside the standing collar of the bodice with its ruched edge showing at the top. Small at first, this frill was later to grow to the ruff.

HOSE

Women wore as an equivalent to drawers, or pants, hose shaped like the outer garment of the name worn by men. Mary, Queen of Scots wore "jersey white hose . . . next her legs". There is no way of knowing how they looked, but the high rounded curves of the hips seen in pictures of women wearing kirtles unsupported by farthingales give a very good idea of the outline of these garments. (See also Venetians, p. 183.)

PETTICOAT

The next garment in the order of its putting on is the petticoat. This garment was attached either permanently or by "points" (see p. 192) to a garment rather like a camisole. The petticoat was long enough to fall to within a few inches of the ground, was about two and half yards round the hem, and was always lined. Those used for warmth were very heavy. Frequently two or more petticoats were worn, of different materials and colours and of different lengths.

When the skirt, or "half-kirtle", was opened down the front, the top petticoat was exposed and became an important part of the costume and, as such, was extremely decorative. It was frequently made of velvet, or satin, tissue or tufted taffeta, and trimmed with gold and silver lace or braid. Sometimes it was pinked to show the contrasting lining, or guarded (i.e., trimmed with bands) with velvet or exquisite lace or even with pearls or precious stones. Sometimes, when not visible in this way, it hung below the kirtle hem in scallops trimmed with spangles or gold lace. (A beautiful example of this can be seen in the portrait of Anne Vavasour between pp. 184-185.)

STAYS

The stiffness of appearance that was so characteristic of the fashions of Elizabethan women was obtained by means of stays (corsets) under the bodices and frames under the skirts. The stays consisted of a tight linen bodice with slots into which strips of wood or whalebone, called "busks", were inserted and tied with laces, or "busk points". Sometimes the entire garment was of whalebone, leather, or even iron. An "iron bodyes" is still to be seen in the Victoria and Albert Museum in London, as are also a number of wooden busks beautifully carved. At the Folger Shakespeare Library in Washington, D.C., there may be seen a corset that possibly belonged to Queen Elizabeth.[1]

[1] A photograph of this corset appears in the *National Geographic Magazine* for September, 1951, p. 423.

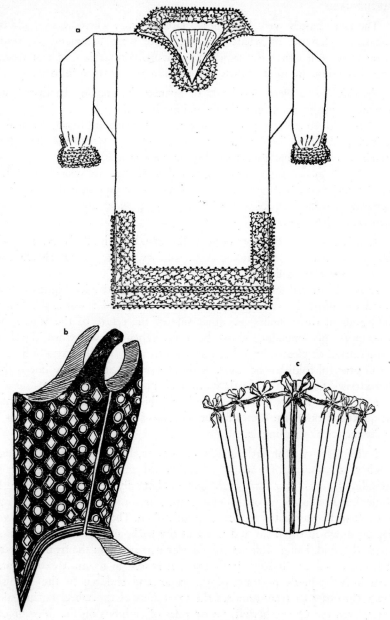

a Linen smock embroidered in silk and gold thread. *b* Iron corset. *c* Linen body
with busks fastened with points

FARTHINGALES

The skirt frames were known as "farthingales". These were made of rushes, wood, wire, or whalebone, and were worn to extend the skirt. There were no less than five types, if not actually in fashion, at least worn, at the same time. In order of their introduction, they were as follows:

Spanish. There were two types of Spanish farthingale, the first more generally worn by the Court, the second by the middle classes.

a. A skirt containing a series of cane or whalebone hoops gradually increasing in circumference from waist to feet over which the dress was stretched so tightly that not a wrinkle or crease was to be seen.

b. A bell-shaped cage of rushes, wood slats, wire, or whalebone. This type caused a rounded swell just below the waist and extended the skirt suddenly about a foot above the hem. This type does not appear to have been worn after 1580.

French. This was the most popular farthingale with all classes. Though there were many modifications, there were two types to which allusion is most frequently made.

a. A roll, or bolster, stiffened with wire or stuffed with bombast, tied round the waist. It was full in the back and tapered towards the front, ending about three inches on either side of the centre of the waist, the tying tapes only extending across the front. When this was worn, the skirt was gathered or pleated into the waistband to allow for the extra bulk and fell in graceful folds to the floor. A slight curve-in at the knee line is the characteristic feature of the kirtle worn over this type of farthingale.

b. A roll, or bolster, at the back only, forming a shelflike bustle, leaving the sides and front of the dress straight. This was known as a "half", "demi-", or "semicircled" farthingale.

Italian. This type of farthingale was worn exclusively by the Court and nobility. It consisted of a wood or iron wheel worn round the waist and extending from eight to forty-eight inches. Naturally the length and breadth of the skirt had to allow for this extension. The abrupt angle of the hip line was softened by a pleated frill or loops of ribbon. The wheel is often shown tipping down in the front and rising at the back, and sometimes it is not equal all round, being wider at the sides or narrowing in the front. In spite of being called an "Italian" farthingale, it is seen in its most extravagant form in Velazquez's portraits of the ladies and children of the Spanish Court. In order to accommodate the extensions of the wheel farthingale, ladies, even the Queen herself, sat on piles of cushions on the floor or on joint stools. Later, towards the end of the sixteenth century, the special "farthingale chair" came into use (see p. 71).

KIRTLE

This is the name given to the dress, which consisted of a bodice and a skirt, or "half-kirtle". In the portraits of the 1540s this garment is shown "closed", or fastened down the front from neck to hem, and this type of dress was usually worn with the Spanish farthingale. Later, one or two portraits show an "open half-kirtle" with a handsome petticoat showing from waist to hem. The kirtle was elaborately trimmed, slashed, guarded, or braided, and frequently the bodice was of different material and colour from that of the half-kirtle.

FOREPART AND STOMACHER

From 1590 to 1600 the kirtle is frequently shown opening all down the front, and there appear two elaborate accessories: the stomacher, or "placard", filling in the opening of the bodice, and the "forepart" filling in the opening of the half-kirtle. These triangular pieces, which seldom matched the kirtle, were, of course, detachable and allowed for variety by introducing different coloured notes to the same basic garment. They were made over foundations of pasteboard, or, as in the case of the stomacher, stiffened with busks, and were usually of very costly materials embroidered, pinked, trimmed with gold and silver lace, spangles, oes, bands of gold, silver braid placed straight or diagonally, and even precious stones and pearls. The forepart and stomacher, if both were worn, did not always match, and this again allowed for further variety in colour and texture. At one time it seems to have been fashionable to "veil" the stomacher "with smoky lawn" to add subtlety to the general effect. The subdued sparkle of gorgeous jewels and decorations seen through the very fine black veiling must have been very beautiful at close range. Over the forepart, or especially over the closed kirtle, aprons were worn by women of fashion from 1550 to 1640. When worn with a closed kirtle, these were in a way equivalent to the forepart, and again were extremely costly and decorative, usually being made of exquisite handmade lace or embroidered lawn or a combination of both.

SLEEVES

Variety seems to have been the most outstanding quality of the sleeves of the period, and, since they, like the forepart and stomacher, were often detachable, they could be changed from day to day.

So many types of sleeves are seen in contemporary portraits and referred to in contemporary plays that it will be necessary to examine them in detail.

Down Sleeve. A long, fairly full sleeve usually attached to, and belonging

S.S.P—L

a, b Spanish farthingale, front and side views. *c* Petticoat and kirtle over Spanish farthingale. *d* Italian wheel farthingale. *e* Kirtle over Italian farthingale

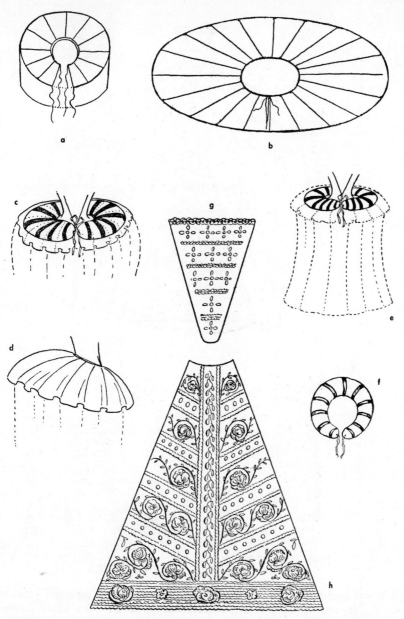

a, b Two types of Italian wheel farthingale seen from above. *c, d* French farthingale, front and side views. *e* French farthingale showing line taken by kirtle. *f* French roll farthingale showing increased size at the back. *g* Stomacher. *h* Forepart, or placard

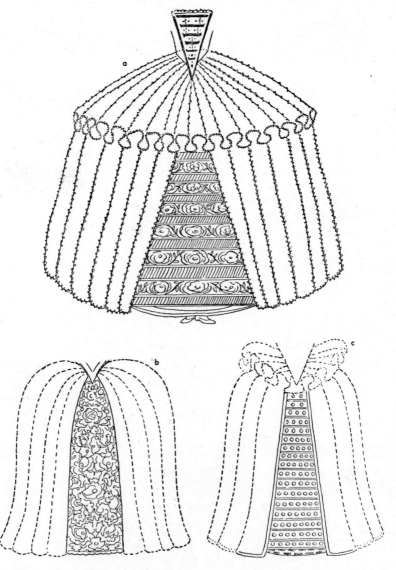

a Wheel farthingale, open kirtle, forepart, stomacher, and petticoat. *b* French farthingale, open kirtle, and forepart. *c* French farthingale, open kirtle, showing petticoat

to, an undergarment, such as smock or partlet, the latter being equivalent to the modern blouse. The down sleeve was nearly always worn with side and hanging sleeves.

Undersleeve. A separate sleeve attached to the armhole of the kirtle and worn under a short-sleeved robe. As the lower part was frequently the only part seen, it was known as a "half-sleeve" or "foresleeve". Sometimes it was actually a half-sleeve covering only elbow and forearm and drawn on like a long glove.

Trunk, or Farthingale, Sleeve. A bulky sleeve tapering towards the wrist and having the shape of a cannon. The top part was extended by means of wire, reed, or whalebone; hence, the name "farthingale" sleeve. It was usually padded and slashed or pinked, or both. (See Petruchio's description of such a sleeve at the head of this chapter.) This sleeve was fashionable only until the late 80s, but a modified form was worn by country women until 1600.

Side Sleeve. A long open sleeve attached round the armhole of gown or robe and meeting in front at the shoulder but falling open from there to a line just below the knee. Often it was of the same material as the gown or robe, but always it had a lining of a contrasting texture or colour. When it fell to the floor, it was known as a "hanging" or "pendant" sleeve.

Rolls, or Wings. All separate sleeves were attached to the armhole of kirtle, gown, or robe by passing a length of tape, braid, or ribbon through holes in the sleeves and corresponding holes in the armhole, each piece of tape, etc., being tied in a bow. These "points" were hidden by "rolls", or "wings", which resembled rounded epaulets and were part of the bodice. Wings were padded or stiffened, slashed or banded, or adorned with bows or loops of ribbon and frequently with jewelled ornaments.

Sleeve-hand. Material of the sleeve that extended beyond the hand in the form of a gathered frill or a circular or pointed flare.

Cuff. A simple fold of linen turned back over the sleeve or a small ruff at its edge. No doubt this was originally the cuff of the smock pulled down to show below the sleeve or turned back over it. As time went on, cuffs were separate attachments and became more and more elaborate and costly.

GOWN

The equivalent of the gown today is the topcoat, and, although it was, early in the sixteenth century, as today, associated with outdoor wear, it later became also a further adornment to formal indoor attire. It was a neck-to-hem garment worn over the kirtle, and there were several distinct types.

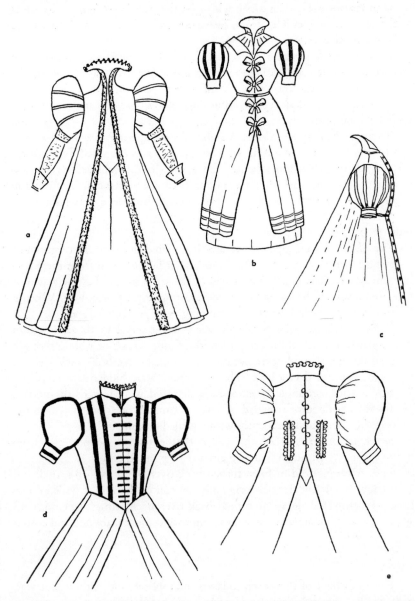

a Dutch, or "round", gown. *b*, *c* Variants of round gown. *d* Italian gown. *e* Flanders
gown

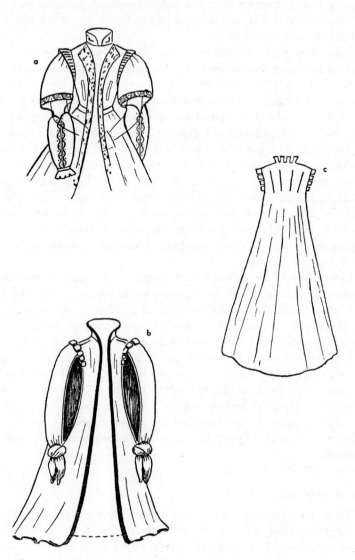

a French gown. *b* French robe. *c* Loose gown

Dutch Gown. Known also as the "round gown", this garment was closed or partly closed down the front and had elbow-length puffed sleeves.

Flanders Gown. This was rather like the Dutch gown but had a fitted bodice and stand-up collar.

Italian Gown. The distinctive feature of this gown was the two bodices, one over the other, the top one being slashed to reveal the under one.

French Gown. This type of gown had a very full skirt, high wings on the shoulders, and hanging sleeves. It was elaborately trimmed, pinked, slashed, guarded, embroidered, or decked with gold or silver lace. This gown, when worn indoors for splendour of formal attire, was referred to as a robe.

Nightgown. This garment, which was worn over the kirtle for warmth, had nothing in common with its modern namesake. It was worn equally indoors and out, in the daytime and at night, and by both men and women. It was an ankle-length coat with long sleeves. Great variety was seen in the collar, which ranged from a simple standing collar of fur to a large one falling in shawl-like folds over the shoulders. A very elaborate type of "nightgown", made of costly material and handsomely trimmed, was worn for very stately occasions.

Loose Gown.[1] This garment was worn over the kirtle but without the support of a farthingale. It hung, as its name suggests, from neckline to floor and completely hid the contours of the figure. Sometimes a long, closed sleeve was attached to the armhole under the high wings, but when it was worn informally, the sleeves of the smock or those of the kirtle were used. Originally used for warmth and informal wear, it later became an outdoor as well as an indoor garment, and was even worn by ladies to Court functions. This practice evidently resulted from King James's request that the enormous farthingales be not worn at Court masques as they cut down the seating capacity at these functions.[2] It says something for the popularity of the loose gown that Queen Elizabeth had nearly a hundred of them in her wardrobe.

Cloak and Safeguard

These two garments were used exclusively for outdoor wear. The cloak, or long cape, was worn for warmth and for the protection of clothes when travelling. The safeguard was a voluminous overskirt worn on horseback. This latter garment was often worn with a short waist-length cape.

---

[1] A beautiful example of a loose gown may be seen at the South Kensington Museum in London, and a photograph of this garment will be found in Linthicum, M. Channing, *Costume in the Elizabethan Drama*, p. 183.
[2] *Ibid.*, p. 182.

HEAD AND NECKWEAR

Rail. This term is used to describe (*a*) a square of material folded shawl-wise and worn round neck and shoulders; (*b*) a veil worn over the back of the head and bowed with wire into two arcs at the shoulder-line; and (*c*) a cape of waist length worn over the smock at night.

Ruffs and Collars. Starting with the ruched edge of the smock showing above the kirtle collar, the ruff had a humble beginning. Its rival, the Medici collar, began in a similar fashion, the kirtle collar being opened and turned back on each side and the smock collar following the same line. On a collar-less kirtle, a stand-up collar of lawn appeared, and this may have been the collar of the smock or partlet. All three types are seen in the early part of the sixteenth century, but are mentioned here since they were retained by country women and the more humble townswomen and female servants up to and even through the period under consideration.

It was usual for ladies to display their bare bosoms until marriage, and the great open Medici collar was frequently worn by unmarried ladies of the Court and nobility. Only portraits of the period can give an adequate idea of the variety and magnificence of this frame, which shows off the beauty of the women to such advantage. The Virgin Queen seems to have worn a great number of the various forms of neckwear, and in an engraving of a portrait of her, painted possibly about 1594, she is seen wearing a small closed neck ruff and the great arching rail together with a magnificent threefold Medici collar (see Frontispiece).

From 1590 to 1610, both open and closed ruffs became more and more elaborate and extravagant and showed greater variety in their make and ornamentation. The introduction of starch was in part responsible for the increased circumference and the intricate "setting" of ruffs. The rise of this collar behind the head was achieved with the aid of a wire frame known as a "rebato", or "supportasse" (see p. 193). The more and more extravagant trimming of gold, silver, and exquisite handmade lace and embroidery and the adornments of pearls were part of the whole trend towards fabulous display.

The closed ruffs of every variety grew larger and larger until, we read, one woman had to have a spoon two feet long in order to eat her soup.[1] By 1610, a simple collar having flaring lapels and known as a "whisk" came into fashion. At first it was fastened at the throat and allowed to spread out on either side beyond the shoulder-line; later it was brought down to the centre of a very low-cut bodice, completely covering the shoulders and rising behind to cover the back of the neck.

In nearly every case the sleeve-hands or cuffs followed the general

[1] Stephenson, Henry Thew, *Shakespeare's London*, p. 36.

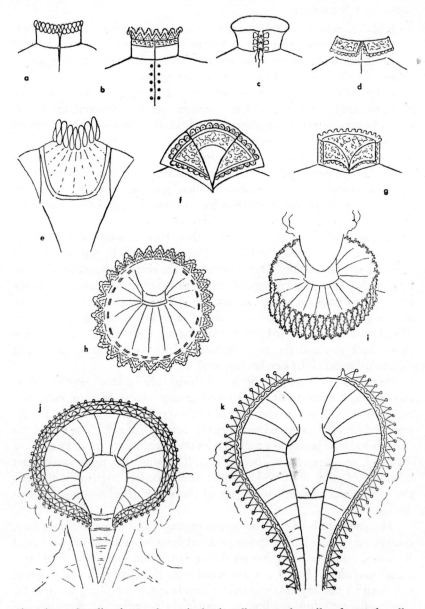

a, b, c, d Smock collar shown above the kirtle collar. *e* Partlet collar. *f, g* Kirtle collar opened to show turned-back smock collar. *h, i* Closed ruffs. *j, k* Open ruffs

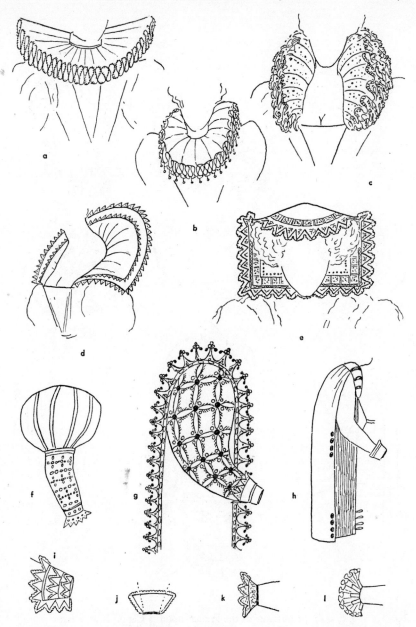

a, b Closed ruffs. *c* Open threefold ruff. *d* Whisk. *e* Shade and open ruff combined.
f Undersleeve, or half sleeve. *g* Farthingale sleeve with hanging sleeve. *h* Side sleeve.
i, j, k, l Cuffs

a, b, c, d, e, f Variants of the French hood. *g* Cap. *h* Beaver hat

a French hood. *b* **Beaver** hat worn over a cap. *c* Spanish cap. *d* Taffeta pipkin. *e* Shade
f Cap

pattern and ornamentation of the neckwear—with the closed ruff a border of ruching being worn, and with the open ruff, a deep turned-back cuff with trimming similar to that of the ruff.

Kerchief. A veil covering the head, sides of face, and neck.

Chinclout, or Muffler. A square of material worn over the chin. It seems to have been worn exclusively by women of the lower classes.

Scarf. A long narrow piece of silk, lawn, cypress, etc., used by women to shield their faces from the sun. It was often given as a favour to lovers.

Wimple. A square or rectangle of linen folded over the head, the sides of the face, and the neck. It was used by women in mourning and is seen today in nuns' head covering.

Tippet. A scarf worn round the neck.

Hats and Head Coverings. It has already been said that rapidly changing fashion was one of the predominant characteristics of costume during the time of the first production of Shakespeare's plays. The most abrupt change in the fundamentals of attire occurred between 1585 and 1590, and nowhere is this more evident than in the hairdressing and headgear of women. Smooth hair, held in place by fillets of ribbon and discreetly covered by hoods, coifs, or cauls, covering the head and sides of the neck, gave place, in the world of fashion, to frizzed or crimped hair piled on wire frames, the excessive use of false hair, and the constant application of dye of all colours. Across the top of this elaboration, women wore, in the house, wreaths of artificial flowers, borders of lace, lawn, and circlets of gold and silver set with precious stones. Strands of hair tied with a succession of satin bows, each one having a jewelled ornament or brooch at its centre, were not uncommon (see the portrait of Anne Vavasour between pp. 184–185).

The back of the head was often covered by a small cap resembling a baby's bonnet, embroidered with gold and silver thread or coloured silks. When the hair was not built up, the caul of medieval times was still worn. It consisted of a hair-net made of gold thread or braid crisscrossed to form a lattice mesh, and was frequently lined with gold tissue or yellow taffeta to give the effect of blond hair beneath. To these caps and cauls a "shade" or "shadow" (something like an eyeshade only turned down flat on the forehead in the middle) was added for outdoor wear to protect the face from the sun. These shades were usually made of starched linen, lawn, or lace, but wired taffeta, satin, or velvet were also used. Occasionally a wimple seems to have served the same purpose as a shade, and the use of black velvet masks as protection both from the sun and from undesirable attentions of strangers was a common occurrence, especially in public places such as the playhouses.

The shade seems to have gone out of fashion about 1590, when women wore either hats of beaver, taffeta, or velvet with high crowns and small brims, like the men, or small Spanish caps shaped like a porringer or basin, with a bunch of feathers on top or at the side. The taffeta pipkin, often referred to, was a large crown pleated into a narrow brim which dipped down to a point on the forehead.

LEG AND FOOTWEAR

Stockings. Hand-knit stockings in silk and wool were worn early in the sixteenth century, and in 1566 we hear of Queen Elizabeth's "silk-woman" being paid for six pairs of black silk knitted stockings. By 1590 a knitting machine was being used, but the price for stockings remained high, a fact accounted for by the decorations, which consisted of the inter-lacing of gold and silver thread and embroidered clocks, or "quirks". Since skirts were long, we have no way of knowing whether women wore dyed stockings to match or to contrast with their costumes, but it is certain that men did. Not until the ankle-length skirt came in about 1600 were the stockings visible. Woollen stockings were worn by the poor and middle classes, and my lady seems to have worn them also for warmth when travelling and as a protection for the silk ones worn beneath.

Garters. Although unseen in women's attire garters were lavishly orna-mented. They consisted of strips of taffeta, cypress, or lace, and were edged with lace of all kinds, knitted strips of crewel being used by the less opulent. With the garter tied below the knee the stocking was turned in to form a roll above the knee.

Boots and Shoes. For riding and outdoor wear women wore high laced boots which came above the calf and had thick soles and a low heel. They were made of leather or velvet and were topped with fur or lace.

A heavy shoe with a cork sole that sloped from two inches at the heel to one inch at the toe was worn for walking in wet and muddy weather, but later an imported fashion introduced the Venetian chopine, a stilt-like over-shoe having a cork base often five to six inches high. Its popularity seems to have been brief, possibly owing to the extreme difficulty of walking in it.

Indoors, the pump was worn by men and women alike. It was usually made of soft leather with a rounded or slightly pointed toe and was without a heel. For adornment it was slashed and pinked and sometimes had latchets tied with ribbon bows on the instep. By 1600 it had become a square-toed, heeled shoe adorned with rosettes ("raised roses") of beautiful gold, silver, or thread lace, sometimes edged with pearls. Pumps, when heelless and made of silk, velvet, or cloth, were known as "slippers"; the term "pump" seems to have applied only to the heavier type made of leather or heavily lined velvet.

The pantofle, a mule, was worn over pump or slipper for outdoor protection at first, but later became so ornamental that it was worn over the slipper indoors for elaborate or formal attire.

THREE CONTEMPORARY DESCRIPTIONS OF WOMEN'S COSTUMES

1590. Here is a description of a costume worn by Queen Elizabeth's woman Fool. As she was a jester, it gives some idea of the type of garment associated with professional entertainment.

. . . a gowne of changeable silk grograine, with a pair of sleeves and stomacher of white satin fringed with gold lace; a petycoat of changeable tuft-taffeta with three gold lace [three rows of gold braid] about the bodyes carnation satin.[1]

It is interesting to notice that here the gown takes the place of the kirtle.

1599. While there are many descriptions of, and allusions to, parts of costume in Shakespeare's plays, there is only one full description of a woman's dress. It occurs in *Much Ado about Nothing*, III, 4. Hero is being dressed for her wedding, and her flattering waiting woman tells her that her gown is worth ten of the Duchess of Milan's, which was

"Cloth o' gold, and cuts, and laced with silver, set with pearls, down sleeves, side sleeves, and skirts round, underborne [over a farthingale?] with a bluish tinsel."

1617. Here is the description of a courtesan seen in the audience at the Fortune theatre.

This lady's bodice was of yellow satin richly embroidered, her petticoat of gold tissue with stripes, her robe of red velvet with a raised pile, lined with yellow muslin with broad stripes of pure gold. She wore an apron of point lace in various patterns; her head-tire was highly perfumed and the collar of white satin beneath a delicately-wrought ruff.[2]

Men's Costume

The attire of Elizabethan men was as rich, as costly, and as lavishly embellished as that worn by their womenfolk. In fact, in some instances, men may be said to have surpassed women in extravagance and eccentricity

[1] Stopes, (Mrs.) C. C., *Shakespeare's Environment*, pp. 273-274.
[2] This description by Chaplain Busano of the Venetian embassy, who was accosted by the woman, is quoted by Alfred Harbage in *Shakespeare's Audience*, p. 100.

when it came to the choice of material, colour, and cut of their clothes. It is interesting to think that the pictorial appeal of Shakespearean productions lost nothing from the fact that there was, in every play, a predominantly male cast. As a result, it will be of the utmost importance for the modern producer to pay particular attention to every characteristic of Elizabethan male attire.

Shirt

The men's shirts did not differ greatly from the women's smocks except that, since they were displayed when the doublet was removed, they were more lavishly embroidered or trimmed.[1] As in the case of the woman's smock, the collar might show above the standing collar of the doublet or be turned down over the edge of it, and it developed later into ruffs and falling bands respectively.

Waistcoat

Over the shirt a waist-length close-fitting garment known as a "waistcoat" was sometimes worn. It might be with or without sleeves and seems to have been worn for warmth, being usually padded or quilted. It might also have served as a foundation for the doublet when it was made of stiff material or inserted with stays, and have helped to maintain the creaseless effect so important to a man of fashion.

Doublet

The garment corresponding to the woman's bodice was cut to fit closely to the figure. An exception was the peasecod-bellied doublet which had, over the abdomen, a protuberance shaped like a pea pod with the curved end hanging over the girdle.[2]

Made of rich materials, the doublet was fastened from the standing collar to the waistline with buttons, often of beauty and value, and trimmed with pinking or slashing that revealed the contrasting lining; with braid; with panes (see p. 182) of contrasting material; with lace of gold, silver, or thread; and, often, with combinations of all these. The sleeves were separate and, so, changeable, giving variety in colour, texture, and trimming to the same doublet. The wings (see p. 165), which started as piccadills to hide

---

[1] Two remarkable examples of these garments can still be seen: one an actual garment of the late sixteenth century at the Victoria and Albert Museum in London, and the other a pictured representation in the portrait of the actor Nat Field, which hangs in the College of God's Gift, Dulwich, London.

[2] This may still be seen in the traditional costume of Punch in the Punch and Judy Show.

S.S.P.—M

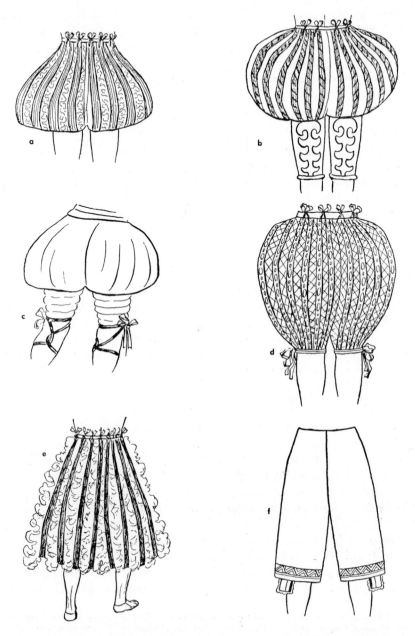

a Paned trunk hose. *b* Paned trunk hose and canions. *c* Trunk hose, canions, and cross-gartering. *d* Venetians. *e* German slops. *f* Open hose

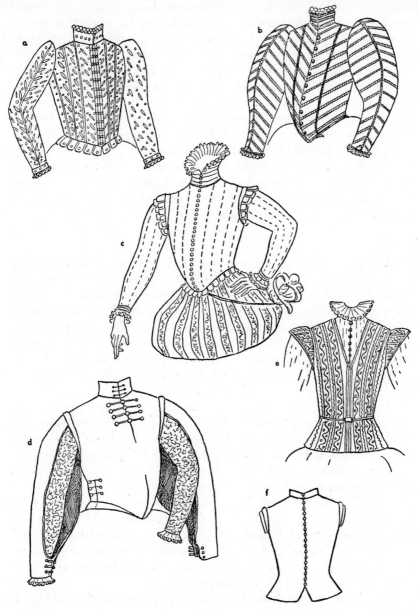

a Slashed and pinked doublet with piccadills. *b* Peasecod-bellied doublet. *c* Slashed suède doublet with piccadills. *d* Jerkin with peasecod belly and hanging sleeves. *e* Velvet jerkin. *f* Leather jerkin

the points fastening the sleeves, later became slashed rolls or stiff, peaked epaulets. Sewed to the waistline were doublet "skirts" of varying lengths, these sometimes being so short that they hardly showed below the girdle. Frequently they were composed of piccadills whose edges either met or overlapped. Apart from their decorative value they served to hide the points that fastened hose to doublet. These points, when made of satin ribbon and tagged with aiguillettes might be tied in bows round the waistline and so become a decoration in themselves. Trimmings running obliquely across sleeves and on each side of the front fastenings were fashionable. Panes over contrasting linings were also popular.

The sleeves, except for great variety in colour, fabric, and trimming, remained unchanged throughout the period. With only slight padding they conformed to the shape of the arm. The "cannon" sleeve and the full "bishop" sleeve were out of fashion by 1580.

JERKIN

A garment worn over the doublet and generally conforming to it in cut was known as a "jerkin"; the skirts of this garment were, however, always longer than those of the doublet, and sometimes consisted of two or three skirts, one over the other, of varying lengths. The sleeves were attached at the armhole and showed great variety, some of the types being short puffs to the elbow; hanging sleeves; sleeves worn over, and following the line of, the doublet sleeves; and "dummy" sleeves, straight or shaped pieces of material hanging from the armhole, which could be fastened round the arm at wrist and elbow with loops and buttons.

The jerkin was sometimes buttoned all down the front, but more often had only a slit halfway down the chest to allow for its being pulled over the head. Slits, or open side seams with buttons on one side and loops on the other, allowed further freedom in putting on a jerkin, and the buttoning of these slits then gave a closer and neater fit to the garment. This means of getting a closer fit, and at the same time of adding a decorative note, was also seen in the bodice of the French robe worn by women. Although the jerkin was doubtless originally worn for warmth, it would seem to have been frequently worn for show, since in most portraits it appears unfastened.

The name "jerkin" also applied to a strictly utilitarian garment made of leather which was worn beneath armour, or as part-uniform by military officers (see p. 179) and gentlemen-in-waiting.

The Court, or dress, jerkin was made of silk, velvet, or cloth and was as lavishly trimmed as the doublet. One Court jerkin is known to have been made of scented suède, ornately slashed and pinked, with one short skirt over one long one.

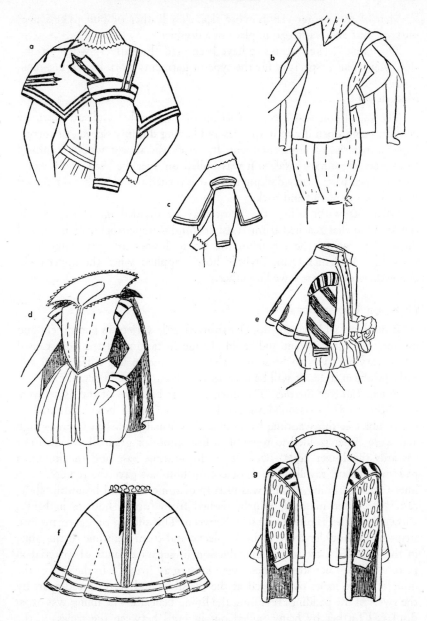

a A mandilion worn "collywestonward" (side to front). *b* Mandilion with hanging sleeves. *c* Mandilion. *d* Short French cloak. *e* Spanish coat. *f* Spanish cloak. *g* Dutch cloak

Men of the poorer classes wore sleeveless leather or buff jerkins over shirt, or shirt and waistcoat, in place of a doublet.

The name "jacket" seems to have been used alternatively with "jerkin" and "waistcoat", especially for the type of garments worn by serving-men.

MANDILION

The mandilion was a type of jerkin that resembled a tabard worn by heralds, being open down both sides and having dummy sleeves, or merely flaps of material to represent them. Its wear was almost wholly confined to soldiers or military officers. It was pulled on over the head, and it seems to have been particularly dashing to wear it turned round so that the sleeves hung down the front and back.[1]

Garments worn below the waist may be divided into two separate types: those that reached from waist to thigh—upperstocks, or hose; and those that covered the leg from the thigh downward—netherstocks, or stockings. A further term, "whole hose", applied when the upperstocks and netherstocks were sewed together.

HOSE, OR UPPERSTOCKS

It has been said that the doublet showed little variety in general cut and outline, but the constant and rapid change in fashion in the hose caused many varying styles to be seen at the same time in late Elizabethan and early Jacobean times. It will be necessary to discuss these in detail.

Round Hose, or Breeches. The most popular breeches of the 1590s were the short, puffed or stuffed variety known as "round hose". Moored to the doublet at the waistline by points, they usually reached to mid-thigh and were either padded to resemble a flat onion, or gradually swelled out towards the lower edge. Between a close-fitting base and the lining, a padding of hair, ravelled wool, or cotton bombast gave the required outline. Over the lining, which was usually of some rich and beautiful fabric, came the outer material, which, slashed from top to bottom in bands, allowed the underlining to be seen between. This slitting of a garment into strips from shoulder to wrist in the sleeve and from waistline to thighline in the hose led later to the introduction of separate bands of material in place of the former strips. These were known as "panes". In the case of the doublet, these panes overlapped at the waistline and were spread apart by the swell of the padding, revealing the lining beneath. The lining was often displayed further by being pulled out in puffs between the panes. In the dress of the Court and nobility, these panes were highly ornamental, being

---

[1] The famous painting of Sir Philip Sidney in the National Portrait Gallery in London shows this so-called "collywestonward" wearing of a military mandilion.

slashed or pinked, embroidered or guarded, or even edged with goldsmith's work or studded with jewels. A slight variant of the round hose was the short trunks, in which the padding was omitted and the hose fell in soft overlapping folds.

Slops. Though the term "slops" was sometimes applied to the various types of round hose, it certainly referred more specifically to German slops, which came into fashion in the 1590s and lasted, with modifications, until the Commonwealth. In place of padding in these garments, a very voluminous lining was used, large, soft puffs of which were pulled out between widely spaced panes. In some cases this lining was so long that, although the panes might reach only to the mid-thigh, the loose flopping puffs hung down to and often below the knee. A strange variant of this was slops which fitted skin-tight over the buttocks with the panes and puffs starting below this line and reaching to the calf of the leg.

Venetians. Close-fitting breeches reaching to, and fastened close at, the knee, had been popular as early as 1560, but the increasing exaggeration of all normal lines of the figure had, by 1595, caused this garment to be padded or wired in such a way that the legs resembled a pair of bellows, being peg-topped or pear-shaped. Later, instead of being stretched over padding, these breeches were gathered or pleated at the waistline and fell in soft folds. (It is possible that modified venetians were worn by women under their petticoats; if so, the fashion came from Italy.)

Open Hose. An equivalent of these breeches is seen today in pedal-pushers. They consisted of long shorts reaching to below the knee. They were worn throughout the period, but mostly by the middle classes, and by servitors, sailors, and the like.

Galligaskins. These were wide unpadded knickers reaching to, and fastened closely at, the knee.

Canions. These stocking-top extensions (also known as "canons") covered the thigh and may or may not have been attached to the hose. They seem to have been made of every kind of material and were frequently embroidered or trimmed.

NETHERSTOCKS, OR STOCKINGS

There seems to have been little difference between the stockings of men and those of women of the Court and nobility. A much longer stocking, however, was needed by men wearing round hose when canions were not worn.

A thick knitted legging was worn over the stockings for protection by horsemen, or at any time when a high boot was worn. The term "hose" as applied to stockings may have started with these footless stockings, which were known as "boot hose".

GARTERS

The garters worn by men were, since they were often visible, more ornate than those worn by women. When canions were worn, invisible garters attached to them seem to have been merely a leather strap and buckle. When open hose were worn, the actual band of the garter was invisible, but the ends hung below the breeches and were fringed, embroidered, or edged with gold, silver, or thread lace. There was a time, early in the period, when tights were attached by points to a girdle or sewed to the hose.

FOOTWEAR

For light footwear, men wore pumps, slippers, and pantofles; for sports, travelling, and soldiering, a great variety of splendid and ornate high boots or top boots. The soft slipper made of cheverel leather was often pinked, slashed, or jagged, and showed a contrasting lining.

OUTER GARMENTS

To the garments already considered must now be added those that were worn over all this finery for the purposes of warmth and yet further show. Of the types in common use we shall consider only those that are likely to be used in the plays—three of them short and two of them long. (See also Nightgown, p. 168.)

Dutch Cloak. The so-called "Dutch cloak" was really a waist-length coat worn until 1620. It was usually guarded and had sleeves, but the arms were never inserted in these, and, draped carelessly over the shoulders, it was worn by men and women alike.

Cassock. By 1590 this type of short coat was worn only by working classes of town and country. It consisted of a loose-sleeved, thigh-length garment fastened or girdled at the waist.

Coat. Worn in place of a cloak, the coat was a closed, waist-length garment with down or side sleeves.

Gaberdine. This was a long closed garment that fitted the upper part of the body but had fairly full skirts below the waist. It was belted at the waist and usually had side sleeves. It seems to have been worn by all classes, but is most usually associated with the merchants.

Cloak. Up to 1594 a short cape had been fashionable, but the long circular French cloak took its place and remained in fashion up to Carolinian times. Cloaks, worn by both men and women, were, like the rest of the

Sir Philip Sidney (1577). Artist
unknown

National Portrait Gallery

Sir Walter Raleigh (1588). Artist
unknown

Preston Davie, Esq.

Lady Anne Vavasour (*c.* 1600–1605). Artist unknown

Supposed portrait of Queen Elizabeth. Artist unknown

Queen Elizabeth dancing with the Earl of Leicester. Artist and date unknown

Lord de L'Isle and Dudley

a Gaberdine. *b* Open robe. *c* Open fur-lined robe. *d* Closed robe

attire of Court and nobility, extremely beautiful and costly, and, in the case of the men, worn in many graceful or fantastic ways: over one shoulder and under the opposite arm, the surplus length being draped over forearm or tucked into the girdle; suspended from the back of the neck with one end brought forward under the arm and flung over the opposite shoulder, etc.

ROBE

These magnificent garments were often of an official, ecclesiastical, or professional character, and thus were most frequently worn by men of middle age or advanced years. Made of sumptuous velvets, satins, silks, and broadcloth, they were guarded with contrasting material, banded with gold or silver braid, and often lined with rare and expensive fur. They were sometimes worn open to display the costume underneath, but there seem to be an equal number of portraits showing them closed and, in some rare instances, caught at the waist by a girdle. Such robes are to be seen today in the Lord Mayor's robe, the judge's scarlet and ermine robe, the cardinal's robe, the many robes of academic and professional institutions, and the robes worn by kings and courtiers on state occasions.

NECKWEAR

The neckwear of men was as varied as fashion or whim could suggest. However, among elderly men, as in the case of the robe, a conservative clinging to the fashions of an earlier day persisted. The upstanding collar of the doublet, which had originally been topped by the pulled-up collar of the shirt, now had an edge of stiffened piccadills round the neck, and, supported by this edge, a ruff band was worn. It varied from a small ruching to a six-inch-deep ruff. This came into fashion about 1570 and was worn consistently by some men until 1620. At the same time another type was worn that evolved from the turned-down shirt collar. It was known as the "falling band", and consisted of an open collar sewn into the top of the upstanding doublet collar and falling to the collar-bone. These two types of neckwear in their simplest forms were contemporaries for about the same span of time.

All the whims of fashion in neckwear that came and went were variations of these two basic styles. The ruff band, starched and set in double S lines, was known as the "organ-pipe ruff" and was fastened in front with band strings or was left open with the strings hanging down. Unstarched and allowed to fall in unstudied folds, it was known as the "ruff à la confusion". About 1590, it grew to huge dimensions and had to be starched and supported by a stiff frame, making the wearer's head appear to be resting on a large plate. The falling bands became more and more elaborate, being embroidered with coloured silk, spangles, and oes, adorned with cutwork or black-work, and edged with gold, silver, or thread lace. In some portraits as many as four falling bands are seen, worn one over the other, all graduating in size so that four differently trimmed edges are visible. A blending of the two styles is seen in the French fall, consisting of a ruff which, instead of standing out at right angles, fell down all round the supporting doublet collar. It is seen in various forms—with merely flattened sets so that the throat is seen; hanging down to the middle of the chest in front and short behind; or hanging at an equal length all round and edged with point lace. All ruffs, of whatsoever type, had either double, treble, or even quadruple layers of material, and the starching and setting of these allowed for great variety. In 1610, the whisk, a wide-open falling band, very stiffly starched and edged with costly lace, came into fashion and continued to be popular for over twenty years.

As in the case of women's bands, men's cuffs followed the general line and ornamentation of the neckwear, being small ruffs or ruching when a ruff band was worn, and turned-back cuffs when a falling band was worn.

SCARF

The silk scarf, worn diagonally across the chest and knotted at the waistline, was part of military officers' insignia and appears in many portraits of military men of the period.

HEADWEAR

Variety again is the outstanding feature of men's headwear during this period. Medieval flat caps were still worn by apprentices, and the three-cornered cap was worn by city merchants and by some members of the professions. A round close-fitting cap with the brim turned up flat against the head all round was known as a "nightcap", but, although it was worn in bed, it was also street wear for aged men and invalids. The Monmouth cap was a round brimless cap with a high tapering crown, worn by sailors and soldiers.

A high conical hat known as a "copatain" seems to have been of Eastern origin. It was sensational and attractive enough to be popular with courtiers and to figure as a decorative head-dress in the Court masques.

Beaver hats, of every size and shape, were worn only by the extremely wealthy, but a substitute made of rabbit fur was common. Felt, velvet, satin, and taffeta were popular materials for all kinds of hats. Trimming

a, b Flat caps. *c, d* Monmouths. *e* Nightcap. *f, g* Copatains. *h, i* Felt hats. *j, k* Velvet hats

a, c, e, h Felt hats. *b, d, f, g* Beaver hats

consisted of plumes, gold lace, and braid, with gold chains or cables round the base of the crowns and jewelled ornaments, brooches, buttons, and medals adorning the brims.

Trimmings & Accessories

BUTTONS

Apart from their use for fastening garments, buttons were used as trimming on almost all clothing, including hats. They ranged from simple bone or horn to gold studded with precious stones and were of countless sizes and shapes.

CODPIECE

There are allusions in the plays to one article of strictly male attire. This is the appendage called a "codpiece", which was fastened by points in the front of the hose. It consisted of a padded cushion adorned with ribbon or slashed to show contrasting lining, and, though it was frequently for show, it seems to have had a bag behind this showy exterior which could serve as a pocket or purse. In spite of reference to it in Shakespeare's plays, it seems to have gone out of fashion by 1590. The Scottish sporran is perhaps a modified survival of the codpiece.

In stating that this one accessory was worn exclusively by men, we underline the fact that all other adornments, with the possible exception of the fan, were worn equally by both sexes. In an age of men of virility and action, this is, at first, a quite astonishing revelation, until we remember that contrast between refinement of thought and violence of action, between fastidiousness of personal adornment and grossness of manners, characterized many men of the period, and that it was in no way detrimental for heroes of war and adventure to appear in fripperies and gewgaws that are considered today exclusively as part of female attire.

FANS

The most popular type of fan used by ladies of the Court consisted of tufts of graduated ostrich plumes set in gold and jewelled handles, sometimes having a miniature in the centre and sometimes a small mirror. However, the open-and-shut oriental type was also popular, as is testified by its appearance in many portraits of the period.

FURS

Many kinds of fur were used to border gowns at hem and sleeve, and many gowns worn in cold weather were fur-lined throughout. Martin, miniver, and sable were worn by the wealthy, and even the city merchants, as we can see in the Holbein portraits, wore collars and deep cuffs of fur as far back as the time of Henry VIII. A fur neckpiece, finished with head and paws set with gold and jewels, was very fashionable for women. Ermine seems to have been worn exclusively by nobility and royalty.

GIRDLE

Apart from necklaces, pendants, miniatures in beautiful and costly settings, brooches, rings, earrings, and chains, another important article of jewelry was the girdle. Those worn by ladies encircled the waist, but had suspended chains of varying lengths to which were attached mirrors, fans, purses, pomanders, and even muffs. Portraits of royalty show girdles of goldsmith's work set with many kinds of precious stones and having extensions down to the hem of the kirtle, from which are suspended magnificent pendants. A simple ribbon girdle, to which the fan alone was attached, was frequently used.

Men wore buckled leather girdles over doublet or jerkin for sports or with armour, but for dress or state occasions they wore girdles of gold, silver, embroidered leather, silk, or velvet, set with precious stones or pearls. At one side and well towards the back was the hanger consisting of one or two straps hooked to the girdle and ending in a plate or pad to which was buckled the scabbard of sword or dagger, or both. Sometimes the plate was hooked directly to the girdle without intervening straps. Sometimes the straps were passed through the panes.

GLOVES

For dress occasions, gloves were made of soft cheverel leather, heavily scented. The deep gauntlet cuffs were embroidered in coloured silks, seed pearls, oes, or precious stones, and edged with linked bands of gold or silver braid, or lace-edged and trimmed with spangles or pearls. The two outer edges of these cuffs had extensions of ribbon loops.

GUARDS

These were bands of material laid on or edging garments. They were usually of a colour and material that contrasted with that of the garment itself. Guarded clothes were not worn by the fashionable after the first half of the sixteenth century, but were still seen on the middle-class provincials, footmen, and stewards. As part of the trimming of official and professional robes, guards have never gone out of fashion.

HANDKERCHIEFS

Used solely for adornment, the handkerchief was made of lawn, silk, and even velvet, edged with gold, silver, or thread lace, and sometimes embroidered in coloured silk in strange and beautiful pictorial designs. The equivalent of the modern handkerchief was the humble "muckinder".

MUFFS

The flat, pillow-shaped muffs in sable, martin, and other rare and expensive furs were used almost exclusively by royalty, but those made of felt, velvet, or satin, and padded for warmth were fairly common. Muffs for show, made of tissue, silk embroidered with pearls and trimmings of all kinds, were used by the lords and fops of the Court of James I.

OES

Usually the term "oes" referred to metal eyelet holes sewed in designs or at regular intervals all over the material of a garment. The name also applied to small gold or silver sequins.

PICCADILLS

The borders of scallops or tabs known as "piccadills" were sewed round the armholes of doublets, at the edges of sleeves, the neckline of doublets, and the waistline of bodice. Elongated piccadills often formed the skirts of doublets. The name also applied to the stiffened tabs or wire frames round the neck of the doublet that served to support the French fall and the closed ruff.

POINTS

Thongs of leather, linen, silk braid, tape, or ribbon, known as "points", were used to fasten garments together. Holes set in pairs, in the two garments to be connected, were placed over each other and the points threaded through and tied in a bow. The tags were of metal, either simple and inexpensive or of gold and precious stones. These latter were visible and used for ornamentation and were known as "aiguillettes". The only survival of this type of fastening is the staylace and the shoelace.

POMANDER

The pomander was a ball compounded of aromatic herbs, essences, and oils, which, placed in an openwork golden case, was suspended from a chain round the neck or from the girdle round the waist. It not only imparted fragrance to the wearer, but was inhaled to counteract bad odours.

PURSES

In a pocketless age, the purse was indispensable. It consisted of a small bag with a draw-string at the top and was made of the same soft leather as the gloves or of embroidered velvet, silk, or cloth.

RAISED ROSES

The rosettes of beautiful lace, sometimes edged with pearls, that adorned the toe or straps of shoes were known as "raised roses"—an adornment, Hamlet reminds us, much affected by the players.

REBATO

The linen- or silk-covered wire frame known as a "rebato", or sometimes as a "supportasse", rose at the back of the neck and supported the high open ruff, or Medici collar, worn by women.

SLASHING

As the name implies, slashing consisted of cuts in material to show the lining of a garment. Small round punctures were referred to as "pinking", long slits as "slashing" or "scissoring", or, when the edges of the slits were like a saw, as "jagging". To prevent ravelling, the longer cuts were made on the bias, and it was not uncommon for a garment to have thousands of these slits. It says much for the close weaving and durability of fabrics that such garments have survived in excellent condition down to today.

III

Costume in Modern Shakespearean Production

Polonius: "Costly thy habit as thy purse can buy,
But not express'd in fancy; rich, not gaudy."
Hamlet, I, 3

THE PRODUCER of a Shakespearean play can, with the foregoing information for reference, proceed with assurance to the choice of fabrics, colours, and line.

It will be as well to study first the approximate date of the first performance of the play under consideration. Although scholars, in many cases, disagree as to these dates, there is usually a variation of only a few years—never enough to affect the costuming of a play appreciably. Since few authorities place presentation of the earliest plays at dates prior to 1590, it will be safe to consider that most, if not all, of the plays were first presented between 1590 and 1613.

Most of the outstanding changes in costume occurred between 1570 and 1590, and by this latter date the period of exaggeration had set in. Although there was great variety of fashions in the clothes worn at any one time, certain prevailing trends made their appearance in 1595 and continued to the end of the century. On the accession of James I in 1603, however, a great change took place, and it is here that care must be taken in costuming the plays that were presented at and after that date. The Jacobean fashions, though showing the same basic garments, vary considerably in line from Elizabethan fashions, and it is probable that stage costuming underwent a complete revolution as a result of the designs made and used by Inigo Jones for the Court masques.

Exaggerations of fashion that were both grotesque and uncomfortable,

194

such as the peasecod doublet, the huge wheel farthingale, and the enormous starched ruffs, should be modified to suit the comfort and dignity of the actor, and to prevent undue accent on costume, which is, after all, only an adjunct to the play. To risk lines—possibly whole scenes—being "lost" because the audience is gaping with astonishment at unusual spectacles of any kind is poor stagecraft. The exception to this is, of course, the costuming of the clowns, whose exaggerated and eccentric garments are legitimate comedy props. In some cases this not only prepares the audience for the farcical note that the clown introduces but helps to underline the plot. For instance, Launcelot Gobbo in *The Merchant of Venice* appears as the "Jew's man" in patched and threadbare clothes and explains, as one of his reasons for leaving Shylock to join the service of Bassanio, that the latter gives "rare new liveries". Bassanio, on taking him into his service, gives orders that his livery is to be "more guarded"—that is, more trimmed with guards—"than his fellows". All this can lead up to the re-entrance of Launcelot dressed for the trip to Belmont, and here the exaggerations of ruff, hat, sleeves, etc., which we can imagine he would add to his livery, can point up comic dismay on the part of Bassanio and helpless laughter, when he first appears, on the part of Gratiano and Lorenzo. Bassanio, wishing to appear with all splendour and dignity as a suitor for the hand of the Lady of Belmont, has already had to subdue the loud jocularity of Gratiano, whom he reluctantly allows to accompany him to Belmont, and Launcelot with his mountebank parody of fashion is the last straw.

The wooden or metal stays, the multiplicity of garments, and the heavy padding and stuffing of bodice and hose must, of necessity, be modified unless we are seriously to hamper the actor's movements and subject him to acute discomfort. *The braced appearance, however, is essential and must be maintained*, but this can be done by using whalebone or plastic corset busks inserted, at widely spaced intervals, into the linings of body garments, and these linings, in turn, can be widely laced to give smoothness of fit while allowing for ventilation. Multiplicity of garments can be suggested by attaching different-coloured strips of varying fabrics, one below the other, to the sleeves and hems of closed gowns and kirtles. Padding should be of the lightest, the best for hose and French farthingales being bran. In many cases it will be found that tissue paper can be used, in the upper part of the cannon sleeve, or to fill out high, soft-crowned hats, for instance.

Ruffs, though they can be shallower than those actually worn in Elizabethan times, must be crisp, and should be worn at rehearsal to enable the actors to get used to them. If they prove a handicap to free and vigorous movement, falling bands for the men and open ruffs for the women can be used.

Assembling a permanent wardrobe for a Shakespearean repertory company is a far less expensive undertaking than it at first appears to be. Since sleeves, panes, foreparts, and stomachers are detachable, many changes in appearance can be given to the same basic garments.

Neutral colours, such as grey or tawny, or even black or white, for doublets and kirtles, will allow for the use of bright colours in the parts mentioned above. Changes in these accessories, when they are of conspicuous colours, will give an effect of an entire change of costume. The basic hose, on the other hand, should be of some light or bright colour in order to suggest that the puffs showing between the panes are, as they originally were, the lining of the hose. The sets of panes should be sewed to elastic waist- and leg bands so that they can be pulled up over the basic hose and so expedite changes.

Cloaks can be reversible, one side being of a light bright colour and lustrous surface, such as primrose or watchet (pale blue) satin, and the other side of a dark, rich colour with a dull surface, such as murrey (mulberry) velvet or cloth.

Further touches of colour can be added, for the sake of variety, by way of such accessories as fans, muffs, handkerchiefs, hats, head-dresses, and the trimming of gloves and shoes. The introduction of coloured starch in the second half of the sixteenth century led to the wearing of red, blue, purple, green, and yellow ruffs, and it would be correct to use cuffs and ruffs to add a further colour note to costumes. There is no doubt, however, that white bands make for freshness and even brilliance of general appearance in Elizabethan costume. Laundering and setting of bands is, of course, a constant expense, and special care must be taken in their wear and storage. A flat circular band of tarleton worn over the top side of the closed ruff will prevent soiling from the make-up on chin and neck; this is inexpensive and can be renewed every time the ruff is worn. Flat boxes for open ruffs and cuffs and circular hat-boxes for closed ruffs will help to keep them fresh and crisp for a considerable time, but it would be well to have a supply of the flat unstarched falling bands and ruffs *à la confusion* in case of need.

Robes, capes, cassocks, and gaberdines can be made reversible, and even the skirt, or half-kirtle—since it has to be lined—can, if carefully made, be turned inside out to serve as two separate garments.

A few "nightgowns" (see p. 168) in dark rich colours for the men and one or two "loose gowns" (see p. 168) in pale colours for the women are essentials. A white or light-coloured loose gown will be needed for Juliet in the balcony scene (*Romeo and Juliet*, II, 2), for Lady Macbeth in the sleep-walking scene (*Macbeth*, V, 1), for Desdemona in the murder scene (*Othello*, V, 2), and for Queen Katharine in the vision scene (*Henry VIII*, IV, 2).

Children should be dressed, as they were in the period, in clothes that are, in every detail, the same as those of adults.

For the lower classes the garments should be of inexpensive materials and of subdued colours, and should have only guards or buttons for ornament. French hoods in tarleton, over which may be worn a straw hat, a closed kirtle of one colour, with reduced or semifarthingale, and an apron, will be appropriate for the women, and a fustian cassock or gaberdine with flat woollen cap for the men.

Armour usually presents the greatest difficulty and expense—difficulty in making and expense in hiring. There are, however, two points to keep in mind that are of help. Owing to the discovery and use of gunpowder, armour in Shakespeare's time was on the decline,[1] the description of the Ghost in *Hamlet* as armed "from top to toe" being, in fact, an historical touch.[2] Moreover there was no uniformity of military costume either for officers or men. A minimum of body armour, such as gorget (a steel collar covering the throat and upper chest) and cuirass (breastplate) together with the morion, or handsome "comb cap" helmet, heavy leather high boots, and gauntlet gloves, would be sufficient for the leaders of the armies in the chronicle plays; while leather jerkins, venetians, broad-brimmed hats or possibly burgonets,[3] would suffice for the rank and file. Military men appearing in civilian life indicated their calling by the gorget (see the portrait of Sidney facing p. 184), the mandilion, and the lieutenant's scarf.

MAKE-UP

The amateur actor attempting make-up for a Shakespearean character for the first time would do well to study paintings and sculpture and brass rubbings that represent persons of all classes of the Elizabethan and Jacobean periods. For the make-up of kings and ecclesiastics such representations as those in *English Medieval Painting* by Borenius and Tristram will be helpful. For the remarkable effects that can be obtained by present-day make-up, see pairs of photographs of the same actor in different parts, between pages 128–129.

---

[1] Full armour made in steel, engraved, embossed, or gilded, and with the body parts made to resemble elaborate long-skirted jerkins were, however, worn for Court pageantry.

[2] If the ghost wears a long cloak, the complete armour can be suggested by the burgonet and gorget alone.

[3] A metal helmet that covered head, cheeks, and neck, with a "fall", or eyeshade, attached to the front.

Books for Reference & Reading[1]

BECK, WILLIAM L., *Gloves, Their Annals and Associations: A Chapter of Trade and Social History*, Hamilton, Adams and Co., London, 1883.

BORENIUS, TANCRED, and E. W. TRISTRAM, *English Medieval Painting*, Harcourt, Brace and Company, Inc., New York, 1926. The illustrations in this book are useful for costuming and make-up, especially of the English kings.

*★BROOKE, IRIS, and JAMES LAVER, *English Costume from the Fourteenth through the Nineteenth Century*, The Macmillan Company, New York, 1937. Arranged in decades. See 1580–1590, 1590–1600, 1600–1610, 1610–1620. Very fine, clear drawings by Iris Brooke. Authoritative and concise.

CHAMBERS, (Sir) EDMUND K., *The Elizabethan Stage*, 4 vols., Oxford University Press, New York, 1923. For apparel of players, see Vol. I, pp. 63, 348, 352, 358, 362, 371; Vol. II, pp. 131, 168, 184, 215, 228, 243, 245, 248, 254, 256; Vol. IV, pp. 199, 204, 217, 237, 240, 241, 304.

——, *Shakespearean Gleanings*, Oxford University Press, New York, 1944. The chapter "On the First Illustration to 'Shakespeare' " gives an account of the only extant contemporary picture of the costuming of a Shakespeare play—*Titus Andronicus*. The picture is reproduced as frontispiece.

DAVENPORT, MILLIA, *The Book of Costume*, 2 vols., Crown Publishers, New York, 1948. See the end of Vol. I and the beginning of Vol. II. Interesting, informative, and well illustrated.

★English Historic Costume Painting Book, No. 6, "Elizabeth and James, 1558–1625", Winsor and Newton, Ltd., London, 1947. Although designed for children, this booklet is of value to the producer for its clear line drawings of the costumes of men, women, and children of all classes and for the chart giving colour and colour combinations of the period.

GAYLEY, CHARLES MILLS, *Plays of Our Forefathers and Some of the Traditions upon Which They Were Founded*, Duffield and Company, New York, 1907. Excellent illustrations of angels, devils, and symbolic figures taken from old frescoes, pictures, illuminated manuscripts, etc.

HARBAGE, ALFRED, *Shakespeare's Audience*, Columbia University Press, New York, 1941. See Chap. 4 for costume of women in the audience, including the clothes of a courtesan at the Fortune Theatre as described by Chaplain Busino of the Venetian embassy (page 100).

HARRISON, G. B., *England in Shakespeare's Day*, Methuen & Co., Ltd., London, 1928. Selections from contemporary sources. For descriptions of dress, see pages 15–16 (King James's concern for clothes); 88–89 (from "The Defence of Connycatching", 1592); 225–227 (from William Harrison's *Description of England*, 1577); 227–228 ("Follies and Fashions", a poem by John Lane, 1600).

[1] An asterisk (★) indicates a book that is of especial practical value in costuming.

HENSLOWE, PHILIP, *Diary*, edited by WALTER WILSON GREG, 2 vols., A. H. Bullen, London, 1904–1908. The most important contemporary source for authentic accounts of all that pertained to stage costume in the Elizabethan playhouse. Vol. I, Text; Vol. II, Commentary.

*KELLY, FRANCIS M., *Shakespearian Costume for Stage and Screen*, Walter H. Baker Company, Boston, 1938. An analysis of costume of all classes for the period 1560–1620. Excellent chapter on the "nice conduct "of period costume. Nine plates and ninety-three line drawings.

——, and RANDOLPH SCHWABE, *Historic Costume: A Chronicle of Fashion in Western Europe, 1490–1790*, Charles Scribner's Sons, New York, 1928. A very good guide. (Notice a figure on the title page of a man wearing every item of exaggerated costume of the period and topped by an ass's head.)

*KÖHLER, CARL, *A History of Costume*, edited and augmented by EMMA VON SICKART, G. Howard Watt, New York, 1930. One of the best guides to the cutting of patterns for the various articles of clothing.

LAWRENCE, WILLIAM J., *Speeding Up Shakespeare*, The Argonaut Press, London, 1937. See Chap. 1, "On the Underrated Genius of Dick Tarleton". Fine illustration of Tarleton, giving an excellent idea of the costume of clowns.

——, *Those Nut-cracking Elizabethans*, The Argonaut Press, London, 1935. For a devil's costume, see reproduction of a title page of a public masque, "The World Tost at Tennis," page 13.

*LINTHICUM, CHANNING M., *Costume in the Drama of Shakespeare and His Contemporaries*, Oxford University Press, New York, 1936. Details of costume—colours, textiles, and trimming, with special reference to their mention in plays of the period. Fine halftone illustrations of extant garments in various museums.

MACQUOID, PERCY, "Costume", *Shakespeare's England*, Vol. II, Chap. 19, Oxford University Press, New York, 1932. Excellent for reference and for illustrative material.

*MORSE, H. K., editor, *Elizabethan Pageantry: A Pictorial Survey of Costume and Its Commentators from c. 1560–1620*, special spring number of The Studio, The Studio Publications, Inc., New York, 1934. The clarity of detail and the diversity of styles of many classes seen in the fine halftone reproductions of contemporary portraits make this book an indispensable source for the costuming of Shakespeare's plays.

MUSEUM OF FINE ARTS, BOSTON, Bulletin for April, 1942, Vol. XI, No. 238. Excellent photographs of late-sixteenth-century garments in the Museum's collection.

National Geographic Magazine, September, 1951. On page 423 is a photograph of an actress putting on a corset (property of the Folger Shakespeare Library, Washington, D.C.) that possibly belonged to Queen Elizabeth.

NATIONAL PORTRAIT GALLERY, London, Reproductions of Elizabethan portraits in the Museum's collection. A catalogue of the portraits with prices of reproductions and post-cards may be obtained from the Museum (St. Martin's Place, Trafalgar Square, London, W.C.2). There are several fine reproductions of Elizabethan portraits in the catalogue itself.

Portraits of the following Elizabethans are suggested as especially valuable for costume details: Queen Elizabeth; Mary, Queen of Scots; the family of Sir

Thomas More, showing the change in costume in four generations; Sir Henry Lee; Sir Francis Walsingham; Lord Burghley; Robert Cecil, Earl of Salisbury; Robert Dudley, Earl of Leicester; Robert Devereux, Earl of Essex; Sir Philip Sidney; Sir Walter Raleigh; Sir Richard Grenville; Sir Francis Drake.

NICOLL, ALLARDYCE, *Stuart Masques and the Renaissance Stage*, George G. Harrap & Co., Ltd., London, 1937. Many drawings of costumes from the Court masques, useful in costuming Shakespeare's late plays—*Cymbeline, The Winter's Tale*, and *The Tempest.*

*NORRIS, HERBERT, *Costume and Fashion*, 6 vols., J. M. Dent & Sons, Ltd., London, 1938. See Vol. III, Book II, *The Tudors: 1547-1603.* An indispensable source for all that pertains to the costume of all classes. Very fully illustrated in colour, half-tones and black and white. Patterns; details of design; how to adjust various articles of attire; how to make and set ruffs; hairdressing and cut of beards, etc.

PALLISER, (Mrs.) BURY, *The History of Lace*, revised under the editorship of M. JOURDAIN and ALICE DRYDEN, Sampson Low, Marston and Co., Ltd., London, 1902. Spendid illustrations of lace aprons, caps, and bands.

PLANCHÉ, JAMES ROBINSON, *A Cyclopaedia of Costume or Dictionary of Dress*, 2 vols., Chatto & Windus, London, 1876, 1879. Vol. I, The Dictionary; Vol. II, A General History of Costume in Europe. One of the finest reference books for information and illustrative material.

REDFERN, W. B., *Royal and Historic Gloves and Shoes*, Methuen & Co., Ltd., London, 1904. Fine photographic plates of gloves and shoes from the time of Elizabeth.

*REINHARDT, HANS, *Holbein*, translated from the French by Prudence Montagu-Pollock, William Heinemann, Ltd., London, n.d. These magnificent reproductions in sepia and colour, though illustrating costumes of an earlier date, are yet a source for all those garments that did not change for nearly a hundred years. Robes, both private and official, have never been more beautifully painted. Special attention is drawn to the portrait of "A London Merchant", on page 45, for the costume and make-up for Shylock.

REMINGTON, PRESTON, *English Domestic Needlework*, The Metropolitan Museum of Art, New York, 1945. Fine photographs of articles of Elizabethan costume from the Museum's collection.

*REYNOLDS, GRAHAM, *Costume of the Western World, Elizabethan and Jacobean, 1558-1625*, George G. Harrap & Co., Ltd., London, 1951. Descriptions and reproductions of some of the most distinguished portraits of the period, several in colour.

RYE, WILLIAM BRENCHLEY, editor, *England as Seen by Foreigners in the Days of Elizabeth and James the First, comprising translations of the two Dukes of Wirtemberg in 1592 and 1610, both illustrative of Shakespeare. With extracts from the travels of foreign princes and other copious notes, an introduction, and etchings*, John Russell Smith, London, 1865. For comments on costume, see pages 7-8, 69-70, 71, 89-90.

Shakespeare Survey, edited by ALLARDYCE NICOLL, Vol. I, University Press, Cambridge, England, 1948. For contemporary illustration of the costuming of *Titus Andronicus*, see page 32.

SIMPSON, PERCY, "The Masque", *Shakespeare's England*, Vol. II, Chap. 26, Oxford University Press, New York, 1932. See illustrations of Inigo Jones's masque

costumes. These could be copied for use in the last comedies of Shakespeare—
Cymbeline, The Winter's Tale, and *The Tempest.*

SIMPSON, PERCY, and C. F. BELL, editors, *Designs by Inigo Jones for Masques and Plays at Court,* University Press, Oxford, 1924. Large clear reproductions of costumes in colour and in black and white suitable for use in the staging of Shakespeare's late plays—*Cymbeline, The Winter's Tale,* and *The Tempest.*

STEPHENSON, HENRY THEW, *Shakespeare's London,* Henry Holt and Company, Inc., New York, 1906. Amusing and informative descriptions of Elizabethan costume. The account of a lady getting dressed (in Chap. 1) is especially delightful.

STOPES, (Mrs.) C. C., *Shakespeare's Environment,* George Bell & Sons, Ltd., London, 1914. Authentic descriptions of the costumes of Queen Elizabeth's Court entertainers—fools, dwarfs, etc.

STOW, JOHN, *A Survey of London,* reprinted from the text of 1603 with an introduction and notes by Charles Lethbridge Kingsford, 2 vols., Oxford University Press, New York, 1908. Contemporary account of official dress and colours and cost of fabrics and furs.

Velazquez, Oxford University Press, New York, 1943. This superb publication depicts the magnificent exaggerations of costume in the Spanish Court. These fashions were to appear as influences in Elizabethan costume. See Plate 70 for a fine and rare example of a "guard", worn by Queen Isabella in this equestrian portrait.

VICTORIA AND ALBERT MUSEUM, Department of Engraving, Illustration and Design, *Catalogue of Rubbings of Brasses and Incised Slabs,* classified and arranged by Muriel Clayton, London, 1929. One of the most authentic sources for Elizabethan costume of the gentry and middle classes. Prints of these rubbings may be obtained at very reasonable rates by applying to the Victoria and Albert Museum, South Kensington, London, S.W.7.

——, *Elizabethan Embroidery* (Book 5). Photographs of articles of Elizabethan clothing. This pamphlet, too, can be obtained from the Museum, or from The British Library of Information, Rockefeller Plaza, New York.

VON BOEHN, MAX, *Modes and Manners,* translated by Joan Joshua, 4 vols., J. B. Lippincott Company, Philadelphia, 1932–1936. See Vols. II and III for fine illustrative material in colour and in black and white.

*WALKUP, FAIRFAX PROUDFIT, *Dressing the Part: A History of Costume for the Theatre,* Appleton-Century-Crofts, Inc., New York, 1938. A practical guide to the cutting of garments and all requirements for their making.

WALLACE, CHARLES WILLIAM, *The Evolution of the English Drama up to Shakespeare,* G. Reimer, Berlin, 1912. Here an interesting account may be found of the wearing of clothes from the royal wardrobe by the boy actors and by university students.

WATKINS, RONALD, *On Producing Shakespeare,* Michael Joseph, London, 1950. A book that both professional and amateur producers will want on their shelves. For skilful adaptations of Elizabethan fashions to modern stage production, see Maurice Percival's delightful drawings.

WELLES, ORSON, and ROGER HILL, editors, *Everybody's Shakespeare,* three plays edited for reading and arranged for staging (*Julius Caesar, The Merchant of Venice, Twelfth*

Night), The Todd Press, Woodstock, Ill., 1934. See the many marginal sketches for costume suggestions.

WHANSLAW, H. W., *The Bankside Stage-book*, Wells Gardner, Darton & Co., Ltd., London, 1924. Useful drawings of various Elizabethan costumes: Court lady, page 178; peasant, page 179; queen and ladies, page 180; lawyer and doctor, page 185 gentleman and manservant, page 189; pupil, schoolmaster, nobleman's son, page 190; courtiers, page 191; soldiers, pages 194–196.

WILSON, JOHN DOVER, compiler, *Life in Shakespeare's England: A Book of Elizabethan Prose*, Penguin Books, Inc., New York, 1949. See Part II, Chap. 5, "Dress and Fashion", for contemporary comments and accounts of costume of the period.

★WINTER, CARL, *Elizabethan Miniatures*, Penguin Books, Inc., New York, 1943. Exquisite coloured reproductions showing the beauty and diversity of head- and neckwear.

MAKE-UP

Max Factor's Hints on the Art of Make-up, Booklets 7, 8, and 9, Shakespeare's Characters. These booklets will be sent on application to Max Factor Hollywood and London (Sales) Ltd., 16 Old Bond Street, London, W.1.

Modern Make-up by Stein, M. Stein Cosmetic Company, New York. A chart for straight and character make-up is included. This pamphlet, with chart, will be sent on application to Funk and Co., 36 South State Street, Chicago, Ill.

Paint, Powder, and Make-up by Ivard Strauss, Barnes & Noble, Inc., New York, 1938. See especially pages 199–203 on Shakespearean make-up.

Stage Makeup by Richard Corson, Appleton-Century-Crofts, Inc., New York, 1949. This recent book with a new approach to aesthetic values and techniques bids fair to revolutionize the whole theory of make-up. It contains many excellent photographs of make-ups, including several for Shakespearean characters.

Part Four

Music & Dancing

I

Music in the Early English Drama

If ever a country deserved to be called "musical" that country was
England in the sixteenth and seventeenth centuries.

Edward W. Naylor, *Shakespeare and Music*

IN WINCHESTER CATHEDRAL, sometime before the end of the
tenth century, there was introduced into the Easter Service an enactment of
the encounter of the three Women with the Angel at the door of the empty
tomb, based, partly, on customs already known on the Continent.
"Quem queritis in sepulchro, o Christicole?" sang one of the "bretheren".
"Jesum Nazarenum crucifixum, o caelicola!" responded three other
"bretheren".

It was a momentous innovation. Out of this simple duologue sprang the
English drama and, as we see, it took its initial step *accompanied by music*.

The inclusion of antiphon and canticle in the dramatization of Church
festivals and liturgy continued in the centuries that followed and accompanied the further development of the mysteries when they went out at the
West Door. When Latin was replaced by the vernacular in medieval plays,
Church music was still played and Latin hymns sung during their performance. Nor was this music an irrelevant flourish. In the cycles of the Corpus
Christi festival there was a deliberate use of music to enhance and intensify
the spoken word. Already it was realized that the moods induced by music
prepare the mind for the reception of the imaginative. It was of great
histrionic importance to have discovered that music invested the speaker and
the action of the play with an other worldness. It made human representation
of God and the saints, if not convincing, yet in some strange way acceptable.
God speaks to the fallen Adam and Eve in the Garden to the accompaniment
of "mynstrelles playinge"; Adam and Eve sing an English lyric; choirs of

205

angels sing liturgical hymns, and shepherds sing carols. This last heralded the final replacement of Church music by folk songs. The next step was marked by the welding of words and music into an interrelated whole. The ornamental lines that characterized the Church music of the time were replaced by simple melodies that conformed to the sense and emotion of the words in progression and mood.

In 1515, John Heywood became Court Singer to Henry VIII. A musician of breeding and education, he brought fresh life into Court entertainment, and under his direction music and drama advanced together towards a new and important form. Taking the by now static morality play, he shook life into flat abstractions by substituting for the bloodless figures of Truth, Chastity, Envy, and the like, contemporary men representative of trades and professions talking together. Lively and secular, the "interlude", so-called, sought to entertain rather than to moralize, and its racy, topical dialogue frequently served to introduce the singing of rounds, part songs, and madrigals, some of which served as accompaniment for dancing.

It is possible that during the time that Heywood was attached to the Court a more developed form of instrumental music as accompaniment to these songs and dances was introduced, and the interlude began to develop into a form that was to reach unparalleled magnificence and beauty as the Court masque.

As drama dropped the ferule and took up the baton, comedy, fortified by situation and plot, found that humorous songs added swing and exuberance to humorous dialogue, and the first English comedies, *Ralph Roister Doister* and *Gammer Gurton's Needle*, came romping in to the accompaniment of rousing songs, dances, and entr'acte music.

The year 1560 saw indigenous comedy giving place to neoclassical comedy and tragedy, the latter bringing in an importation from Italy. This was the *intermedio*, or "dumb show", which, preceding the acts, symbolized or elucidated the plot of the scenes to follow. It was performed in mime to the accompaniment of instrumental music at first, and later included both song and dance.

Taking threads from the interlude and neoclassical comedy and tragedy, John Lyly now gathered them into his skilful hands and wove a new and delicate pattern of interrelated music and drama. An author and skilled musician, and possibly Assistant Choir Master to the singing boys of St. Paul's, Lyly employed his talent and opportunities in writing prose comedies of five acts for the young choristers, which not only served to show their acting ability, but allowed for the introduction of exquisite vocal and instrumental music as an integral part of the play. These musical comedies, performed for the Queen and Court in the beginning, later became one of the most agreeable attractions to the select audiences of the private theatres and, as already mentioned, a serious rival attraction to the professional companies in the public playhouses.

Briefly, the association of music and drama from the earliest times remained unimpaired through all the vicissitudes of dramatic evolution. Music had supplied the solemn chants for the liturgical tropes and mystery plays, the atmosphere and songs in the moralities, the rollicking rounds and songs in the interludes and early comedies, the mysterious and haunting background for the dumb show of neoclassical tragedy, and the lilting loveliness for the Children's comedies.

Before considering the part that music played in Elizabethan stage production, it is well to recall that, during the six centuries when music had been attendant on the drama, she had also had a life and career of her own outside the theatre, and that the era that saw the full flowering of England's greatest poetry and drama saw also unrivalled achievement in vocal and instrumental music.

There is an exuberance that springs from a sense of national well-being which, pervading the minds of men of all walks of life, finds an outlet in the communal arts. From 1588 the growing awareness of national integration, security, and development resulted in thirty years of stability, in which time a rapidly widening culture had time to develop. In that time the abundant outpouring of creative energy in the fields of music, poetry, and drama marked, both in magnificence and in magnitude, the highest achievement of national genius.

Musical composition now became an art practised by those whose talent and training entitled them to be considered professional musicians; at the same time the knowledge and performance of vocal and instrumental music became more widespread among amateurs of every social class than at any other time before or since.

Music everywhere! In the fields, cottages, taverns, and city streets the poorest and least privileged sang ballads, rounds, and part songs. Trades and crafts of every kind were carried on to a perpetual accompaniment of singing. Citterns hung in the barbers' shops that the waiting customers might play and sing to pass the time. Nor was this an inconsequential warbling out of sheer lightness of heart; from the refugee weavers singing their metrical psalms to the drunken tinkers singing a canon in three parts, all showed skill in performance.

The burgher class, waxing fat on steadily increasing mercantile prosperity, could afford to study music under professional tutelage and to spend time acquiring the skill and artistry requisite for the performance of extremely difficult and complex madrigals and instrumental music.

There had been a time when music had been considered an effeminate pastime by the young man of fashion, but now it was an art to be cultivated if he was to take his place with distinction among his equals. The "after-dinner" period in many upper- and middle-class households became a time for the performance of exquisite part singing, with all members of the household, including servants, joining in. Singing a part "at sight" and improvising on stringed instruments was expected of the educated, and failure to acquire these accomplishments reflected upon breeding and upbringing.

At Court, not only were the ladies in waiting expected to be skilled musicians, but the Queen herself was a performer and patron of the art. Following the custom of her father, Elizabeth, on her accession, included in her household staff 17 trumpeters, 6 sackbutists, 3 drummers, 2 flute players, 2 lutanists, 1 rebeck player, 8 viol players, 2 harpists, 2 virginal players, 8 men singers, 6 singing children, 9 minstrels, 7 "musician strangers", 8 interlude players, who sang, and 2 makers of instruments.

The recognition of the educational value of music is seen in its acceptance as an alternate examination subject at Cambridge from those seeking fellowships; in the encouragement of the practice of chamber music and madrigal singing among the faculties and students of the universities, and as part of the educational training of royalty and nobility.

Many "virtuous" properties were attributed to music, such as its power to cure sickness, melancholy, and madness, to subdue tempestuous passions in man and beast, and even to revive the dead.

The Pythagorean system treating of the "music of the spheres", whose grave and sweet music sounded through the universe although inaudible to human ears, was taken very seriously by the classical students, and its acceptance is stated and implied by Shakespeare and many contemporary writers.

Like the actors, the professional musicians now enjoyed the patronage of the Court and nobility with the result that their social status improved. All of them, or nearly all of them, started their careers as choir-boys in the royal and university chapels. At the age of thirty, or thereabouts, a musician could present an original composition, along with testimonials of his musical study and practice, to the universities, and upon these proving adequate could without further examination receive his degree of Bachelor, or even Doctor, of Music. A further honour, much valued by musicians, was admission to the fellowship of the Gentlemen of the Chapel Royal, a membership which, however, does not seem to have included any regular duty to the royal household.

A great many of the famous musicians of the period who were, or were willing to become, Protestants, became organists in the English cathedrals, while those who remained true to the "old religion" occupied honoured positions in cathedrals and courts on the Continent. Their less illustrious fellows were choir-masters and organists in churches and chapels; choir-men, musical entertainers, and tutors in noblemen's houses in England and abroad and even in the houses of the wealthy middle classes.

Musicians were no less versatile than most professional men of the time. A few were Doctors of Medicine, several were dons at the universities, some studied and practised law, a few were poets, and several were clergymen. The most outstanding example is perhaps Thomas Campion, who studied law, was a poet and playwright, a classical scholar, a musician of outstanding ability in technical knowledge, while all the time following his profession as a Doctor of Medicine.

Along with the men of talent and, in many cases, genius, there were other musicians who, as descendants of the medieval minstrels, were without educational advantages or regular means of livelihood. Classed with strolling players as common vagrants, despised as social outcasts, these men, in spite of the fact that they could and did obtain noblemen's patents, wandered over the countryside eking out a bare existence by playing at fairs and festivals. Those who drifted to London were more fortunate in finding employment in the comparatively permanent haunts of tavern and playhouse. Their one-time fellows in adversity, the players, who now basked in the security afforded by the building and organizing of the playhouses, became their occasional employers, and these musicians and those actors whose training and ability made them acceptable musicians for public performance supplied the music for the Elizabethan theatre[1]. Of ill repute, these strolling musicians received their full share of censure, not only from the Church and the Puritans, but even from the theatres, and allusions to their thriftlessness and impudence are as numerous in plays as they are in sermons, those of Shakespeare being no exception.

Here, then, is the all-pervading interest in, and performance of, music in the social life of the time, and, once realized, the reflection of it in the plays is no longer a matter for wonder. It explains why thirty-two of the plays have allusions to music or instruments or performers and why there are no less than 300 stage directions for music in the plays as a whole.

The claim that Shakespeare's plays were full of topical allusions is strongly supported by the constant emphasis that he places on the musical life of his day. Every type of musician familiar to the time is here represented.

---

[1] In England, the employment of orchestras in "legitimate" theatres to supply overture and entr'acte music still continues, and outside, entertaining the theatre queues, the less-fortunate descendants of the strolling musicians "pass the hat" as they have ever done.

For instance, we find the drummers and trumpeters who supplied martial and formal music for warlike and state occasions; the groups of players of stringed and small wind instruments attached to royal and noble households; the soloist, who often combines his musical profession with that of professional jester; the bands of strolling musicians hired for special occasions; the young men of fashion and nobility representing the cultured interest in music as well as the skill in its performance. There are the groups of huntsmen and shepherds who burst into song, the lady in waiting who sings to her own lute accompaniment; the skilled musician (although this is a disguise) who is employed by the wealthy merchant to train his daughters, and, finally, trained children who appear as soloists, duettists, and in chorus in at least three of the comedies. But the portrayal of types of musicians is not all. Current beliefs in regard to music are expressed: belief in the Pythagorean theory of the "music of the spheres" and belief in the healing properties of music. Here, in music, was an element familiar to his audience that Shakespeare saw as a dramatic device of tremendous potency, and that he used to aid exposition as well as to impart delicate suggestion.

II

Music in the Playhouse & in Modern Production

DUKE ORSINO: "That piece of song,
That old and antique song we heard last night:
Methought it did relieve my passion much,
More than light airs and recollected terms
Of these most brisk and giddy-paced times."
Twelfth Night, II, 4

LIVING IN an age when music was a part of the everyday life of all social classes, Shakespeare's audience must have consisted of people accustomed to music in church, at work and play, at all civic and royal ceremonials, at festivals, feastings, and funerals. There is little doubt that most of them could sing or play, or both, and that all were capable of appreciating select, as well as popular, music. It is safe to surmise then that at places of public entertainment such an audience would not only expect but demand music. In meeting this demand in the public playhouses, the managers had also to remember that the more select, and remunerative, part of the audience was accustomed to the beautiful music supplied at the private theatres by the child actors. Finally there was the long-established tradition of music as an indispensable part of dramatic performance.

In the early days of innyard productions with meagre and precarious money returns, music could consist of little more than rolling drums, blaring trumpets, and the pipe-and-tabor accompaniment of the terminal jig. When better days arrived with the building of the theatres, there was still one omission that was in direct contrast to the custom of the private theatres. This was the opening of the play with no more overture than three blasts on a trumpet to herald the Prologue, while at Blackfriars the children played for an hour or more before the play began. The omission may have been partly owing to the custom, on the part of the audience, of singing old songs and "calling" for old tunes at the beginning and end of acts. We know that this was done in the case of *Summer's Last Will and Testament* when it was performed in 1593. But we do not know if this was customary in the case of Shakespearean performances.

In a modern production it would be as well to include an overture consisting of songs and incidental music used in the production. It would serve to evoke the mood of the play and would give a chance to introduce Elizabethan music to those members of the audience whose ears are un-accustomed to its form and tonal quality.

Following the Elizabethan custom of only one intermission, entr'acte music can be introduced, nor need this be limited to instrumental music—in the comedies, at least—for it is certain that such an interval frequently saw the performance of songs and group dancing by members of the company.

Whether the modern director will want to go so far as to conclude with the jig is doubtful. He may consider that such a coarse and boisterous note would be a fitting end for such plays as *The Comedy of Errors, The Taming of the Shrew*, or *The Merry Wives of Windsor*, but it is doubtful if any but the professional vaudeville comedian could carry it off with the requisite bounce and dash.

The music in the plays consists of three general types:

1. Martial and "state" music played by wind and percussion instruments
2. Songs unaccompanied or accompanied by strings
3. Incidental music played on various instruments to accompany dance, action, or spoken word.

Mention must be made here of "still music". This was background music to help create a special atmosphere, and, as no mention of it is usually made in the lines, it is believed to have been played by invisible musicians in the third-balcony level. One exception occurs in *Richard II*, V, 5, where reference is made to the invisible music heard in the prison.

The suggestion that the greater part of this music was supplied by members of the company is based on the fact that by far the best lyrics were sung by boys playing female roles, with the clowns a close second, the latter, as part of their professional stock-in-trade, singing to their own instrumental accompaniment. Two other facts support the idea, one being the known ability of some of the members to play various instruments, and the other, that it seems to have been customary, in Henslowe's company at any rate, for many musical instruments to be included in lists of properties.

Since it is doubtful whether independent musicians would have played on any but their own instruments, it seems safe to conclude that these were used by the actors.[1]

That opportunities were made for outstanding or unusually gifted members to show their skill is seen by the introduction of the Welsh song sung by a boy in *1 Henry IV*, III, 1 (see p. 116); the love song sung to his own lute accompaniment by the supposedly aged Pandarus in *Troilus and Cressida*, III, 1; and the self-accompanied song performed by the Lady in Waiting in *Henry VIII*, III, 1. The unusually large number of songs and the playing of various instruments required of Ariel in *The Tempest* is possibly accounted for by the fact that about 1611–1613 young men who had been trained as vocalists and instrumentalists in the Children's companies were being taken into the company of the King's Men. Another interesting idea, made convincingly clear by William J. Lawrence,[2] is that the plays of *As You Like It* and *A Midsummer Night's Dream* as we have them today may not be the versions seen on the public stage, but especially adapted and augmented versions used for a special performance at the wedding of Henry, Lord Herbert, to Anne Russell, the Queen's favourite Maid of Honour, at the home of the bride's mother at Blackfriars, June 16, 1600. It is known that the Queen was present. It is known that these two plays were performed as part of the festivities. It is also known that another play was performed by the Children of Paul's. What more possible, and probable, than that the Children would be available for the singing parts in the adult plays and that most of the lyrics were especially inserted for them to sing. The same thing may be true of *The Merry Wives of Windsor*, which was written most probably for a command performance at Windsor Castle, for here again the Children of the Chapel Royal would be on hand to perform the fairy song and dance in the final act.

For the accompaniment to dances and entr'acte and incidental music there is no doubt that the actors employed the small bands—"noises", as they were called—of musicians that were available for hire in and round about the City. For Court performances such music would be supplied by the musicians of the Royal Household.

Here then are the ways in which the demand for music in the Elizabethan playhouse was met: by the actors themselves, by the talented and trained Children's companies for Court performances, by a later inclusion of some of them into the public-playhouse companies, and, for occasional productions, by the hiring of special groups of professional musicians.

[1] We have to remember, of course, that Henslowe ran pawnbroking as a side line, and it is just possible that some of these instruments may have been held as security for loans.
[2] See Lawrence, William J., "A Plummet for Bottom's Dream", *Shakespeare's Workshop*, pp. 75–97.

With musical ability as common as it was, all demands could no doubt be met with ease in Elizabethan times; but today the producer of a Shakespearean play will have difficulty in finding actors who can play or sing, or both. It is possible that he will be faced with the alternative of having an actor trained to sing and play or a musician and singer trained to act. Dance and incidental music will, of course, have to be supplied by a group of musicians. In this event, it would be fortunate indeed if they could play this music on the Elizabethan instruments for which it was written, or on suitable facsimiles of these instruments. A glance at the tables on pp. 215–219 will enable those not already familiar with Elizabethan instruments to take the first step towards achieving such a delightful objective. As a last resort, this music may be supplied by an off-stage gramophone. Fortunately there are many excellent records of Elizabethan music available, some of which are performed on the instruments of the period. (See Recordings Available for Use in Elizabethan Stage Production, pp. 292–298.)

Elizabethan Musical Instruments

Instrument	Description	Substitute or facsimile	Use
		PERCUSSION	
Bells	Large iron bell	Institutional bell; might be purchased from builders who do demolition work, or from a foundry or store	Tolling for the dead; sounding an alarm; striking of a clock
	Small bells set on stands and struck with a mallet	Tubular bells suspended from a stand and struck with a small hammer	Chiming of church bells for weddings, festivities, holidays, coronations, christening, etc.
Cymbals		Modern cymbals	Although there is no mention of this instrument in the stage directions, they are mentioned in the text as being part of the uproar heard off stage in *Coriolanus*. Possibly they were used when a clashing noise was required in battles off stage, and certainly the clang would be effective as an accompaniment to rolling drums when thunder, storm, and the like were represented. Their shivering—made by hitting their edges with a mallet—would also be suggestive for supernatural scenes
Tabor	A hoop of wood with parchment stretched over one side only. Usually played with one wooden stick	Tambourine with metal clappers removed, or a small hand drum used in jazz bands	Used in conjunction with a pipe to accompany rustic dances, the marching of masquers, and entrances and business of clowns (see Pipe)

Elizabethan Musical Instruments (continued)

Instrument	Description	Substitute or facsimile	Use
Tambou-rine	Similar in appearance to a modern military side drum, hung over one shoulder or round the neck and played with two wooden sticks	Modern military side drum. For "muffled drum" the sticks are padded with heavy cloth	Military marches; dead march. In combination with trumpets for entrances of royalty or nobility in war scenes, for alarums and retreats, to drown noise of traps and "machines", and as a dramatic device to drown unwelcome speeches, such as appeals and curses

WIND

Instrument	Description	Substitute or facsimile	Use
Bugle	Large bent military bugle	Modern military bugle	For martial soundings and courtly ceremonials. (This instrument together with the trumpet was most frequently used in the plays)
Cornet	A hollowed tusk, or wooden representation, covered with leather, slightly curved, and sometimes having squared sides	Cornet	Sometimes used in place of a trumpet; also used to accompany songs and dances of a lively character
Fife	Same as the modern fife	Fife	Used with drum for the marching of soldiers, for masquers, for apparition scenes, and for dumb shows
Hautboy	Conical wooden tube, with six holes in front, a thumb hole behind, and a double reed in the mouthpiece. The instruments were also called "shawms" and sometimes "waits". Usually played in "consorts" of four different sizes	Although the modern oboe is the descendant of this instrument, it is hardly a suitable substitute, for the Elizabethan hautboy was so shrill that it was used with drums and trumpets to make an impressive or confused noise. The bugle, or even the trumpet, would be a better substitute	Used by watchmen; to accompany ceremonial action; to "bring in a banquet", and with drums for "noise" off stage

Elizabethan Musical Instruments (continued)

Instrument	Description	Substitute or facsimile	Use
Horn	A long, circular-wound brass tube with a flaring bell	English horn, which is an alto oboe	Used for hunting scenes, and usually heard off stage
Pipe	A small pipe with three holes. Played with one hand while the other beats time on the tabor, which is suspended from the wrist of the hand that plays the pipe. (See Tabor.) Sometimes the pipes were quite large	It is possible to purchase these, but a flageolet, or even a whistle can be used as a substitute	Used by clowns for jigs, and by rustic minstrels for rural festivities and merrymaking
Recorder	A flute with a whistle mouthpiece, seven finger holes, and one thumb hole. Played in a "consort" of four, the instruments varying in size and pitch and known respectively as "treble", "alto", "tenor", and "bass" recorders. Sometimes one treble recorder would be accompanied by a consort of strings. (See Viol)	Have come into favour again and can be purchased from any musical-instrument store or firm	Used for "still music"; to accompany supernatural action; when a mood of gentle melancholy is to be evoked; for love scenes; and as an accompaniment to solo singing
Sackbut	Same as the modern trombone. Frequently used in "broken" music, that is, in conjunction with other types of instruments, such as lutes, harpsichord, viols, and cornets. These small orchestras were also known as "broken consorts"	Trombone	Used for the three blasts that heralded the Prologue but inappropriate for the purpose today, a cornet or trumpet being less harsh and strident. It seems strange that this instrument and the noisy hautboy should have been used for the stately *Grand Bal*. (See Pavan)

Elizabethan Musical Instruments (continued)

Instrument	Description	Substitute or facsimile	Use
Trumpet	Coach-horn type having no keys	Trumpet	Used for courtly and martial ceremonials. (The most frequently used instrument in the plays as a whole)
		STRINGED	
Cittern[1]	An instrument of four double strings played with a plectrum, resembling a flat-backed mandoline	Mandoline, guitar, or dulcimer	Used to vamp accompaniments for songs. Also in small orchestras composed of various kinds of instruments. (See Sackbut)
Lute	Usually a six-stringed instrument, the lower five strings being in pairs. The *chanterelle*, or sixth string, was single, and upon this the melody was played while the lower five supplied the accompaniment There were many types of lutes. The above describes the most common, known as the "treble lute". The alto lute and the bandore had no *chanterelles* and played only chordal accompaniments The bass lute was very large and had additional strings on a second head	Treble lute—guitar Alto lute—guitar Bandore—guitar or dulcimer Bass lute—harp There are modern lutes and lute-guitars and also lute players, but, in spite of the recent revival of interest in the instrument, they are all rare	For song accompaniments and for "still music"
Viol	A six-stringed instrument played with a bow. It came in three sizes, which corresponded in pitch to treble, tenor, and bass voices; the last was known as the "viola da gamba"	Treble viol—violin Tenor viol—viola Bass viol—cello	For song accompaniments both on and off stage. Also played on or off stage in conjunction with other instruments forming a small orchestra for dancing, for "music", "soft music", and "still music". Sometimes a consort of viols did, and can, accompany a treble recorder

[1] Not mentioned in the stage directions, but so common that their inclusion, as properties or actual instruments, is inevitable.

Elizabethan Musical Instruments (continued)

Instrument	Description	Substitute or facsimile	Use
Virginals[1]	A small, oblong keyboard instrument having strings that were plucked by quills when the pianolike keys were struck	The strange rustling tinkle can be fairly faithfully reproduced by placing one or two layers of tissue paper over the strings of a small spinet piano	There is no reason to believe that this instrument was ever used in the public playhouses, and there are no stage directions referring to it. Its use in the private theatres, however, is certain, and it is more than likely that it was used in the late plays, performed in the Blackfriars theatre, such as *Cymbeline*, *The Winter's Tale*, and *The Tempest*. This instrument started as a kind of dulcimer, known as a "psaltery", and it may be that the "psalteries" of *Coriolanus*, V, 4, really refers to virginals

[1] The harpsichord, though larger and more complex than the virginals, was similar to them in the method of tone production and, hence, in tone quality. Recently it has again come into favour. (See lists of virginal and harpsichord recordings, pp. 296-297.)

III

The Dance in Early England

CAPULET: "Come, musicians, play.
A hall! a hall! give room, and foot it, girls."
Romeo and Juliet, I, 5

THE DANCE in England has a long history. Accounts of dancing to vocal accompaniment at feasts, funerals,[1] bridals, wakes, and May Day and harvest festivals go back to the twelfth century, and there is no doubt that these in turn are references to very old and long-established customs. The earliest type of dance was processional and ritualistic and dated back to pre-Christian times, and from this progressive dance and the round dance, which took place round some sacred object, such as a stone, tree, or fire, all country or folk dances are derived. The pagan origin of these ceremonial dances is seen in the use of garlands and posies in their performance and the now rare horn or antlered head-dress worn by the men, pointing to fertility rites of agrarian and pastoral communities. The processional dances survive in the Sir Roger de Coverley, or the Virginia reel, and many "figures" of folk and ballroom dances. The best example of the round dance survives in the Maypole dance of rural England. It is likely that we have the music and words to a thirteenth-century round in "Sumer is i-cumen in", which might easily have been used for the Maypole dance. As might be expected from songs and dances having their origin in fertility rites, the theme of love

---

[1] It is still the custom in Flanders to dance at the funeral of a young girl, and Ravel's "Pavane for a Dead Infanta" suggests that he might have come across some reference to this custom in Spain.

and wooing is found frequently in the words of many dance songs,[1] and this in turn suggests the origin of men and women dancing in couples. The oldest dance that has survived in unbroken sequence is the morris dance, which, as an offshoot of the grim sword dance, may have been part of the ancient rites of human sacrifice. That it is sometimes danced from one place to another[2] points to its processional origin; that the dancers wear white and wave handkerchiefs suggests ritual costume; the blackened faces of some of the mummers who form part of the background suggest the use of ashes from the sacrificial fire, and the bells on the legs and arms of the dancers serve to imitate the clashing of swords used in the even earlier dance from which the morris is derived. Associated with May Day festivities, it is still to be seen at other times of the year in country districts all over Europe.

From the early folk dances came all the dances of Elizabethan times. From the processional type came the "hay" of the country folk and the pavan of the Court; from the "round", circular group dances of all classes; from the wooing dances, all folk and Court dances performed by men and women in couples; and from the morris dance, folk mummings that brought the rough humour and buffoonery to medieval miracles and mysteries, Elizabethan comedy and tragedy, and survive as part of folk festivals down to our own day. It is interesting to note the transition of folk dances to Court dances. The former were introduced into castle and Court by professional minstrels, gleemen, and tumblers, and there underwent changes and expansions—changes in the form of moderation and stylization, and expansions by way of sophisticated elaboration. By Shakespeare's time there were everywhere in England the two distinct types of dancing, that of the folk and that of the Court, and though the Court introduced elements of folk dancing into the masques, there is little or no sign of the folk using Court dances in their holiday-making. However, the public theatre was the one place where the two elements mingled and were seen by all classes. The rollicking folk romps, the stately Court dances were all introduced into Shakespeare's plays and, together with many allusions to the dances and dance music of the time, reflect the popularity of dancing among the social enjoyments of the day.

---

[1] According to Sir Edmund K. Chambers, a wooing chanson of "Transformation" is sung by harvesters and by lace-makers at the pillow (*The Mediaeval Stage*, Vol. I, p. 170). This recalls Count Orsino's lines in *Twelfth Night*, II, 4:

> ". . . Come, the song we had last night.
> Mark it, Cesario; it is old and plain;
> The spinsters and the knitters in the sun,
> And the free maids that weave their thread with bones,
> Do use to chant it."

[2] It will be remembered that Will Kempe, a member of Shakespeare's company, danced a morris from London to Norwich.

As might be expected in a country where music was an art practised by all social classes, dancing was an inevitable corollary. Dance tunes were used extensively as a basis for elaborate compositions, and the music of contrasting dance forms being grouped into a certain order by musicians gave rise to the suite, which later led to the sonata. In the *Fitzwilliam Virginal Book*,[1] one of the most famous collections of music compiled at the time, we find that, out of something like 300 compositions, 134 are dances; that over half the songs are dance songs, and that nearly all the airs used for elaborate instrumental compositions are those of popular dance tunes.

Before considering the plays from the point of view of the music and dance required by the stage directions and suggested by the text in the plays of Shakespeare, it will be necessary to describe Elizabethan dances and give directions for their performance. (See next chapter.)

---

[1] Discussed by Dr. Edward W. Naylor in *An Elizabethan Virginal Book*.

IV

Steps of Elizabethan Dances

Good fellows must go learn to dance,
    The bridal is full near-a,
There is a Braule come out of France,
    The trick'st you heard this year-a;
For I must leap, thou must hop,
    And we must turn all three-a,
The fourth must bounce it like a top,
    And so we shall agree-a;
I pray thee, Minstrel, make no stop,
    For we will merry be-a.

From an old ballad printed in London in 1569 and quoted by
W. Chappell in *Popular Music of the Olden Time*, Vol. 1, p. 243

BEFORE WE consider the steps of Elizabethan dances, we must take into account the manner in which they are danced. Every dance has its characteristic mood and is, in part, an elaborate mime of a prevailing emotion.

Court Dances

The Court dances were of two general types: *basse* dances, in which the feet were close to the ground with steps consisting of glides or walking steps, and *haute* dances, where running, skipping, hopping, and leaping were introduced. Of the first type by far the most famous was the pavan.

PAVAN

Mood: ceremonial dignity and grave pride.

Time: 2/2 or 4/4, the dance beginning solidly on the first beat.[1]

Instruments: drum and human voices, or drum and wind or stringed instruments or both. For tabulation of the drum rhythm for the pavan, see *Orchesography* (ARBEAU), p. 58.

Steps:

1st beat: The gentleman has the lady on his right. He takes her left hand in his right hand, holding it on a level with her waist. Together they take one step with the right foot, and, although the step is forward, they make a slight curve toward the right, the left knee is slightly bent, and the body swings with a slight undulation of the hips.

2nd beat: The left foot is brought up to the right foot; then follow a rise on the toes and a return to standing level. (The step and the joining of the feet on the 1st and 2nd beats are known as a "right single".)

3rd beat: A forward step is taken to the left, with the left foot making a slight curve toward the left, the right knee being bent slightly, and the hips swinging toward the left.

4th beat: The right foot joins the left; then follow a rise on the toes and a return to standing level. (These two movements on the 3rd and 4th beats are known as a "left single".)

5th beat: One step to the right.

6th beat: One step to the left.

7th beat: One step to the right.

8th beat: The left foot joins the right; then follow a rise on the toes and a return to standing level. (These four movements on the 5th, 6th, 7th, and 8th beats are known as a "right double".)

The dance continues with a left single, a right single, and a left double again, followed by a right single, a left single, a right double, and so on. From this it will be seen that two singles, followed by a double, comprise the entire dance as far as the steps go.

Variety in the pavan comes with the directions the steps take, for it may be danced forward in a steady progression; backward with the gentleman behind the lady, guiding her by the hand; forward and backward so that

---

[1] This is sometimes difficult on the stage, and it is suggested that the first strain be played through once in order that the dancers may get into place and become familiar with the tempo, at the same time making the sweeping bows to one another and the company that always precede the *basse* dances.

the dancers stay practically in one spot;[1] to alternate sides; with the gentleman dancing round his standing partner; or with the gentleman dancing alone towards the centre of the floor, bowing to the lady on the opposite side of the room—presupposing that the couples surround the outer edge of the dance floor—then dancing back and bowing to his partner. (Suggestions for turning the pavan into a set dance by means of combining these steps into various figures have been made by Mabel Dolmetsch in *Dances of England and France*, pp. 86–88. In this same work the sequence of steps that compose the Long Pavan is also explained, on pp. 97–101.)

The slow processional form of the pavan known as the *"Grand Bal"*[2] was danced on stately and ceremonial occasions, such as a ball at Court or in the house of a great noble, especially when royalty was present. Dancing very slowly and with grave decorum, the couples encompassed the room two or three times, bowing to the distinguished hosts and guests as they passed the dais on which they were seated. On such occasions the dancers were arrayed in splendid costumes, the ladies with costly gowns sweeping the floor, the gentlemen in plumed hats with their jewelled swords lifting their magnificent cloaks behind.[3]

As might be expected, the pavan was frequently used in the Court masques, especially for the entrance of gods, goddesses, kings, emperors, and the like. On such occasions the music was livelier and the tempo faster than that used for the *Grand Bal*. Another type, known as the *"passamezzo"*, was quite gay in mood, light in step, and moderately fast in tempo. Last of all and farthest removed from the solemnity of the processional pavan was the *Pavane d'Espagne* (Spanish Pavan), which became very popular towards the end of the sixteenth century. One figure of this dance is given below, and it will be seen that, though there is some influence of the stately walking dance still lingering, the mood is entirely altered, being one of tripping liveliness. For this reason it will, perhaps, lend itself to stage presentation far better than the earlier forms of the pavan.

Spanish Pavan

Mood: gay and vivacious.

Time: duple time at a tripping pace.

Instruments: drum and wind and stringed instruments.

[1] For a description of this movement used for a special dance in *Love's Labour's Lost*, see page 266, and for a dance in *Much Ado about Nothing*, see page 273.

[2] A modified form of this survives in the Grand March that usually precedes a formal ball in America. The term "prom" for academic balls evidently derives from this promenade.

[3] This would seem to substantiate the belief that "pavan" is derived from the Latin *pavo* (a peacock), but it must be remembered that there was an ancient dance of Padua known as the "padoaua" from which it may have derived.

S.S.P.—P

Steps:

Introduction
 1st beat: Left single.
 2nd beat: Left single.

Main dance
 1st beat: Raise the left foot in front and lower it.
 2nd beat: Raise the right foot in front and lower it.
 3rd beat: Spring to the left.
 4th beat: Bring the feet together.
 5th beat: Raise the right foot in front and lower it.
 6th beat: Raise the left foot in front and lower it.
 7th beat: Spring to the right.
 8th beat: Bring the feet together.
 Repeat the main dance three times.

Finale
 1st beat: Raise the right foot in front and lower it.
 2nd beat: Raise the left foot in front and lower it.
 3rd beat: Raise the right foot in front and lower it.
 4th beat: Bring the feet together.

Music for the Pavan

"Belle Qui Tiens Ma Vie" in *Dances of England and France* (DOLMETSCH), p. 88.

"Belle Qui Tiens Ma Vie" (in four parts, instruments or voices, with drum rhythm indicated throughout) in *Orchesography* (ARBEAU), pp. 58–59.

BULL, JOHN, "St. Thomas Wake", G minor (for piano), published by G. Schirmer, Inc., New York.

——, "St. Thomas's Wake", pavan *en suite* (see footnote [1] p. 227), in *Shakespeare and Music* (NAYLOR), pp. 194–195.

BYRD, WILLIAM, "The Earl of Salisbury's Pavan", in *Dances of England and France* (DOLMETSCH), p. 96.

——, "The Earl of Salisbury's Pavan", A minor (for piano), published by G. Schirmer, Inc., New York.

CHAMBONNIÈRES, JACQUES CHAMPION DE, "L'entretien des Dieux", G minor (for piano), published by G. Schirmer, Inc., New York.

DOWLAND, JOHN, "Lachrymae Pavan", in *Dances of England and France* (DOLMETSCH), pp. 90–93.

"The Lord Zouche's Masque", in *Dances of England and France* (DOLMETSCH), pp. 93–94.

"Processional Pavan", in *Dances of England and France* (DOLMETSCH), p. 85.

"La Rote de Rode" (pavan), in *Dances of England and France* (DOLMETSCH), p. 85.

TOMKINS, THOMAS, "Pavana", in *An Elizabethan Virginal Book* (NAYLOR), pp. 16–19.

GALLIARD[1]

Mood: blithe, dashing, and brisk.

Time: 3/4, six quarter notes played in two bars of triple time.

Instruments: drum and wind and stringed instruments.

Steps: The simple basic steps are five light running steps—left, right, left, right, left—followed by a leap and, on the sixth beat, a return to position, one foot slightly in advance of the other.

The dance starts with the gentleman taking his lady's hand and bowing to her and to the company as he removes his hat; the lady in the meantime acknowledges this *révérence* by inclining her head as she bends both knees with one foot well behind the other. They now dance the five steps followed by the leap on the part of the gentleman and a slight jump on the part of the lady. When they have circled the dance floor once or twice, they pause at the top of the floor; the gentleman bows, the lady curtsies and then dances alone to the bottom of the floor, where she turns and stands facing the gentleman, who has followed her and who now performs a series of carefully rehearsed steps, known as "passages", before her, turning first one shoulder and then the other towards her as he does so. She once again dances alone to the top of the room, and again the gentleman follows and again displays his agility in a series of passages before her, after which they bow to one another and the gentleman leads the lady to her chair and, bowing before her, thanks her for the honour she has done him.

(A variation[2] of the above can be performed in which the lady is given more opportunity to dance. After the usual dance round the room has been accomplished, the couple dance to the middle of the floor and there divide, one going to the top of the floor, the other to the bottom. They now turn and face one another, and, both curving to the right, advance towards each other, pass, and take each other's places, after which they return, pass, and go to their original places. The passing and counterpassing is performed with grace and restraint by the lady and with vigour and agility by the gentleman. Throughout, the couple face one another, and in order to do this they take the line of an elongated *S*, which means that together they form a figure *8*. As they advance they naturally dance forward, but after they pass one another they turn and dance the rest of the steps backward and in this way follow the rule of always being vis-à-vis.)

The variations of the basic steps of the galliard are innumerable, since

[1] When the galliard followed the pavan, sometimes the same melodic theme was used for each; it was then known as "pavan *en suite*". See Music for the Pavan (p. 226).

[2] Suggested by Cesare Negri (1604), who is quoted by Mabel Dolmetsch in *Dances of England and France*, p. 107.

not only are there endless combinations that can be used, but they can be augmented further by the introduction of any new steps that the gentleman cares to devise, the brilliance and dash of these innovations being part of the display.

Two Examples of Galliard Steps

Passage I

1st beat: Spring on the right foot and hop on it.

2nd beat: Bring the left foot up and with the toe touch the toe of the right foot.

3rd beat: Spring on the left foot and hop on it.

4th beat: Bring the right foot up and touch the toe of the left foot.

5th beat: Leap in the air and come down lightly on the toes with one foot slightly in advance of the other. (This is known as "posture".)

6th beat: Rest in posture position.

The leap varies according to the skill and strength of the dancer, in some cases being high enough to allow a scissors movement of the legs while in the air or even a double rotation of the whole body, in others being no more than a modest leap with feet together.

Passage II

1st beat: Spring on the right foot and hop on it.

2nd beat: While hopping on the right foot, raise the left foot in front to about knee height.

3rd beat: Spring on the left foot and hop on it.

4th beat: While hopping on the left foot, raise the right foot in front to about knee height.

5th to 8th beats: Repeat the first four beats.

9th beat: Leap. Posture.

10th beat: Rest in posture position.

The variations of this step consist of raising the foot *across* the hopping leg both in front and behind; of kicking first the right foot and then the left up in front without hopping; of kicking to the sides; of kicking up behind. Where the movements are fast and furious, the leap and posture need not be introduced on *every* fifth and sixth beat but can be delayed for eight or even sixteen bars if desired. In order to make these directions useful for stage production, there are included here three passages that combine very effectively for purposes of display.

A Suggested Sequence of Passages

Passage I

1st beat: Raise the right foot while the left foot hops.

2nd beat: Raise the left foot while the right foot hops.

3rd beat: Without hopping, kick forward first with the right foot, then with the left.

4th beat: Without hopping, kick backward first with the left foot, then with the right.

5th beat: Leap.

6th beat: Posture.

Passage II

1st beat: Raise the right foot across the back of the left leg while the left foot hops.

2nd beat: Raise the left foot across the back of the right leg while the right foot hops.

3rd beat: Raise the right foot across the front of the left leg while the left foot hops.

4th beat: Raise the left foot across the front of the right leg while the right foot hops.

5th beat: Leap.

6th beat: Posture.

Now dance the final passage (Passage III) in double time.

Passage III

1st beat: Raise the right foot in front while hopping on the left foot. Raise the left foot in front while hopping on the right foot.

2nd beat: With the right foot raised in front, give a jump and change feet so that the left is raised. With the left foot raised in front, give a jump and change feet so that the right is raised.

3rd beat: Without hopping, kick the right foot in front and then the left. Without hopping, kick the right foot behind and then the left.

4th beat: Hop on the left foot and kick across in front with the right. Hop on the right foot and kick across in front with the left.

5th beat: Leap high enough to clap the heels together.

6th beat: Posture.

The transition from folk to Court dancing is nowhere so obvious as in the galliard, the basic steps of which are all found in the morris dance.

The retreating of the lady and following of the gentleman and the display
of masculine prowess—for there is no doubt that the passages call for strength
and endurance—point to an even older "wooing dance", which, in turn,
may have originated from the mating display of certain birds.

CINQUEPACE

A more vigorous form of the basic steps of the galliard is seen in the
cinquepace, and this can be used in place of the galliard steps in all parts of
the dance exclusive of the passages.

Mood: gay, even boisterous.

Time: 3/4 at a brisk pace.

Instruments: drum and wind and stringed instruments.

Steps:

1st beat: Hop on the right foot while raising the left foot in front—
about knee height.

2nd beat: Lower the left foot a little in advance of the right one; hop on
it while raising the right foot.

3rd beat: Lower the right foot a little in advance of the left foot; hop
on it while raising the left foot.

4th beat: Lower the left foot a little in advance of the right foot; hop on
it while raising the right foot.

5th and 6th beats: Leap in the air, returning to the floor on the toes with
one foot slightly in advance of the other (5th and half of the 6th
beat). Rest (second half of the 6th beat.)

Music for the Galliard and Cinquepace

BULL, JOHN, "St. Thomas's Wake", in *Shakespeare and Music* (NAYLOR), pp. 195–196.

BYRD, WILLIAM, "The Earl of Salisbury's Galliard" in *Dances of England and France*
(DOLMETSCH), pp. 110–113.

——, "Galiarde", A minor, published by G. Schirmer, Inc., New York.

DOWLAND, JOHN, "Captaine Digorie Piper: His Galiard", published by the Oxford
University Press, New York.

——, "The King of Denmark's Galiard", published by the Oxford University Press,
New York.

"Gagliarda Tamburina" (16th-century lute MS. from the Dolmetsch Library), in
Dances of England and France (DOLMETSCH), pp. 117–119.

"Galliarde ' la Lyonnaise" (published by Pierre Allaigant, 1530), in *Dances of England
and France* (DOLMETSCH), pp. 122–123.

HASSLER, HANS LEO, "Gagliarde", in *Pre-classic Dance Forms* (HORST), p. 29.

MORLEY, THOMAS, "Frog Galliard", in *Dances of England and France* (DOLMETSCH),
pp. 127–128.

OYSTERMAYRE, JEHAN, "Galliard", in *An Elizabethan Virginal Book* (NAYLOR), pp. 22–24.

Airs of traditional and contemporary galliards will be found in *Orchesography* (ARBEAU), pp. 82, 83, 86–89, 91–93, 96, 98–102.

CANARY

Another wooing dance that was very popular at the Courts of Elizabeth and James I was called the "canary", and, although it is thought to have been named for the Canary Islands, the supposed place of its origin, the basic steps are part of an ancient folk dance common to all European nations.

Mood: wooing and devotional on the part of the gentlemen and modestly receptive on the part of the ladies.

Time: duple time, that is, 2/4 or 6/8.

Instruments: drum and wind and stringed instruments.

Steps: Each gentleman takes his lady by the hand, and together they dance to the end of the dance floor, using a light running step or skip, as in the hay. The gentlemen now dance backward down the room with the same light running step; they then advance dancing as before, until they stand before their ladies. They then dance the following measure of six beats while the ladies stand watching them.

1st beat: Tapping the ground with his left foot, he raises his right foot and lowers it.

2nd beat: Springing on the left foot, he brings the right heel against the left heel.

3rd beat: Springing on the right foot, he brings the left heel against the right heel.

4th beat: Tapping the ground with the right foot, he raises his left foot and lowers it.

5th beat: Springing on the right foot, he brings the left heel against the right heel.

6th beat: Springing on the left foot, he brings the right heel against the left heel.

This measure is then repeated, after which the gentleman bows, takes the lady's hand, and together they dance back to the place from whence they started, using the same step as before.

Music: There is an air for the canary to be found in *Orchesography* (ARBEAU), p. 151, and another in *Popular Music of the Olden Time* (CHAPPELL), Vol. I, p. 358.

LAVOLTA

This dance is of the same general form as the galliard since it is a *haute* dance in triple time with elevation on the fifth beat and a rest on the sixth. But there all resemblance ends, for the lavolta is danced by couples in close contact in a very limited space.

> *1st beat:* The gentleman, who is facing the lady, springs forward on his left foot, raising his right foot.
>
> *2nd beat:* With his right arm round the lady's waist and his left hand beneath either her bust or the point of her stomacher, he takes a fairly long step on the right foot, turning his right shoulder to the lady at the same time. The lady now places her left arm round the gentleman's neck and with her right hand holds down her dress.
>
> *3rd beat:* The gentleman, with his left thigh beneath the lady's "rump" (to quote Arbeau), now lifts her as high as possible.
>
> *4th, 5th, and 6th beats:* The lady is returned to the floor, and both she and the gentleman, with feet together, pause for two beats.

This covers a three-quarter turn. In four such movements the couple arrives back at the spot from which they started after having made a very small circle. For this reason the dancers soon become very giddy, and it is as well to make circles to the right and left alternately.

It is almost impossible to visualize this elevation of the lady without having actually seen it. Fortunately we have a revealing picture of Queen Elizabeth dancing a lavolta with the Earl of Leicester (facing p. 185).

In spite of royal participation, this dance was considered vulgar by the élite, and the young Capriole in Arbeau's *Orchesography* suggests that it is not either "beautiful or decent, unless you are dancing with some buxom serving wench".

Music for Lavolta

"Air of a Volta", in *Orchesography* (ARBEAU), p. 106.
BYRD, WILLIAM, "La Volta", in *Dances of England and France* (DOLMETSCH), p. 132.
MORLEY, THOMAS, "La Volta", in *An Elizabethan Virginal Book* (NAYLOR), p. 48.
   The lavolta can also be danced to quick-time galliard music.

COURANTE

Another dance that was popular at Court in Shakespeare's day was the courante. Here again we have an example of a country dance being adapted for courtly performance and, since the basic steps are the same as those of the pavan, with running and jumping in place of the walking steps, we must conclude that they both sprang from the same original country dance.

Mood: light, swift, and lively.
Time: quick 3/4 time.
Instruments: drum and wind and stringed instruments.
Steps:
1st beat: Spring to the right on the right foot; bring feet together.
2nd beat: Spring to the left on the left foot; bring feet together.
3rd beat: Take three light running steps—right, left, right.
4th beat: Bring feet together.

As in the pavan, this dance can go progressively forward, or backward and forward, or even sideways, depending on inclination or the dancing space available.

Music for the Courante

CHAMBONNIÈRES, JACQUES CHAMPION DE, "Courante", in *Pre-classic Dance Forms* (HORST), p. 46.
"Corranto" (anonymous), in *Dances of England and France* (DOLMETSCH), pp. 142–143.
"English Corranto" (16th century; anonymous), in *Dances of England and France* (DOLMETSCH), pp. 134–135.
FRESCOBALDI, GIROLAMO, "Corrente", published by G. Schirmer, Inc., New York.
HOOPER, EDMUND, "Corranto", in *An Elizabethan Virginal Book* (NAYLOR), pp. 35–36.
LULLY, JEAN BAPTISTE, "Courante", published by G. Schirmer, Inc., New York.
"Sir John Hope's Currant" (16th century; anonymous), set by ARNOLD DOLMETSCH, in *Dances of England and France* (DOLMETSCH), p. 136.
"Traditional Air of the Courante" in *Orchesography* (ARBEAU), p. 109.

ALLEMANDE

Mood: grave, rather ceremonious, with a touch of sentiment.
Time: duple.
Instruments: drum and wind and stringed instruments.
Steps: This is a processional dance with couples holding each other's two hands, gravely pacing one couple behind the other in a long line. The dance consists of three walking steps—left, right, left— with the right foot raised in front on the fourth beat. A series of these "doubles" is followed by a pair of "singles" (see p. 224) in which, instead of closing the feet, the foot is raised forward.

There would be little difference between this dance and the pavan except for one unique feature which characterizes the allemande, that is, the division of the dance into three parts by intervals during which the music stops and the partners engage in conversation. When the music starts again, it becomes quicker and gayer, so that the third and final dance is very bright and performed at a brisk tempo.

As the name suggests, this dance came from Germany, but the changing mood of the three parts suggests a later French influence. There was, indeed, a form known in France, paradoxically enough, as *"allemande française"*.

Music for the Allemande

"Allemande" (anonymous; 16th century), in *Dances of England and France* (DOL-METSCH), pp. 145–146.

"Allemande Nouvelle", Clavier Tablature Book of Bernard Schmid (1577), in *Dances of England and France* (DOLMETSCH), pp. 157–158.

BULL, JOHN, "The Duke of Brunswick's Alman", published by Williams, London.

——, "The Duke of Brunswick's Alman" (from the *Fitzwilliam Virginal Book*), in *Dances of England and France* (DOLMETSCH), pp. 149–150.

BYRD, WILLIAM, "The Queen's Almayne" (from the *Fitzwilliam Virginal Book*), in *Dances of England and France* (DOLMETSCH), pp. 151–152.

HOOPER, EDMUND, "Alman", in *An Elizabethan Virginal Book* (NAYLOR), pp. 31–32.

JOHNSON, ROBERT, "Alman" (from the *Fitzwilliam Virginal Book*), in *Dances of England and France* (DOLMETSCH), p. 148, and *An Elizabethan Virginal Book* (NAYLOR), p. 137.

LULLY, JEAN BAPTISTE, "Allemande", published by G. Schirmer, Inc., New York.

BRANLE, OR BRAWL

The word "branle" applies to a series of dances coming from various parts of France. Having similar basic characteristics, these dances evidently sprang from a common source, but, as improvisations were made, various districts evolved their own particular forms, and these forms in turn took on a local habitation and a name. One feature they have in common, that of being danced *sideways*, for which reason they can be danced in one long line or in a ring. There is no need to discuss more than a few forms of the branle here, and these will be limited to those suitable for stage presentation. The outstanding difference between the various forms seems to be one of mood: for instance, the *Branle Simple* and the *Branle Double* are both sober and dignified dances; the *Branle Gai* is sweet, with subdued gaiety; and the *Branle Bourgogne* is lively, with a certain degree of innocent high-spirited abandon.

Branle Simple

Steps:

1st beat: Fling the left foot sideways, rest on it and bring the right foot up to it.

2nd beat: Fling the left foot sideways, rest on it and bring the right foot up to it.

3rd beat: Fling the right foot sideways, rest on it and bring the left foot up to it.

4th beat: Fling the right foot sideways, rest on it and bring the left foot up to it.

Branle Double

Steps:

1st beat: Fling the left foot sideways, rest on it and bring the right foot up to it.

2nd beat: Fling the left foot sideways, rest on it and bring the right foot up to it.

3rd beat: Fling the right foot sideways, rest on it and bring the left foot up to it.

4th beat: Fling the right foot sideways, rest on it and bring the left foot up to it.

5th beat: Raise the left foot toward the front; lower it.

6th beat: Raise the right foot toward the front; lower it.

7th beat: Bring the feet together.

8th beat: Rest.

In some districts the branle was danced with a rough vigour. One of these forms, the *Branle du Haut Barrois*, is said to have been danced only by peasants, but what is most interesting is that it was also danced by courtiers in masques where they were impersonating rustic characters such as shepherds. In fact it is more than likely that the dance in *Henry VIII* danced by the King and his courtiers on their arrival at Wolsey's palace disguised as shepherds was the *Branle du Haut Barrois*. (See suggestions for dances in *Henry VIII*, p. 244.)

Branle du Haut Barrois

Mood: quick, lively, even boisterous.

Time: duple.

Instruments: pipe and tabor.

Steps:

1st beat: Spring to the left with both feet off the ground and come down
with the weight on the right foot and with the left foot pointing
out at the side—feet about twelve inches apart.

2nd beat: Repeat, only the left foot, instead of pointing to the side, is
now pointing in front of the right foot.

3rd beat: Spring to the right and point to the side with the right foot.

4th beat: Spring to the right and point in front with the right foot.

5th beat: Spring to the right and come down with the feet together.

6th beat: Rest.

The dance now goes into a second phase that is far more strenuous than
the first.

1st beat: Spring to the left—both feet off the ground—and come down
with the right foot pointing to the side.

2nd beat: Leap in the air.

3rd beat: Spring to the left, the right foot pointing to the front.

4th beat: Leap.

5th beat: Spring to the right with the left foot pointing to the side.

6th beat: Leap.

7th beat: Spring to the right with the left foot pointing to the front.

8th beat: Bring the feet together, rise on the toes, and sink to standing
height.

The entire dance is then repeated but with the first spring being made
to the right.

When a play ends with a dance, this is a very effective one to choose,
for the entire cast can dance it facing the audience, and, since it is danced
sideways, exits can be made *dancing*. On an Elizabethan stage, where a
general exit has to be made, this is a happy means of getting everyone "off"
without delay and without breaking the gaiety of the close.

Music for the Branle du Haut Barrois

There seem to be various opinions as to the actual time of this dance,
but since we know that it was often danced to ballads, it is reasonable to
suppose that it was danced in common time, to the sound of pipe and tabor.
Any contemporary song tune in common time will be appropriate, then,
for the branle, and a good example is to be found in *Popular Music of the
Olden Time* (CHAPPELL), Vol. I, p. 78, where "We be three poor mariners" is
said to be the tune used for the *Branle de Poitou*. Many other traditional tunes
in common time can be found in the same work on pp. 56–97 and 110–243.

Country Dances

The folk dances of England are so numerous that any attempt to discuss them in their entirety in this chapter would be futile, nor would prolonged emphasis on the subject be of direct use to the producer of a Shakespearean play. As in the case of the Court dances, therefore, only those that are called for in the stage directions will be considered.

Lighthearted rustic romping is, naturally, to be found in the comedies only—the grim revelling of the witches in *Macbeth* can hardly be considered as anything but a grotesque and irrelevant interpolation. Country dances occur in *A Midsummer Night's Dream*, II, 2, in *The Merry Wives of Windsor*, V, 5, and in *The Winter's Tale*, IV, 3. The dances that best fit the demands of the text in these plays are the round, or roundel, in the first two, and the hay in the last.

The round, as has been explained, was originally danced round some person or object. In *A Midsummer Night's Dream* this would be the sleeping Titania, and in *The Merry Wives of Windsor*, the sleeping Falstaff. If, however, the sleeper is on the inner stage, as has been suggested in the case of Titania, there will not be sufficient room to dance round her, and it would be better for the Fairies to dance on the middle stage.

SELLENGER'S ROUND

One of the oldest known circular dances, and one that has never fallen out of popular favour, is Sellenger's Round. It dates back to 1450, but is possibly of pagan origin, going back in time to nature-worship ritual. It was, and still is, danced by villagers round the Maypole in May Day festivities. The traditional music for this dance, dating back to the reign of Edward III, has survived, and is to be found in *Popular Music of the Olden Time* (CHAPPELL), Vol. I, p. 69. An arrangement made by William Byrd for *Queen Elizabeth's Virginal Book* will be found in the same volume on page 71. (It is suggested that, though the simple form played on pipe and tabor would be suitable for *The Merry Wives of Windsor*, the more sophisticated arrangement by Byrd, played on harp or harpsichord, would be more appropriate for *A Midsummer Night's Dream*.)

Figure 1: An equal number of couples stand in a ring, take hands, skip to the left for four beats, and then to the right for four beats.
Figure 2: Still standing in a circle, all link arms, skip toward the centre

of the ring for two beats, and then back to their former places on two beats.

Figure 3: Partners now face one another, and each skips diagonally three steps to the right and curtsies or bows, according to the sex of the dancer. This takes four beats, and skipping back to the former position and again curtsying or bowing takes another four.

Figure 4: Partners either join hands or link arms and swing round for eight beats.

Figure 5: All take hands in a circle and skip to the left on four beats and then to the right on another four beats.

Figure 6: They repeat Figure 2 twice.

Figure 7: Now on four beats the dancers form two lines, facing one another with a space in between.

Figure 8: One line stands still while the other line skips toward them on three beats, curtsies or bows on the fourth beat, and then skips back on four beats. The other line now does the same.

Figure 9: They repeat Figure 3.

Figure 10: They repeat Figure 4.

Figure 11: They repeat Figure 1.

These eleven figures can be repeated as many times as desired.

Music: danced in 4/4 time to old song and ballad tunes, for which see *Popular Music of the Olden Time* (CHAPPELL), Vol. I, pp. 56–97 and 110–243.

THE HAY

Little is actually known of this country dance, the steps introduced in the *Branle de la Haye*[1] being a courtly modification of but one feature of it. However, it is admitted by many authorities that the dance nearest in style and figures to the original hay survives in the Sir Roger de Coverley.

Figure 1: Two long lines are formed with the ladies in one line and gentlemen in the other facing each other.

Figure 2: The gentleman at the top and the lady at the bottom advance toward each other with light running steps. They then join right hands with arms extended above their heads, turn round each other, and return to their places.

Figure 3: They repeat Figure 2, using their left hands for the turn.

Figure 4: The same dancers now advance toward each other again;

---

[1] See Arbeau, Thoinot, *Orchesography*, pp. 142–144.

the gentleman bows, and the lady curtsies, and they return to their places.

Figure 5: The top gentleman gives his right hand to his partner (the lady opposite to him in the line) and his left to the second lady in the line, while his partner, after giving him her right hand, gives her left to the second gentleman in the line, and thus they continue, chainwise, down the line until they reach the bottom. They then hold up their joined hands and the joined couples pass beneath and divide, the ladies going one way and the gentlemen the other. The final couple, after having passed under the joined hands, remains and becomes the top couple, and, the two long lines having been again formed, the dance recommences.

Music: For a traditional Sir Roger de Coverley tune, see *Popular Music of the Olden Time* (CHAPPELL), Vol. II, p. 535.

V

Music & Dance in the Plays

FERDINAND: "Where should this music be? i' th' air, or th' earth?
It sounds no more—and sure, it waits upon
Some god o' th' island."

The Tempest, I, 2

THE SEARCH for the authentic musical setting for lyrics and ballads in the plays of Shakespeare reveals the fact that very few of these are actually known; but it is not difficult to find, among the music of the fifteenth and sixteenth centuries, airs which can be adjusted to fit the metrical form of these verses. The abundance of music of the period that has survived, indeed, may be more than a little overwhelming to the producer who is attempting to select suitable music for any one particular play. The suggestions, therefore, that follow are designed to aid his selection, but, be it understood, not to reduce his further search or to curtail his delight in the exquisite music of the time. Further suggestions for the appropriate type of Elizabethan dances, together with their music, are also made, but by no means claim to be all-inclusive.

Histories

The music in the histories is nearly all of a martial character, and, in order to avoid repetition, the musical requirements of each play will not be considered separately. An analysis of the stage directions[1] common to all and suggestions for suitable music and instruments will, it is hoped, be sufficient guide for the modern producer. One exception will be made, however. The far more elaborate music called for in *Henry VIII* will be discussed separately and in detail at the end of this section. Furthermore, four plays will be considered with the histories in view of the predominantly martial character of the music called for in their performance—*Julius Caesar, Troilus and Cressida, Antony and Cleopatra,* and *Coriolanus.* (*Titus Andronicus* is not considered since its performance today is unlikely.)

Alarum

This is usually found in conjunction with "excursions", a term that applies to marching, counter-marching, charging, and retreating of soldiers. It consists of shrill and prolonged blasts on trumpets, accompanied by rapid rolling of side drums. When an uproar is indicated, blows on the kettle-drum and clashing of cymbals may be added. Sometimes the text indicates that "alarum" is sounded by trumpets alone.

Charge (sounded)

This should be sounded by a trumpet. The notes are not known, but the present-day military "charge" (British) could be used.

Fanfare, or Flourish

This is a ceremonial and prolonged passage of trumpets usually preceding the entrance of royalty or nobility. It is generally clearly indicated in such stage directions as "Flourish of trumpets", "Sound a flourish", "Flourish and then hautboys". But it may also have been implied in "English Herald with trumpet". Again, "Enter York with trumpet", *1 Henry VI,* IV, 3, may mean "with trumpeter", or "preceded by a trumpet flourish". The music for a short flourish may be found in *Shakespeare and Music* (NAYLOR), p. 200. For a longer and more elaborate flourish, see "Fanfare for Trumpets" in *Military Music* (KAPPEY), p. 50.

Marches

Dead March. This should be a slow and solemn rhythm played on muffled side drums "on" and, if possible, on kettledrums "off". A tolling bell would

---

[1] Stage directions (for music) quoted in this section are from the Everyman's Library edition of the plays since they are much fuller than those in most other editions—and so more helpful to the producer.

Attention is called to the fact that the scene division of certain plays (for example, *Antony and Cleopatra* and *The Winter's Tale*) varies slightly in different editions, and, consequently, the Everyman's references used here will not always apply exactly to other editions.

S.S.P.—Q

be an appropriate accompaniment. The actual tablature is doubtful, but any of the marches in *Orchesography* (ARBEAU), pp. 29–38, played in very slow time could be adapted for the purpose. It should be used in *Richard II*, V, 6; in *Richard III*, I, 2; and in *1 Henry VI*, I, 1, and II, 1.

Military Marches. Sometimes the directions for a drum march are clearly given, as in "Here sound an English march". "A march afar off", "A march", or "March" alone. Sometimes it is implied by such directions as "Drums and soldiers", "Drums and colours", that entrances are made to march time. The tablature for such marches will be found under "Ancient English Drum March" in *Shakespeare and Music* (NAYLOR), p. 201.

Such directions as "Drums strike up" and "Drums sound afar off" refer to the rapid rolling of side drums.

Parley

For "Trumpets sound a parley", the trumpets would be accompanied by the rolling of side drums. For the music, see *Shakespeare and Music* (NAYLOR), p. 176.

Prologue

Like Chorus, the Prologue is preceded by three long blasts on a trumpet.

Retreat

This would be sounded by a trumpet and, sometimes, as indicated, would be accompanied by drums. The actual notes of "Retreat" of the period are unknown, but the present-day version as used in the British Army could be substituted.

Sennet (often followed by a flourish)

This is a trumpet passage long enough to allow for the business it has to accompany. It is mostly used for processional entrances and exits, and, though no music for this is known, it would not be inappropriate to use a variation on a fanfare. See *Military Music* (KAPPEY), p. 50.

"Still" Music

This is usually sweet plaintive music played on recorders and oboes. In *Richard II*, V, 5, this would be heard throughout the opening speech. "When griping grief", in *Shakespeare and Music* (NAYLOR), p. 187, or "Lachrymae Pavan" by John Dowland, in *Dances of England and France* (DOLMETSCH), pp. 90–93, would both be suitable for this atmospheric type of incidental music.

Supernatural Music

This type of music would be used for background in such scenes as the raising of spirits in *2 Henry VI*, I, 4; to accompany the symbolic scene in *3 Henry VI*, II, 5, when the dead-march drum music could be added to the soft shrilling of flutes or oboes; and in *Richard III*, V, 3, for the entire scene when the apparitions of the murdered arise. No definite tune for this type of music is suggested. It should be as far as possible a series of eerie sounds in a wailing minor key. Flutes and the shivering of cymbals would be effective. Both "still" and "supernatural" music was, without doubt, played behind the curtains of the top, or third-level, gallery.

Tucket

A tucket was a signal for marching used by cavalry troops and played on brass instruments. For a French tucket, see *Shakespeare and Music* (NAYLOR), p. 202.

"Winds his horn"

This direction occurs in *1 Henry VI*, II, 3, and it should be a hunting call, music for which can be found in *Shakespeare and Music* (NAYLOR), p. 203, and in *Military Music* (KAPPEY), pp. 58–59.

Special Directions for Music ("Noise", etc.)

In *2 Henry IV*, II, 4, "Sneak's Noise" is called in to entertain Falstaff and Doll Tearsheet. A "noise" was the term used to designate the small bands of wandering musicians who haunted the taverns, and such a group now plays for this supper-party. They might consist of a couple of fiddles and a clarinet, recorder, or oboe. It would be appropriate for them to play songs that were popular in the London streets at the time, two good examples being "Greensleeves" and "Come live with me". These are both to be found in *Shakespeare and Music* (NAYLOR), the first on page 188 and the second on page 182.

Another direction, in *1 Henry IV*, III, 3, is "Falstaff meets them playing on his truncheon like a fife". This means that he holds his truncheon *across* his lips and imitates a fife with his voice. A very improper song that was highly popular about the time of the production of the play would be just the sort of tune that Falstaff would use for this. It was called "The Carmen's Whistle" and can be found in *Shakespeare and Music*, p. 188.

There are very few songs actually sung in the chronicle plays, but one in *1 Henry IV*, III, 1 is very unusual. It is sung in Welsh by a lady, and the accompaniment is played on a lute by a man. We have no way of knowing what the song was, but it should not be difficult to find a traditional Welsh air to which a contemporary love song could be sung. The accompaniment could be played on a guitar or a dulcimer.

In *2 Henry IV*, V, 3, Silence sings snatches of rollicking songs in a miserable voice with a blank face, but the tunes for these have not survived. He might, however, quaver all these to some popular air, such as, for instance, "Chevy Chace" (also known as "Flying Fame"), which can be found in *Popular Music of the Olden Time* (CHAPPELL), Vol. I, p. 199. (Falstaff, it will be remembered, sings "When Arthur first in Court" to this tune as he enters in *2 Henry IV*, II, 4.)

King Henry V (in *Henry V*, IV, 8) commands a *Non Nobis* and *Te Deum* to be sung. The singing could be started loudly by all on stage, fade on the exit, and continue very softly through the Chorus which opens Act V. Music can be found in Grove's *Dictionary of Music and Musicians*, *Non Nobis* in Vol. II, pp. 642–643, and *Te Deum* in Vol. V, p. 295.

HENRY VIII

Act I, scene 2. "Cornets".

This is unusual, for the flourish here indicated is usually sounded by trumpets. These "entrance" fanfares could be sounded by two heralds, one in either window stage, with fine effect.

Act I, scene 4. "Hautboys".

This could be a sennet of cornets while the banquet is being set and again during Cardinal Wolsey's entrance. The direction of "Drum and trumpet: chambers discharged" could be carried out "off" with a prolonged trumpet blast accompanied by rapid rolling of side drums and single violent bangs on the kettledrum.

"Hautboys. Enter the King and others as masquers habited like shepherds."

A very effective pastoral note could be introduced by the use of pan-pipes, or pipe and tabor for this entrance. The music that is used for the dance a little later could be played.

"They choose [ladies for the dance]. The King chooses Anne Bullen. . . . Music. Dance."

As the King and his courtiers represent shepherds, the most appropriate dance would be the *Branle du Haut Barrois* (see p. 235). Any contemporary tune in common time will be right for this dance music, but by far the most appropriate would be "The Kyng's Masque", which can be found in *Shakespeare in Music* (ELSON), p. 145. This music could be played again for the general exit at the end of the scene, which in turn should be followed by a distant flourish.

Act II, scene 1. "Enter Buckingham from his arraignment".

The procession should enter very slowly to the sound of muffled drums. A tolling bell in the distance should sound throughout the scene. The drums should cease when Buckingham begins to speak and start again only on the general exit.

Act II, scene 4. "Trumpets, sennet, and cornets".

This suggests a flourish of trumpets heard "off", and then the two heralds could appear in the window stages as before and could play a sennet through the business that follows.

Act III, scene 1. "Take thy lute, wench; my soul grows sad with troubles: Sing and disperse 'em, if thou canst".

A singer who can accompany herself is essential here. If an alto lute is not available, a guitar is a good substitute. The song "Orpheus with his lute" is believed to have been written by John Fletcher, and since the original tune has not survived, it would be appropriate to sing it to the melody which Robert Johnson composed for another lyric of Fletcher's called "Care-charming sleep". This can be found in *Melody and the Lyric* (GIBBON), p. 125.

Act IV, scene 1. "The order of the Coronation".

After the flourish of trumpets played by the heralds in the window stages, the choristers are heard singing in the distance. They can sing "O Lord, the Maker of all things", the words of which are attributed to Henry VIII and music to William Mundy. This can be found in *Boyce's Cathedral Music*. Or they might sing "Rex gloriose Martyrum", which can be found in Latin in *Melody and the Lyric* (GIBBON), p. 7, and in English in *The English Hymnal* (No. 183).

The procession follows in the order indicated to the sound of pompous and splendid music. This is one place where a gramophone might be used with very fine effect, since it would be practically impossible to have a group of musicians off stage who could do justice to the type of music required. In the collection of recorded music known as "*L'Anthologie Sonore*", there is a record of Melchior Franck's, "Pavana, Tantz, and Intrada", that would be admirable for this purpose (see p. 295, *The Instrumental Suite at the Beginning of the 17th Century*). This music should die down during the duologue of the First and Second Gentlemen, swell again to a fine crescendo, and fade again on the general exit, after which the heralds should play a final flourish as the scene closes.

Act IV, scene 2. "Sad and solemn music. Vision".

The music should accompany the dance and the symbolic dumb show and die away very gently during the sixteen lines of dialogue which follow. This "supernatural" music should be played by stringed instruments, such as cello, violas, and harp, by musicians hidden in the minstrels' gallery or in one of the window stages. The mime dance is minutely described in the stage directions and needs no further explanation beyond saying that all sections of the mime should be linked by the soft gliding steps of the pavan. In *Dances of England and France*, Mabel Dolmetsch has suggested that the music for this Vision might well be "Lachrymae Pavan" by John Dowland and has included an admirable arrangement of the words and music, pp. 90–93. (See also the score for this music listed on p. 290.) Another appropriate air would be "O Death, rock me on sleep", which can be found in *Melody and the Lyric* (GIBBON), p. 34, and in *Popular Music of the Olden Time* (CHAPPELL), Vol. I, p. 238.

Act V, scene 5

The music already suggested for the coronation scene might well be used for the christening ceremony preceded by the fanfare by the heralds, continuing softly through the dialogue, swelling again on the final exit, the scene closing, as before, with the fanfare of trumpets played by the heralds.

JULIUS CAESAR

Act I, scene 2

The ceremonial music that accompanies the processional entrance in the opening of this scene should be of a florid character. It is not necessary for the musicians to appear on the stage, but they can be directed from the stage when to die down in order that Caesar may be heard. Casca's "Peace ho! Caesar speaks", if called sufficiently loudly, might serve the purpose. Again, Caesar's "Set on; and leave no ceremony out" might be loud enough for them to hear and to play as before, and Casca's "Peace yet again!" for them to stop altogether. Music for processional purposes of the period will be found in *Military Music* (KAPPEY), pp. 73–74. Wind instruments would be best. As the procession passes off stage, a sennet is sounded, according to stage directions, but there seems no reason why the music which accompanied the entrance should not also accompany this exit.

"*Flourish. Shout.*" Offstage.

"*Shout. Flourish.*" Offstage.

The re-entrance of Caesar and his train seems to call for a sennet since one is called for on their final exit.

Act I, scene 3

Drums will be needed for "Thunder" in the opening of this scene and for Act II, scene 2.

Act III, scene 2

At the end of this scene the body of Caesar might be carried out to a dead march on muffled drums (see p. 241). The same might be sounded when the body is brought on stage and again when it is taken off at the end of the scene.

Act IV, scene 2

A drum march is heard off stage, and the drummers come on and continue playing until Brutus and his officers and men have entered. The drum march heard off stage that accompanies Cassius and his soldiers should be different from the one heard for Brutus. For various drum rhythms, see *Orchesography* (ARBEAU), pp. 29–38.

Act IV, scene 3

Lucius sings to his own accompaniment. We do not know what song was sung, but, after hearing it, Brutus says, "This is a sleepy tune", which indicates the type of song it must have been. A song that would fulfil this requirement and be in keeping with the atmosphere of the scene would be "O Death, rock me on sleep". See *Popular Music of the Olden Time* (CHAPPELL), Vol. I, p. 238, and *Melody and the Lyric* (GIBBON), p. 34.

Act V, scene 1

"Supernatural" music might accompany the entrance of the ghost (see p. 243). Drum taps should accompany the marching for positions in the opening of the battle, but Brutus and his army should enter to a drum march.

Act V, scene 2. "Alarum".
Act V, scene 3. "Alarum". "Alarum". "Low alarum".
Act V, scene 4. "Alarum".
Act V, scene 5. "Low alarums"—continuing until Brutus dies; then *"Retreat"* is sounded. For martial music, see pp. 241–243.

TROILUS AND CRESSIDA

Three trumpet blasts should precede the entrance of the Prologue. For descriptions of the martial music mentioned below, see pp. 241–243.

Act I, scene 1. "Alarum" (three times).
Act I, scene 2. "A retreat sounded".
Act I, scene 3.

"Sennet" for the entrance of the warriors to the council. A *"tucket"* for the Trojan herald, Aeneas. Later Aeneas says to his trumpeter, who has evidently entered with him:

"Trumpet, blow aloud,
Send thy brass voice through all these lazy tents,"

and the sounding that follows should be strong and rousing.

Act II, scene 2

Although not stated, there should be a flourish for the entrance of Priam and the Court.

Act III, scene 1

In this scene we have music heard off stage, and a very little later the musicians, still playing, are on the stage. The explanation is obvious. The opening of the scene is on the middle stage, and the curtains of the inner stage are drawn to discover Helen, Paris, and Musicians; Helen and Paris move to the middle stage as they greet Pandarus, leaving the musicians on the inner stage; Pandarus speaks of the music as "good broken music", meaning music played well by different kinds of instruments. Plucked stringed instruments and recorders would be a correct combination, and, if possible, one of the stringed instruments should be a lute or a guitar, which Pandarus later borrows to accompany himself. The music for the opening of the scene could be a popular tune such as "Light of Love" (see *Fifty Shakespere Songs* and *Popular Music of the Olden Time* (CHAPPELL), Vol. I, p. 224) or, if something formal is considered more in keeping with the scene, "A Measure" from the *Giles Lodge Lute Book* (1570), which can be found in *Dances of England and France* (DOLMETSCH), pp. 53–54, would be very charming played by strings and wind instruments. The music for "Love, love, nothing but love" is unknown, but the words can be sung to the tune used for "Come, sweet love, let sorrow cease" if the last six bars are repeated. This tune, well known in Shakespeare's day, can be found in *Popular Music of the Olden Time*, Vol. I, p. 240. At the end of this scene a "*retreat*" is sounded.

Act III, scene 3. "*Flourish*".
Act IV, scene 4. "*A trumpet sounds*".

The trumpet that is sounded is "Hector's trumpet", and this should be an *individual* flourish.

Act IV, scene 5. "*Trumpet sounds*".

There is no need to describe the type of sounding made by Ajax's trumpeter; the lines themselves say all:

> "Thou, trumpet, there's my purse.
> Now crack thy lungs, and split thy brazen pipe:
> Blow, villain, till thy sphered bias cheek
> Outswell the colic of puff'd Aquilon.
> Come, stretch thy chest, and let thy eyes spout blood."

The notes should be those of the Greek camp call—not the same as those of "*Trumpet within*", which come later before Hector's entrance of the Greek Camp, those being "the Trojan's trumpet". The "*alarum*" during the fight is evidently sounded without drums, since a little later the direction is "*Trumpets cease*".

Act V, scene 4. "*Alarums. Excursions*".
Act V, scene 8. "*A retreat sounded*" (twice).
Act V, scene 9

There is no direction for the rolling of drums, but this is evidently an omission since Nestor orders "Peace, drums".

ANTONY AND CLEOPATRA

The entrances of the world-known figures in this play are all preceded by florid trumpet flourishes. It would be as well to use at least three different fanfares for these in order to anticipate the entrances of the three chief characters—Octavius, Antony, and Cleopatra—in the quickly moving scenes. A further one might be used for Pompey.

The various battle scenes are suggested by *"Trumpets sound"*, *"Flourish"*, *"Retreat afar off"*. (For these, see pp. 241–242.)

Act II, scene 7. *"Music plays"*.

A banquet is brought on and arranged to the sound of music. That this music is played *"off"* seems certain since it should be distant enough not to interfere with the dialogue of the servants as they go about their business. It should be stately, ceremonial music ending in a swelling and prolonged *sennet* as Caesar, Antony, and the Captains enter and seat themselves. Suitable sixteenth-century music for this purpose can be found in *Military Music* (KAPPEY), pp. 72–74.

The song sung by the boy at the above banquet is no rollicking drinking song, in spite of the scene which follows, but a hymn to Bacchus, possibly based on a classical model. The music is unknown, but it could be sung to "If all the ages of the earth", a melody composed by Alfonso Ferrabosco in 1609 and used in the splendid *Masque of Queens*. This can be found in *Ayres by Alfonso Ferrabosco the Younger*, or in *Melody and the Lyric* (GIBBON), p. 143. It would seem from Enobarbus's order:

> "All take hands.
> Make battery to our ears with the loud music",

that there is an instrumental accompaniment, and no doubt this was played by wind instruments. "The holding every man shall bear" is an order to everyone to join in the chorus.

At the end of this scene, there is one rather rare stage direction, which consists of the sounding of a flourish *with drums*; if possible this should be sounded by a trumpet accompanied by rapid rolling of side drums.

Act III, scene 10

The *"noise of a sea fight"* in this scene will be more a concern for the property man than for the musicians, and calls only for the side drums and kettledrums to aid in the uproar.

Act IV, scene 3

The strange music heard by the soldiers on guard is described as that of *"hautboys as under the stage"*. If possible this hint should be followed, or a microphone and loud-speaker attachment could be used. In this latter case the music could be placed below the stage or behind one of the pillars. For this eerie sound, wind instruments, such as recorders, clarinets, or oboes, should be used, with a shivering of cymbals to accompany a series of strange and unrelated sounds. Any definite musical form should be avoided.

Act IV, scene 9

There is one stage direction in this scene that might be altered to give dramatic effect. The soldiers are trying to wake the dead Enobarbus, thinking he is only asleep, when *"drums afar off"* are heard rousing the camp. If, instead of drums, a reveille could be sounded by a muted cornet off stage, the tragedy of Enobarbus's death would be touched by even more plaintive irony.

CORIOLANUS

This play has more stage directions for music than any other play of Shakespeare's. It is all, with one exception, martial music that is called for, and most of it is of a robust character; in fact, one direction (Act V, scene 4) calls for a positive uproar of brass, drums, and shouts. (For details on martial music, see pp. 241–243.)

Act I, scene 4. "Drums and colours". "They sound a parley". "Drum afar off".
"Alarum afar off". "Alarum". "Another alarum". "Alarum continues".
Act I, scene 5. "Alarum continues still afar off".

This "still" is explained by the fact that there is no break between scenes 4 and 5, and the alarum in scene 4 is the one *still* heard in scene 5.

Act I, scene 7. "Drum and trumpet".
Act I, scene 9. "Flourish. Alarum. A retreat is sounded". "A long flourish".
"Flourish. Trumpets sound and drums".
Act I, scene 10. "A Flourish. Cornets".
Act II, scene 1. "A Sennet. Trumpets sound". "Flourish". "Flourish. Cornets".
Act II, scene 2. "A Sennet". "Flourish of cornets".
Act III, scene 1. "Cornets", for the entrance of Coriolanus.
Act IV, scene 5. "Music within".

This music is being played at the feast off stage and should be free and gay in contrast with the scene between the surly servants and the disguised Coriolanus on stage. There is a "French March" (1660) in *Military Music* (KAPPEY), pp. 78–79, that would serve the purpose very well and would not seem incongruous in a play so predominantly martial in character. If a milder type of music is required by the producer, "La Magdalena", a *basse* dance for four instruments (1530), would not be too incongruous if played on wind and stringed instruments. This can also be found in *Military Music* (KAPPEY), pp. 19–20.

Act V, scene 4. "Trumpets; and hautboys; drums beat; all together". "Music still with shouts".

Act V, scene 5. "A flourish with drums and trumpets".

Act V, scene 6. "Drums and trumpets sound with great shouts of the people". "Drums and colours". "Exeunt bearing the body of Coriolanus. A dead march sounded".

Tragedies

ROMEO AND JULIET

The traditional three blasts on a trumpet precede the entrance of Chorus to speak the Prologues to Acts I and II, and, though it is not stated, it is more than likely that a ceremonial flourish preceded the three entrances of the Prince.

Act I, scene 4

The gaiety that pervades the "ancient feast" at the palace of the Capulets (Act I, scene 5) is anticipated by the masking scene that precedes it (Act I, scene 4). Here we have two lighthearted young men with their lovelorn companion on the way to gate-crash the masked ball in the palace of their enemies. Accompanied by their torch-bearing pages, we see them pause in the street and, out of sheer high spirits, fire verbal squibs and declaim exquisite poetry. The pages hand them masks and dominoes and, on order, strike up their tabors; now, to the lively drumbeats, all journey round the stage (for this business, see footnote 1, p. 36). If the tempo is duple, Benvolio and Mercutio could use a lively courante step while Romeo could languidly bring up the rear walking in slow time.

Act I, scene 5. "Music plays and they dance".

The boisterous orders of Capulet,

> "Come, musicians, play.
> A hall! a hall![1] give room, and foot it, girls,"

and the fact that during the dance he calls for yet more room and orders the fire to be quenched as the hall has grown too hot, all suggest a dance of vigorous movement and swift pace. For these reasons it might be well to start with a courante, which could then, by altering from duple to triple time,[2] go into a galliard. This latter dance allows, in a remarkable way, for

---

[1] Clear a space.

[2] The time of the courante as given by Arbeau is duple; Mrs. Dolmetsch, however, gives it as triple. If the latter is used, the transition to the galliard will be simple.

the required stage business: Juliet, with the other ladies, can dance her solo across the stage towards the place where Romeo is standing, and, as she comes towards him, he can ask the servingman who she is. While her back is towards him and her partner is dancing his first measures before her, Romeo can speak his praise of her beauty almost in her ear, while she, by a backward inclination of her head, can indicate that she is listening. The quarrel between Capulet and his nephew Tybalt would then occur during the time that Juliet is dancing to the other side of the stage followed by her partner, who dances his second set of measures before her. She could then return again to where Romeo stands, and, after another brief measure danced by her partner, there would be a general *révérence* as the dance concludes. Juliet's partner is surely Benvolio, who has sworn that at this ball he will show Romeo beauties that will eclipse his Rosaline, and now, at the end of the dance, he brings Juliet to Romeo, who takes her hand and leads her to the forestage, where the first love scene takes place. In the meantime music plays softly as the rest of the company break into groups, talking and exchanging bows and pleasantries.

In regard to the music, if the courante is danced in triple time, appropriate ones would be an "English Corranto" of the sixteenth century, which can be found in *Dances of England and France* (DOLMETSCH), pp. 134–135, and two lively ones in *Pre-classic Dance Forms* (HORST), pp. 45–46. If the duple time is used, a pavan played in quick time—a *passamezzo*—would be best. Best of all, however, would be a pavan *en suite*—that is, one that goes into a galliard by a change of time but not of melody. "St. Thomas's Wake" would be admirable for this and can be found in *Shakespeare and Music* (NAYLOR), pp. 194–196. (For a suggested recording of a pavan and galliard, see p. 296, *French Dances of the 16th Century*.)

As to the musicians, they are evidently in sight, but as all floor space is needed for the dancers and the lookers-on, it would be as well to put them on the balcony stage. If possible they should play stringed instruments, such as violins and guitars, with perhaps a recorder or two.

Act II, scene 4

Mercutio sings "An old hare hoar", and, though we have no idea of the tune he originally used, it could be sung to the then-popular air of "The Staines Morris Tune", which can be found in *Popular Music of the Olden Time* (CHAPPELL), Vol. I, pp. 125–126. His exit song with its mocking refrain of "Lady, lady, lady" is evidently the final bars of "There dwelt a man in Babylon" and can be found in *Shakespeare and Music* (NAYLOR), p. 183.

Act IV, scene 4. "Music within".

At the end of this scene, the musicians that are being brought by County Paris to play for his wedding are heard playing off stage. It would be according to custom for them to play a "hunt's up". Moreover, the liveliness of such music would create poignant dramatic irony, since the audience knows that there is to be no joyous bridal for the expectant bridegroom. A "hunt's up" will be found in *Popular Music of the Olden Time* (CHAPPELL), Vol. I, p. 60.

Act IV, scene 5. "Enter Friar Laurence and Paris, with Musicians".

The group of musicians that enters with Paris could be the same as that seen at the Capulets' ball, if we consider that it was, supposedly, a band of independent minstrels hired for special occasions by the nobility. Care must be taken that they carry wind instruments only since one remarks, "Faith, we may put up our pipes and be gone." Peter evidently quotes "When griping grief the heart doth wound," but if he had a mind to sing it, the music can be found in *Shakespeare and Music* (NAYLOR), p. 187.

HAMLET

The usual ceremonial flourish precedes the entrances and exits of the Court in Act I, scene 2 and Act II, scene 2, and there is a *"flourish of trumpets and ordnance shot off within"* in Act I, scene 4, which, the text explains, accompanies the King "as he drains his draughts of Rhenish down". This is again repeated when the King ironically drinks to Hamlet's health in the duel scene (Act V, scene 2). These flourishes should be sounded by trumpets or cornets accompanied by rapid rolling on side drums. For the "ordnance", thumps on the kettledrum will be more effective than firearms.

Act III, scene 2. "Danish march. A flourish".

The Danish march that accompanies the entrance of the Court to see the play has, unfortunately, not survived; however, very appropriate music for processional purposes can be found in *Military Music* (KAPPEY), pp. 78–79.

The *"hautboys"* that accompany the dumb show should emit a shrill screaming sound such as a fife can give, and no attempt at a melody should be introduced.

The three blasts that herald the Prologue should be light in quality—cornets instead of trumpets—and less florid than those used for the Court ceremony.

Act IV, scene 5

The snatches of song sung by Ophelia here and by the Gravedigger in Act V, scene 1, are ballads popular in Shakespeare's day, set to old folk tunes. Fortunately we have a very good idea of these from the fact that many of them were used as the airs for more elaborate compositions by the fine musicians of the time.

Ophelia sings, "How should I your true love know", and goes on to sing three stanzas interspersed with dialogue. This is one of the many ballads that grew up round the pilgrimages to the shrine of Walsingham. The words are a mere echo of a ballad written by Thomas Deloney, a contemporary of Shakespeare. The tune, known as "Walsingham", was used for compositions for the virginals by John Bull and William Byrd, and by John Dowland for a setting for the lute. The simple form of the air, as sung by Ophelia, can be found in *Melody and the Lyric* (GIBBON), p. 47; *Shakespeare and Music* (NAYLOR), pp. 189–190; *Popular Music of the Olden Time* (CHAPPELL), Vol. I, p. 236. The three stanzas, as quoted in the play, may be from different ballads or from different versions of the same ballad, and this would be a skilful indication to an Elizabethan audience of the confusion in Ophelia's mind. That she also sings "Tomorrow is Saint Valentine's Day", a ribald popular song, is another indication of known symptoms in female madness. The music can be found for this in *Melody and the Lyric*, p. 107.

On Ophelia's re-entrance she sings another three lines of the Walsingham ballad, starting, "They bore him bare-fac'd on the bier". Her reference to a song with a refrain of "Down a-down, and you call him a-down-a" is unknown, but it is possible that she only speaks the words in any case. "For bonny sweet Robin is all my joy" is all that is known of a song "My Robin is to the greenwood gone", but the music is extant and can be found in *Shakespeare and Music*, p. 191, and in *Popular Music of the Olden Time*, Vol. I, p. 234. "And will he not come again?" has been recognized as words sung to an old dance tune[1] known as "The Milkmaids' Dump" and, in *The English Dancing Master*, as "The Merry Milkmaids". For the music, see *Popular Music of the Olden Time*, Vol. I, p. 237.

Act V, scene 1

The Gravedigger's song, "In youth when I did love", is a fragment from Lord Vanse's "The Image of Death", to which there are several traditional tunes, two of which can be found in *Popular Music of the Olden Time* (CHAPPELL), Vol. I, p. 217.

---

[1] It is possible that the dance tune grew out of the song version.

Act V, scene 2. "March afar off, and shot within".

At the beginning of Act IV, scene 4, when Fortinbras, a Captain, and Soldiers enter marching, it will be noticed that there is no indication of military music. This is to be explained by the fact that they merely wish to cross Denmark on their way to fight in Poland and have to obtain permission from the King to do so. The point is made doubly clear by the absence of the usual "drums and colours" and by Fortinbras's order to the soldiers to "Go softly on". All this is in direct contrast to the return of Fortinbras and his army after his successful campaign when, on his meeting with the English ambassadors to Denmark—off stage—*"a march afar off and shot within"* are heard. Then Fortinbras enters *"with drum and colours"*.

The *"dead march"* for the final exit should be played on muffled drums. The tablature for this can be found in *Shakespeare and Music* (NAYLOR), p. 201. It goes without saying that this "Ancient English Drum March" should be played very slowly. For *"a peal of ordnance . . . shot off"*, kettle-drums can be used.

MACBETH

Act I, scene 1. "Thunder".

The "thunder" preceding the appearance of the Witches in this scene, and again in scene 3, could be effectively produced by the kettledrum.

Act I, scene 2. "Alarum within".

This is evidently sounded by the trumpet alone and is something in the nature of a flourish heralding the entrance of the King with his sons and attendants.

Act I, scene 3. "Thunder". "Drum within".

For "thunder" use the kettledrum as in scene 1. The "drum within" just before Macbeth's entrance should be made by rapid rolling on the side drum.

Act I, scene 4

A *"flourish"* precedes the entrance of the King and his attendants and accompanies their exit.

Act I, scene 5

A very effective impression could be made if, on Lady Macbeth's line "Hie thee hither", a trumpet could be heard in the distance suggesting that Macbeth is already within sight of the castle and his coming is being heralded by his trumpeter.

Act I, scene 6. "Hautboys and torches".

The musicians, who, with the torchbearers, open the scene, are playing hautboys, according to the text, but surely, had it been possible, bagpipes would have been used, both here and in the opening of scene 7. Their use in a modern production would be correct and effective.

Act I, scene 7. "Hautboys and torches".
See Act I, scene 6.

Act III, scene 1. "Sennet sounded".

Here is another example of the long flourish that accompanies the ceremonial entrance and seating of a Court. A magnificent prolonged flourish may be found in *Military Music* (KAPPEY), p. 50.

Act III, scene 4

Although it is not indicated, a flourish should surely accompany the ceremonial entrance of the Court to the banquet table.

Act III, scene 5. "Thunder" as before for the entrance of the Witches.

(It is doubtful if this scene and parts of Act IV, scene 1, are ever included in modern productions—they are so feeble and so out of key with the rest of the tragedy. William J. Lawrence has offered a solution to the mystery of their existence in the play[1] by proving very convincingly that here was a case of the inclusion of a Court antimasque in a public-playhouse perform-ance. This time, however, it was not a direct borrowing, as in *The Winter's Tale*, but was a third-hand, or twice-removed, revival. An antimasque of witches appears first in Jonson's *The Masque of Queens* given at Whitehall on February 2, 1609. It was then appropriated, with alterations and the inclusion of two songs, "Come away" and "Black Spirits and White", by Thomas Middleton for his play *The Witch*. This play was a complete failure—with the exception of this antic witch scene. After this fiasco, Middleton seems to have been discouraged, for we find him in 1610 revising old plays for the King's Men, Shakespeare having, in all likelihood, retired to Stratford. Small wonder that, when *Macbeth* fell into his hands, Middleton should have thought of the successful antimasque of witches and have introduced

---

[1] Lawrence, William J., "The Mystery of Macbeth: A Solution", *Shakespeare's Workshop*, pp. 24–38.

S.S.P.—R

it with the incongruous scene between Hecate and the Witches and the dance of the Witches after the apparitions in Act IV, scene 1.)

"Music and song within: 'Come away, come away', etc."

One setting for this may be found in Rimbault's *Ancient Vocal Music of England*, where Robert Johnson is given as the possible author. This volume is, unfortunately, available in very few libraries.

Act IV, scene 1. "Thunder". "Music and a song, 'Black Spirits', etc."

The setting of this song has not survived, but in Davenant's version of *Macbeth*, produced about 1663, music was written for the play by Matthew Locke, and some of it survives in rare collections of music published in 1666,[1] 1669,[2] and 1680.[3] In 1689, the "famous" *Macbeth* music was published; this was also accredited to Matthew Locke and is, in fact, published today by Angener & Co. of London as "The Celebrated Music to Macbeth in Complete Score with Accompaniment for the Pianoforte by Matthew Lock, newly arranged by E. J. Loder." However, there always seems to have been some doubt as to Locke's being the composer, and William J. Lawrence has most convincingly supported the idea of Purcell as the composer.[4] Although this music is not in any way typical of that heard in Middleton's revised *Macbeth*, for want of any other, it could be used.[5]

Thunder accompanies the appearance of each apparition. To this might be added the shivering of cymbals and the wailing of flutes. In regard to the dance of the Witches, we can form a pretty good idea of the type of thing it was by turning to Jonson's own description of the dance in *The Masque of Queens*:

... full of preposterous change and gesticulation [being performed] back to back and hip to hip, their hands joined, and making circles backward, to the left hand, with strange fantastic motions of their heads and bodies.

The only music to be considered in Act V is entirely martial in character and consists of the following:

Act V, scene 2. "Drum and colours".
Act V, scene 4. "Drum and colours".

The drums should play an English march here, for which see *Shakespeare and Music* (NAYLOR), p. 201.

[1] "Musick's Delight on the Cittern."
[2] "Apollo's Banquet for the Treble Violin."
[3] "The Pleasant Companion: or New Lessons and Instructions for the Flagelet."
[4] Lawrence, William J., "Who Wrote the Famous *Macbeth* Music?" *The Elizabethan Playhouse.*
[5] Those seeking for representative music of the time will find that which was used for the Witch dances in *The Masque of Queens* in the British Museum (MSS. 10,444ff21421[b]).

Act V, scene 5. "Drum and colours".
Act V, scene 6. "Drum and colours".
Act V, scene 7. "Alarums".

This direction is repeated four times, suggesting a battle off stage.

Act V, scene 8. "Alarums. Retreat. Flourish".

These sound as the victorious Malcolm and his supporters enter *"with drum and colours".*
"Flourish" to follow "Hail, King of Scotland".
"Flourish" at the final exit.

OTHELLO

In spite of the wartime background and the soldier hero, in *Othello* there is none of the martial music usually called for under similar circumstances in Shakespeare's plays. The reason for this is, possibly, that the campaign discussed in the first act is never really undertaken. Again, this omission may have been deliberate with a view to underscoring the domestic quality of the tragedy. The trumpet flourishes are for the most part of the ceremonial kind: in Act II, scene 1, it is Othello's own trumpet call announcing his arrival on the Island of Cyprus; in Act II, scene 2, the Herald doubtless blows a fanfare before reading the proclamation; in Act IV, scene 1, Lodovico's entrance is preceded by a *"trumpet within"*; and in Act IV, scene 2, trumpets *"summon to supper"*.

Act II, scene 3

Iago sings "And let me the canakin clink, clink". The tune for this drinking song is lost, but there are other drinking songs of the period that would serve equally well; for instance, the famous "I cannot eat but little meat", which had been sung in *Gammer Gurton's Needle*, was a very old song but still popular at this time. Two others, "Troll, troll, troll the bowl to me" and "Toss the pot", have both the hearty, carefree tone that would serve to loosen the bonds of Cassio's discretion equally well. The first is a catch and might be caught up by all the drinkers, while the second is obviously sung by a group in unison. In either case Iago could start the first line. The music for the first of these three songs can be found in *Popular Music of the Olden Time* (CHAPPELL), Vol. I, p. 72; for the other two, in *Melody and the Lyric* (GIBBON), pp. 109 and 111.

A little later Iago sings "King Stephen was a worthy peer". These two stanzas are taken from an old Scottish ballad known as "The Old

Cloak", and the tune for this, as pointed out in *Popular Music of the Olden Time*, Vol. II, p. 505, seems to have been a modified form of "Greensleeves", which can be found in Vol. I, p. 230. A later tune can be found in *Melody and the Lyric*, p. 108, and in *Shakespeare in Music* (ELSON), pp. 202–203.

Act III, scene 1. "Enter Cassio and some Musicians".

As we know from the lines of the Clown, these musicians carry wind instruments. On his entrance, Cassio bids them play

"Something that's brief; and bid 'Good morrow, general'."

Arousing someone in the morning with music was known as a "hunt's up", and no doubt took its name from the famous song "The hunt is up" used for that purpose. This would be an excellent tune for the musicians to play on pipes or recorders and was possibly used in the original production. The music may be found in *Popular Music of the Olden Time* (CHAPPELL), Vol. I, p. 60, and in *Shakespeare in Music* (ELSON), pp. 226–227.

Act IV, scene 3

"The Willow Song", sung by Desdemona, is one of the songs originally used in a Shakespearean play that has survived. The words are an adaption of an old ballad known as "The Lover's Complaint". Music and words can be found in *Fifty Shakespere Songs*, in *Shakespeare's Use of Song* (NOBLE), p. 152, and in *Popular Music of the Olden Time* (CHAPPELL), Vol. I, pp. 206–208. An old manuscript of this song has a setting for a lute accompaniment, but, since Desdemona is undressing as she sings and Emilia is attending her, this could not have been used in the play. The informality of the singing, with breaks for dialogue, suggests, as Desdemona says, something that keeps running in her head, and anything so definite as an instrumental accompaniment would destroy this illusion.

KING LEAR

The main action begins with the prolonged sennet that usually accompanies the entrance and seating of a Court for a ceremonial occasion. If music is thought advisable, appropriate marches and procession music can be found in *Military Music* (KAPPEY), pp. 71–74 and 78–79. In the same book a magnificent and prolonged flourish that would serve for the sennet will be found on page 50.

Throughout the play there are the usual "*flourishes*", "*tuckets within*", "*drums afar off*", "*drums and colours*" for the battle scenes, as well as individual flourishes for the King of France and Cordelia, the Duke of Albany and

Goneril, and the Duke of Cornwall and Regan. In Act V, scene 3, when the trumpet sounds three long blasts after the proclamation, these are, of course, played on stage by heralds. The *"trumpet answers within"*, which follows, should be strong and challenging. Music and directions for all this martial music will be found on pp. 241–243.

Act III, scenes 2, 4, 6

The snatches of songs and rhymes sung by Edgar and the Fool should be set to old ballad tunes, and for these *Popular Music of the Olden Time* (CHAPPELL), Vol. I, pp. 56–243, will be the best source of information. One song, sung in part by the Fool in Act III, scene 2, is, if we can judge by the refrain ("With hey, ho, the wind and the rain"), the same as that used for the epilogue song in *Twelfth Night*. This will be found in *Popular Music of the Olden Time*, Vol. I, p. 225, under the title of "When that I was a little tiny boy".

Act IV, scene 7

When "soft music" plays in the hope of restoring Lear to sanity, care must be taken to increase the volume on the line "Louder the music there", as it is here supposed actually to wake him. Any one of the seven pavans in "Lachrymae" (see p. 290) would be suitable music. It should be played, if possible, on a harpsichord or harp, or on a dulcimer with accompanying plucked cello strings.

CYMBELINE

It is noticeable that in this play there are no flourishes, fanfares, or sennets for state entrances, or martial music for the battles. The explanation for this may lie in the possibility that the play was written for Court production and abandoned before performance, and that the text for the first publication of the play, in the Folio of 1623, was taken from the incomplete prompt copy of the abandoned performance. However that may be, the modern producer will add what formal and martial music he considers necessary.

Act II, scene 3. "Enter Musicians".

In this play we have the only indication of an instrumental performance on the stage that is directly followed by a song.

"First, a very excellent good-conceited thing; after, a wonderful sweet air, with admirable rich words to it", is Cloten's instruction to the musicians, and the order is carried out. The "good-conceited thing" could easily refer to a "phantasie" or "toye", types of music introduced by the musicians of the day. One of the well-known "toyes" of the time was by Giles Farnaby, and a "phantasie" that would be particularly appropriate would be "Fantasy for a Chest of Viols" by Thomas Weelkes. (For recordings of "A Toye" by Farnaby, played on virginals, see pp. 296 and 297; of the "Fantasy" as played by the Dolmetsch family, see p. 296.) The instruments used for this performance are referred to by Cloten as requiring "fingering" and as being composed of "horse-hairs and calves'-guts", which seem to indicate that viols were used. The "wonderful sweet air" is, of course, "Hark, hark, the lark". The music for this song is unknown, but it can be sung to the old tune of "Cherrily and Merrily", which will be found in *Popular Music of the Olden Time* (CHAPPELL), Vol. I, p. 285. There is also, of course, the lovely setting by Franz Schubert, but the older tune would be more in keeping with the play as a whole. (The Schubert setting is in *Fifty Shakespere Songs.*)

Act IV, scene 2. "Solemn music".

This, Belarius says, is to be played on "my ingenious instrument", a reference, according to the Furness Variorum edition, to an aeolian harp. If this suggestion is followed, a soft sighing quality of sound may be made with muted strings or by the brushing of harp strings. If an actual air is used, an old-time one of haunting sadness that would be particularly appropriate is "Western wind, when wilt thou blow?" For this, see *Popular Music of the Olden Time* (CHAPPELL), Vol. I, p. 58. This same music might continue softly through the speaking of the dirge, "Fear no more the heat of the sun".

"*Song*". The fact that this lovely dirge is, according to the lines of the play itself, *spoken*, rather than sung, may be explained by the fact that the company was short of singing boys at the time the play was written.[1] The suggestion is borne out by the description of the voices of Arviragus and Guiderius, who speak the dirge, as "broken". Further evidence of the theory is Cloten's suggestion, in Act II, scene 3, that "Hark, hark, the lark" is sung by a eunuch—a line possibly inserted by the playwright to explain the use of a man singing falsetto in place of the usual boy.

Act V, scene 4. "Solemn music".

The apparition scene is enacted to the sound of "*solemn music*", and some of the ghosts appear "*with music before them*", which seems to indicate that not only were the musicians heard, but actually appeared in the appari-

[1] Noble, Richmond, *Shakespeare's Use of Song*, pp. 136–137.

tion. However, a few lines later we have *"Then, after other music, follow the two young Leonati"*, and it becomes clear that passages of music heard off stage precede the entrance of each set of ghosts. Distant music played on plucked strings—harp, dulcimer, etc.—would be effective, and again, as in the *Henry VIII* "vision", the "Lachrymae Pavan" by John Dowland would be an excellent choice of music. For this, see *Dances of England and France* (DOLMETSCH), pp. 90–93, and the score listed on p. 290 of this text.

TIMON OF ATHENS

Act I, scene 1. "Trumpets sound". "Trumpet sounds".

It will be noticed that the entrance of Timon calls for "trumpets" while that of Alcibiades, for a "trumpet" only. The intention may have been to accentuate the pomp and splendour with which Timon surrounds himself, as we see him in the opening of the play. These two fanfares should be entirely different, of course, as they are the individual flourishes of the two men.

Act I, scene 2. "Hautboys playing loud music".

While the "great banquet" is "being served in", "hautboys" play "loud music". The preparations for banquets, which occur frequently in plays of the time, almost always are accompanied by loud music. This at once suggests that the table either came up on the large centre trap or was lowered from "aloft", and that music was used to drown the creaking of the machinery. In any case it adds to the formality and importance of such scenes if a prolonged sennet is played during the business of preparation.

The masque opens with a *tucket* heard "off" and is followed by the entrance, first, of the servant who comes to announce the arrival of the "ladies" and, then, by Cupid to introduce them. The ladies, as Amazons, then enter *"with lutes in their hands, dancing, and playing"*. Although they carry lutes and appear to be playing as they dance, it is doubtful whether this is more than a miming gesture, since Timon bids his own house musicians play a welcome for the masquers, and, later, the second dance is certainly accompanied by hautboys. If this is so, the musicians should accompany the first dance on stringed instruments in imitation of the lutes the Amazons are supposedly playing (guitars and dulcimers could be used if lutes were not available). The music though gay should yet have a certain formality and could be a continuation of the "welcome" music.

This first dance described in the stage directions corresponds, as Dr. Naylor has pointed out,[1] to Thomas Morley's account of an Italian galliard[2]

[1] Naylor, Edward W., *Shakespeare and Music*, p. 111.
[2] Morley, Thomas, *Introduction to Practical Music*, 1597.

which was danced to the singing of the dancers. As the ladies dance alone, it is possible that the introductory steps of the galliard alone are used. The beautiful "Galliard" by Jehan Oystermayre would be suitable music. This can be found in *An Elizabethan Virginal Book* (NAYLOR), pp. 22–24.

> *"The Lords arise from table, with much adoring of Timon; and to show their loves, each singles out an Amazon, and all dance, men with women, a lofty strain or two to the hautboys, and cease."*

The "lofty strain or two" suggests a stately dance of couples hand in hand, and the pavan seems the inevitable choice, but it is possible that this grave dance might seem an anticlimax after the gaiety of the galliard. A suggestion that might meet the situation more suitably would be to dance the pavan in double time, in other words to dance a *passamezzo* or the Spanish Pavan with its livelier movements. Any pavan music played in double time would be appropriate. The tune for the Spanish Pavan has the advantage of having been very popular in Shakespeare's time, and this may be found in *Popular Music of the Olden Time* (CHAPPELL), Vol. I, p. 241.

Act III, scene 5

Although not indicated in the directions, it is obvious that a fanfare should be sounded before the curtains of the inner stage are drawn to discover the Senate in the opening of this scene.

Act III, scene 6. "Music. Tables set out".

Soft, but spritely, music should be played "off" while the banquet is "set out" and the guests are arriving, and this should continue until Timon throws water in the faces of the guests, when it should break off in confusion. Suitable music would be "The Duke of Brunswicke's Alman" by John Bull or "The Queen's Almayne" by William Byrd, both of which can be found in *Dances of England and France* (DOLMETSCH), pp. 149–152.

Act IV, scene 3. "Music afar off". "Enter Alcibiades with drum and fife". "Drum beats".

The usual drum-and-fife music should be used for the entrance of Alcibiades and the drum beat for his exit.

Act V, scene 4. "Trumpets sound".

Alcibiades enters to a fanfare of trumpets and calls for a parley with the words,

> "Sound to this coward and lascivious town,
> Our terrible approach."

The last line of the play, which is

"Let our drums strike,"

calls for a drum march.
All the descriptions of this martial music will be found on pp. 241–243

Comedies[1]

THE TWO GENTLEMEN OF VERONA

Act IV, scene 2. "Who is Silvia?"

It is evident from the text that the song is sung by men's voices accompanied by a consort of stringed instruments. Although it is suggested that they first play a "dump" (a slow mournful dance tune), they actually start with the serenade. That they follow the song with the dump and continue to play it softly through the dialogue which follows seems to be suggested by the Host drawing Julia's attention to some alteration in the music ("Hark! what fine change is in the music!").

The earliest known setting for this song is by Richard Leveridge (1670–1758). A later one by Franz Schubert is better known, of course. Both of these can be found in *Fifty Shakespere Songs*. A very good example of a contemporary dump will be found in *Shakespeare and Music* (NAYLOR), pp. 199–200.

LOVE'S LABOUR'S LOST

Although this is considered the earliest of Shakespeare's plays, there is no doubt that it was revived—"newly corrected and augmented"—for Court presentation at Christmastide in 1597–1598.

The artificiality of the Court characters, who with delicate satire emphasize the contemporary fad for elaborately stylized language, gives an impression of exquisite foppery to all that they say and do, and this in turn should be reflected in the music.

Act III, scene 1

Upon Armado's demand for a song, Moth is indicated as singing, but only the word "Concolinel"[2] gives any hint of his song, if indeed it is a hint,

---

[1] *The Comedy of Errors* has no directions for music. The producer, however, is advised to introduce an overture, entr'acte music, and finale of Elizabethan ballad tunes. See *Popular Music of Olden Time* (CHAPPELL), Vol. I, pp. 56–243.

[2] There is the possibility that this is an aural mistake and that it stands for "Come follow me". This would be an appropriate song for Moth. For this, see *Popular Music of the Olden Time* (CHAPPELL), Vol. I, p. 273.

for it has no connection with any known tune or words. This delightful youngster has an air of precocity and wit that suggests training of a sophisticated kind. He is rather a Child of Paul's than of the playhouse, and it would be in keeping with his evident skill for him to sing some dainty conceit such as Thomas Morley's canzonet "Sing we and chant it". A solo arrangement of this "Ballet for Five Voices" can be found in *Melody and the Lyric* (GIBBON), pp. 86–87. Another possibility is "Sing care away" to the tune of "Heart's-ease" (see *Popular Music of the Olden Time* (CHAPPELL), Vol. I, p. 210).

Act IV, scene 1

Rosaline's

> "Thou can'st not hit it, hit it,
> Thou canst not hit it, my good man."

and Boyet's

> "An I cannot, cannot, cannot,
> An I cannot, another can"

are the words of an old three-man song set to a dance tune. If it could be sung, it would add one more delight to the studied gaiety of the scene. For the music of this, see *Shakespeare and Music* (NAYLOR), p. 193, and *Popular Music of the Olden Time* (CHAPPELL), Vol. I, p. 239.

Act V, scene 2. "Trumpets sound within".

A flourish of trumpets within anticipates the entrance of the masquers. This could be a French tucket. See *Shakespeare and Music* (NAYLOR), p. 202.

Then "*enter Blackamoors with music*". This may mean "with musical instruments" since, later, they are asked by Rosaline to play for the dance, and, apparently only after some delay, "*music plays*".

There is little doubt that it is a stately pavan that they play during the progressive duologues, and that the gentlemen step the measures backward and forward before the ladies, who refuse to dance. In each case, the couple remains at the front of the forestage as long as the duologue lasts and then "progresses" to make room for the next couple. Finally the gentlemen bow to the disdainful ladies and retire.[1]

For one of the loveliest pavans arranged to be sung, or played, in four-part harmony, see "Belle qui tiens ma vie" in *Orchesography* (ARBEAU), pp. 58–59, and in *Pre-classic Dance Forms* (HORST), pp. 12–13. For another fine pavan, by Thomas Tomkins, see *An Elizabethan Virginal Book* (NAYLOR),

[1] This movement of the pavan is described on p. 225.

pp. 16–19. If access to the *Fitzwilliam Virginal Book* is possible, no less than forty-six pavans will be found there. For further suggestions, see p. 226.

The play closes with two contrasting lyrics, "When daisies pied and violets blue" and "When icicles hang by the wall". The original settings for these have not survived. Tuneful settings for them were written by Thomas Augustine Arne, however, and may be found in *Fifty Shakespere Songs*.

THE MERCHANT OF VENICE

The entrances of the Prince of Morocco (Act II, scenes 1 and 7) and the Prince of Arragon (Act II, scene 9) are preceded by flourishes. The opening words of Act III, scene 2, suggest that Bassanio's initial entrance into Belmont has occurred some time before this scene and no flourish is required. In Act V, scene 1, however, his return from Venice is announced by a tucket. If, as already suggested in the discussion of *King Lear*, each important person had his own distinguishing flourish, each of these three suitors should have an individual and characteristic fanfare.

For "flourish" and "tucket", see *Shakespeare and Music* (NAYLOR), pp. 200 and 202.

Act II, scene 6

At the opening of this scene, maskers might enter, revel, and depart to the shrill piping of a fife accompanied by the beating of a tabor. "The Carmen's Whistle" would be an appropriate tune for this and can be found in *Popular Music of the Olden Time* (CHAPPELL), Vol. I, pp. 139 and 140, and in *Shakespeare and Music* (NAYLOR), p. 188.

Act III, scene 2

"Tell me where is fancy bred" is sung by Balthasar to his own accompaniment on, probably, a lute. A guitar or dulcimer will serve equally well today. No music for this has survived, but with a few slight alterations this lyric might be sung to the tune of "Tell me, dearest, what is love". See *Melody and the Lyric* (GIBBON), p. 137.

Act V, scene 1. "Enter Musicians".

The musicians are requested by Lorenzo to "bring [their] music forth into the air", and, although their entrance is indicated in the stage directions, Portia does not know where the music comes from when she enters a little later. This may indicate that the musicians play in the window stage on the same side as that from which she makes her entrance and so are invisible to her. This music which accompanies the lovely poetry of the garden scene is continuous until Bassanio and Antonio enter. The quiet beauty of the scene suggests that this "still" music might have been a pavan. Any one of John Dowland's "seven passionate pavans" in his *Lachrymae, or Seven Tears* would be suitable; or the exquisite old pavan "Belle qui tiens ma vie", to be found in *Orchesography* (ARBEAU), pp. 58–59, and also in *Pre-classic Dance Forms* (HORST), pp. 12–13, would be particularly appropriate.

A Midsummer Night's Dream

As has been stated before, the form in which this play has come down to us is very possibly the one especially arranged for a Court performance. With the décor supplied by the Revels Office and aided by the beautifully trained Children of the Chapel Royal and Children of Paul's, it was in all likelihood a very elaborate affair, introducing more music, singing, and dancing than was possible in the public playhouse.

The masque elements that pervade the whole play should be emphasized by the formality and beauty of the dances even if they are country dances, as some of them undoubtedly are, and by the singing of trained voices, preferably those of children.

The Courtiers, Rustics, Lovers, and Fairies that constitute the four diverse groups that become entangled in the magic of a moonlit wood all have their appropriate music in the text itself, and this can be echoed by instrumental music if inclination and means allow.

It has already been suggested that the play be preceded by an overture composed of all the music that is heard later in the various scenes, but in the case of this play it would perhaps be more effective to use theme music indicating the different characteristics of the four groups. For this a "Suite for Five Brass Instruments" by Johann Pezel would be admirable. The Intrada (1) could be the Clowns' theme; the Allemande (2), the Courtiers' theme; the Courante and Allemande (3 and 4), the Lovers' theme; and the Gigue (5), the Fairies' theme. To mark the nuptial element which pervades the whole play, "The Bells" by William Byrd might be played on a harp— if a virginal is not available—to accompany Theseus and his bride-to-be at the opening of the play, and again, for the blessing of the bridal chambers at the close.

Act I, scene 1

The ceremonial entrance of Theseus and Hippolyta should be preceded and accompanied by a prolonged fanfare.

Act II, scene 1

Puck and the First Fairy could enter to the tune of the Gigue mentioned above played softly, and this could continue until Titania and Oberon enter. There is a musical setting for this duologue composed by Thomas Simpson Cooke that could also be used, although it has nothing of the authentic Elizabethan style. This will be found in *Fifty Shakespere Songs*. Yet another possibility would be Thomas Ravenscroft's "The Urchin's Dance" (1611) in *Melody and the Lyric* (GIBBON), p. 132.

Act II, scene 2. "Come, now a roundel and a fairy song".

There is a direct reference here to the traditional custom of singing the accompaniment to round dances, but since the dance is rapid, light, and nimble, there should be no attempt by the dancers to sing, or the accompaniment will degenerate into a breathless gasp. It could be sung by an unseen choir of children's voices or, better still, by the four special fairies, Pease-blossom, Cobweb, Moth, and Mustard-seed.

As to the music, "Ye spotted snakes" might be sung to the traditional tune of Sellenger's Round, but for a less hackneyed setting for this lovely lyric a dance song called "Millfield" might be used. The music is far older than the words and was doubtless used as the tune for many an old ballad. "Ye spotted snakes" can be sung to this if the last eight bars are repeated for the refrain. For the steps of the round, see pp. 237–238. For the music, see *Popular Music of the Olden Time* (CHAPPELL), Vol. I, pp. 185–186, and *Melody and the Lyric* (GIBBON), p. 67. During this dance the numbers should decrease, as groups go off to do their "offices", until one little one is left alone to "stand sentinel". Perhaps he falls asleep, or perhaps he runs away; at any rate, the Clowns are able to approach "near the cradle of the Fairy Queen" without any alarm being given.

Act III, scene 1

There is no known tune for Bottom's song "The ousel cock so black of hue", but the words can be sung to the old tune of "In Peasecod Time". It is a tune that was often used for the singing of old ballads and, as a folk tune, is just the sort of thing Bottom would sing. This will be found in *Melody and the Lyric* (GIBBON), p. 22, and in *Popular Music of the Olden Time* (CHAPPELL), Vol. I, p. 198.

Act IV, scene 1. "Music".

Titania calls for

"Music, ho! music! such as charmeth sleep,"

and an appropriate tune in response to this command would be "Care-charming sleep" composed by Robert Johnson in 1615. However, a few lines later Oberon says:

"Come, my queen, take hands with me,
And ock the ground whereon these sleepers be,"

and this certainly suggests a rollicking dance. It would, therefore, be more fitting to have the music of such a dance song as "Trip and go" played off stage, very softly, in response to Titania's call and swell out until it becomes a dance song for three voices—Titania, Oberon, and Puck—and fades when Puck says:

"Fairy King, attend and mark."

Not only are the words of "Trip and go" suitable, but this was actually a very popular tune for the morris dance of the time. It is in galliard time (6/8), and, since this dance, beside being a Court dance, was largely made up of morris steps, it would be most appropriate for Oberon and Puck to dance a few "measures" on either side of Titania and for all three to exit using the basic galliard step. For "Trip and go", see *Melody and the Lyric* (GIBBON), p.55, and *Popular Music of the Olden Time* (CHAPPELL), Vol. I, p. 131.

"Horns winded within."

As the voices of the Fairies die away after their exit, a hunting horn is heard in the distance, which gradually increases until Theseus and his train enter. Later Theseus says:

"Go, bid the huntsmen wake them with their horns,"

which suggests that the musicians do not appear on the stage, since, in response to this order, *horns* are heard *within*. For the winding of a hunting horn, see *Shakespeare and Music* (NAYLOR), p. 203, or *Military Music* (KAPPEY), pp. 58–59.

Act V, scene 1

A prolonged fanfare should precede and accompany the entrance and seating of the Court. In direct contrast with this will be the *"flourish of trumpets"* which precedes the entrance of Quince as Prologue. In order to set the stage for the uproarious farce that is to follow, this "flourish" can be a feeble off-key blast from a tin trumpet.

When Bottom asks Theseus if it will please him to *hear* a Bergomask dance between two of the company, he is referring to the rustic dance of

Bergomo peasants which was always danced to a *sung* accompaniment. The little company could sing "Now Robin lend me thy bow" while Pyramus and Thisby dance. This is in duple time, and a parody of the allemand or courante with—in spite of the tempo—some lavolta leaping would be a fitting end to the "tragical mirth". "Now Robin lend me thy bow" can be found in *Popular Music of the Olden Time* (CHAPPELL), Vol. I, p. 80. As the clowns make their exit, the great bell should be heard striking midnight. Theseus speaks as the last note dies away.

Puck's spell-binding words,

"Now the hungry lion roars,"

should be spoken to the soft eerie sound of distant flutes. A tune that might be used very effectively for this would be "How can the tree", to be found in *Melody and the Lyric* (GIBBON), p. 36.

Oberon commands the Fairies,

"And this ditty *after me*
Sing and dance it trippingly."

One explanation of this is found if Titania's words,

"First, rehearse your song by rote," etc.,

are addressed to Oberon for, in that case, it becomes plain that Oberon sings first and then all repeat the song, taking hands and dancing at the same time. Here again Ravenscroft's "The Urchin's Dance" would be delightfully appropriate. (See *Melody and the Lyric*, p. 132.)

Oberon's final speech could be spoken to the same spell music that accompanied Puck's

"Now the hungry lion roars"

and could fade away slowly as the Epilogue is spoken. Again, as suggested above, this blessing of the bridal chambers could be spoken to the faint and lovely sound of "The Bells" by William Byrd played on a harp, or to the record No. 14 of *L'Anthologie Sonore*, where it is played on the virginals (see full details on p. 296).

(A setting for "Through the house give glimmering light" was composed by William Luiley and can be found in *Fifty Shakespere Songs*. But this is lacking in the robust quality of Elizabethan music. It is, however, tuneful and sweet.)[1]

---

[1] If Mendelssohn's incidental music is preferred to the above suggestions, care should be taken to omit the hackneyed Wedding March, which would call attention to the anachronistic note in a Shakespearean production.

THE TAMING OF THE SHREW

Although this play contains many references to music, there are only two stage directions that actually call for music. They both occur in the Induction, one being where a hunting horn is heard off stage, the other the flourish that heralds the players. For the hunting horn, see *Shakespeare and Music* (NAYLOR), p. 203, or *Military Music* (KAPPEY), pp. 58–59. For the trumpet flourish, see *Shakespeare and Music*, p. 200, or *Military Music*, p. 50. For the snatch of song "Where is the life", sung by Petruchio in Act IV, scene 1, see *Popular Music of the Olden Time* (CHAPPELL), Vol. I, p. 236.

AS YOU LIKE IT

Act I, scene 2. "Flourish".

This announces the entrance of Duke Frederick and his lords. The wrestling match should be accompanied by a roll of side drums.

Act II, scene 5. "Under the greenwood tree".

For this song Amiens either plays his own accompaniment or sings it without instrumental music. For an old traditional tune, dated somewhere about 1450, to which this song may have been sung, see *Melody and the Lyric* (GIBBON), p. 56. See also *Shakespeare in Music* (ELSON), p. 63, for the music described as "the oldest setting of these words" and "very popular in the seventeenth century". The parody of it given by Jaques should also be *sung*, no matter how inferior the actor's voice.

Act II, scene 7. "Blow, blow thou winter wind".

This song, also sung by Amiens, should be accompanied since the Duke has commanded,

"Give us some music, and, good cousin, sing."

The original tune for this lyric has not survived. The most frequently used setting is a modern one composed by William Arms Fisher, to be found in *Fifty Shakespere Songs*.

Act III, scene 3

Touchstone's exit song, "O sweet Oliver", was sung in 1584 to the tune of "The hunt is up" and can be found in *Melody and the Lyric* (GIBBON), p. 31.

Act IV, scene 2

"What shall he have that kill'd the deer?" is sung by a man and a male chorus, and it would not be inappropriate for Amiens to be the soloist. There is an old setting in *Melody and the Lyric* (GIBBON), p. 111.

Act V, scene 3

"It was a lover and his lass" is one of the few songs in the plays that has an authentic contemporary setting. This duet was composed by Thomas Morley and can be found in *Fifty Shakespere Songs*; in *Melody and the Lyric* (GIBBON), p. 112; and in *Shakespeare in Music* (ELSON), pp. 192–193.

Act V, scene 4

Hymen's speech has obviously a background of "still" music, but "Wedding is great Juno's crown" is sung. The musical setting is unknown, but it would be possible to use "Triumph now with joy and mirth" by Thomas Giles, and this same air could be played softly for the "still" music. It can be found in *Melody and the Lyric* (GIBBON), p. 62.

"A dance."

The *Branle du Haut Barrois* would be especially effective for this exit dance (for reason, see p. 236).

MUCH ADO ABOUT NOTHING

The mood of triumph, resulting from a safe return from a successful war, in which the play opens can be emphasized by martial music. Drum marches and trumpet flourishes can be heard in the distance, then grow nearer and finally end in a prolonged flourish as Don Pedro, Don John, and train enter.

Act II, scene 1

As in *Love's Labour's Lost*, the formality of the dialogue sequence suggests progressive movement, and, although the cue for *"music"* comes after this, it is more than likely that the couples are actually dancing as they speak. In any case it would be an excellent opportunity to dance the pavan. The slow, stately walk would not detract from the dialogue, and the advance and retreat movements would allow each couple to stay in the middle of the forestage as long as their duologue lasted, and then to "progress" to make room for the next couple. When Beatrice says, "We must follow the leaders", the music could change into triple time, and the galliard could be danced.

An excellent example of a pavan, which, by altering the time from duple to triple time, becomes a galliard, may be found in *Shakespeare and Music* (NAYLOR), pp. 194–196. As in *Romeo and Juliet*, the musicians can be either to one side of the middle stage or in the balcony in order to give all possible space to the dancers.

Act II, scene 3. "Enter Balthasar with music".

"Music" here refers to the instrument that Balthasar will later use to accompany himself, evidently, if we can judge from Benedick's reference to "sheeps' guts", one of the fiddle family. Since he sings to his own accompaniment, a "kit" would be most convenient (see footnote, p. 281). At the stage direction *"air"*, he apparently plays the melody before beginning the song itself.

The setting for this song, "Sigh no more, ladies", composed by Thomas Ford may not have been the original one, but it is almost certain to have been used in a Court revival of the play. If this is true, it was sung by three voices. (Could it be possible that Don Pedro and Claudio joined Balthasar in warbling this lyric as part of the deception played on the listening Benedick?) As a solo, this setting is far from satisfactory, and, unless it can be arranged to a contemporary "ayre", it would be best to use the one composed by Richard John Samuel Stevens or, even, the tuneful setting made by Sir Arthur Sullivan. Ford's arrangement for three voices may be found in *Melody and the Lyric* (GIBBON), p. 117; the other two, in *Fifty Shakespere Songs*.

Act V, scene 2

"The God of Love" could be sung to Thomas Campion's "Shall I come, sweet love, to thee?" It goes without saying that Benedick sings very inexpertly and cracks on the final notes. This air can be found in *Melody and the Lyric* (GIBBON), p. 95.

Act V, scene 3

This scene presents a problem. Although it suggests all the solemnity of a mourning ritual, the audience knows that Hero is not dead and that there is no cause for mourning, and, moreover, although the scene takes place in a church and the ritual is performed by Christians, a pagan hymn is sung! Many producers get round these difficulties by cutting the scene. This is a pity for it is dramatically effective, and it is possible to include it and at the same time to touch the ironic comedy of the scene with a delicate hand. There is a tune to which "Pardon, goddess of the night" can be sung, known as "Hymn for a Widower, or Widow, delivered from a troublesome yokefellow". It was written by George Wither and is set to a hymn tune known as "The Lamentation", which in turn is to be found in Thomas East's *The Whole Booke of Psalmes* (1592), and, more accessibly, in *Melody and the Lyric* (GIBBON), p. 163.

Act V, scene 4

A dance to the music of pipes closes the play. On a modern stage this dance would bring down the final curtain, but on an Elizabethan stage it is necessary for everyone to exit at the end of the play. In both cases the branle would be the dance most suitable for a finale. The fact of its being danced sideways would allow the entire company to face the audience, as in a final "call", and on an Elizabethan stage the dancers could divide in the middle, and each side could exit dancing through the two side doors.

Since the last line of the play reads "Strike up, pipers!" the music must be played by pipes of some kind, preferably recorders. Many airs for branles can be found in *Orchesography* (ARBEAU), pp. 113–146. (See also those listed on p. 236 of this book.)

THE MERRY WIVES OF WINDSOR

Act I, scene 4

Mistress Quickly sings "And down, down, adown-a" to appear at her ease in a difficult situation. This refrain could be from "The Baffled Knight", in *Melody and the Lyric* (GIBBON), p. 54, or from "Cold's the wind and wet the rain" from Dekker's *The Shoemaker's Holiday*, which can also be found in *Melody and the Lyric*, pp. 99–100, and in *Popular Music of the Olden Time* (CHAPPELL), Vol. I, p. 278.

Act III, scene 1

Parson Evans, in a stage of nerves bordering on hysteria, sings part of Marlowe's "Come, live with me", into which he confusedly inserts a line from Sternhold and Hopkin's Old Version of Psalm 138. Two possible musical settings for this can be found in *Shakespeare and Music* (NAYLOR), pp. 181–182. The first of these, Dr. Naylor points out, is a corrupt form of the old tune of "Walsingham". If this were used, it might have been a further indication to an Elizabethan audience of the muddled state of mind of the singer.

Act V, scene 5

The dance song "Fie on sinful fantasy!" can be set to John Dowland's then-popular "Frog Galliard", which can be found in *Melody and the Lyric* (GIBBON), p. 60, and in *Popular Music of the Olden Time* (CHAPPELL), Vol. I, p. 129. The tune will have to be played twice for the first eight lines of the poem, with a further repeat of the last eight bars to fit the final couplet. This dance song is certainly performed round Falstaff, and the steps and figures of Sellenger's Round would be admirably suited to the scene. (For steps and music, see pp. 237–238.)

MEASURE FOR MEASURE

Act IV, scene 1

"Take, O, take those lips away" sings the boy to Mariana in the desolation of the "moated grange". This lyric, which may have been written by John Fletcher,[1] was set to music by John Wilson and published in 1653 in *Select Music, Ayres, and Dialogues*. The melody can also be found in *Melody and the Lyric* (GIBBON), p. 123, and in *Shakespeare in Music* (ELSON), pp. 167–168. There is nothing in the text to suggest that the song was accompanied unless there is a hint from Mariana, in her lines,

> "I cry you mercy, sir; and well could wish
> You had not found me here so musical,"

that she was playing for the boy to sing. It would certainly add to the poignant beauty of the little scene if one or the other, preferably the boy, could play the accompaniment.

ALL'S WELL THAT ENDS WELL

The usual ceremonial flourish of cornets heralds the entrances of the King in Act I, scene 2; Act II, scene 1; Act III, scenes 1 and 3; and Act V, scene 3. For this, see *Shakespeare and Music* (NAYLOR), p. 200.

Act III, scene 5. "A tucket afar off".

For this, a French tucket should be sounded, which will be found in *Shakespeare and Music* (NAYLOR), p. 202. When the troops pass with "*drum and colours*", a march should be played by the drums. For this, see *Shakespeare and Music*, p. 201.

---

[1] Noble, Richmond, *Shakespeare's Use of Song*, pp. 88–91.

Act IV, scene 1. "Alarum within".

This would be a rapid rolling of side drums heard "off".

"A short alarum within."

TWELFTH NIGHT

Act I, scene 1

The music played for the Duke's delectation is evidently performed by a group of his own musicians and, furthermore, they are evidently "discovered" as the play begins. This would mean costuming a number of musicians for this one opening number—a costly procedure. There seems no reason why the music should not be heard "off" if the Duke can address his orders to them convincingly enough to suggest that they are in an adjoining room.

According to Dr. Naylor,[1] the piece they performed could have been "The Lord Salisbury, his Pavin" by Orlando Gibbons, which has in the last strain a "dying fall". It will be remembered that the Duke requests them to repeat this strain. This pavan may be found in the modern reprint of *Parthenia* edited by MARGARET H. GLYN, and in *Dances of England and France* (DOLMETSCH), p. 96.

Act II, scene 3. "O mistress mine".

A contemporary setting for this song is credited to Thomas Morley, and the melody was later used for a composition for the virginals by William Byrd. It can be found in *Melody and the Lyric* (GIBBON), p. 113, and in *Shakespeare in Music* (ELSON), pp. 209–210. Feste should accompany himself on a guitar or mandolin.

With one exception the catches and snatches of ballad and the like sung by Sir Toby are all extant and may be found as follows:

"Hold thy peace"—a catch for three voices: *Melody and the Lyric*, p. 110; *Shakespeare and Music* (NAYLOR), p. 192; *Shakespeare in Music*, p. 211; and *Fifty Shakespere Songs*.

"Three merry men are we": *Melody and the Lyric*, p. 79; *Shakespeare and Music*, p. 182; *Shakespeare in Music*, p. 214; *Fifty Shakespere Songs*.

"Tilly vally, lady! There dwelt a man in Babylon": *Shakespeare and Music*, p. 183.

"Farewell, dear heart": *Shakespeare and Music*, p. 183; arranged with all the bits of dialogue, in *Shakespeare in Music*, pp. 216–218, and in *Fifty Shakespere Songs*.

[1] Naylor, Edward W., *Shakespeare and Music*, p. 105.

"O, the twelfth day of December" is probably the opening line of the old ballad of Musselburgh Field and could be sung to any ballad tune.

Act II, scene 4. "Music plays".

This direction follows the Duke's command

"Seek him [Feste] out, and play the tune the while."

The tune played is, therefore, the one to which "Come away, Death" is sung shortly after. No tune for this has survived, but it is evident from the Duke's references to it as "old and antique" and "old and plain" that it was a traditional ballad air. With very little alteration it can be sung to such old airs from *Popular Music of the Olden Time* (CHAPPELL) as "Dulcina", Vol. I, p. 143; "Was ever man so tost in love", Vol. I, pp. 171–172; and "In sad and ashy weeds", Vol. I, p. 202.

Act V, scene 1

The epilogue song, "When that I was and a little tiny boy", can be found in *Shakespeare in Music* (ELSON), pp. 321–322, and in *Popular Music of the Olden Time* (CHAPPELL), Vol. I, 225. (For the use of part of this song in *Lear*, see p. 261.)

THE WINTER'S TALE

In the first three acts of this play there are no directions for music, nor is its use indicated in the text, though doubtless the usual three blasts of the trumpet herald the entrance of Chorus after Act III. With the entrance of Autolycus in Act IV, scene 2, however, the play shifts into another key, and music, of one kind and another, occurs frequently throughout the act.

Act IV, scene 3

With a bound, Autolycus comes rollicking on singing "When daffodils begin to peer". The tune this was sung to might have been any one of the popular ballad airs of the time, and with all the contemporary tunes that are extant it should not be hard to find one that is suitable. Perhaps "Heart's-ease" would be about as good as any. It had already been used for the words of a song in Thomas Rycharde's *Misogonus* in 1560, and it is as a setting to this song that it appears in *Popular Music of the Olden Time* (CHAPPELL), Vol. I, p. 210.

The music to Autolycus's exit song, "Jog on, jog on the footpath way", is known to have been the traditional air of "Hanskin", and this may be found in *Shakespeare and Music* (NAYLOR), p. 185; in *Melody and the Lyric* (GIBBON), p. 104; and, together with a special note on the popularity of the tune, in *Popular Music of the Olden Time*, Vol. I, pp. 211–212.

Act IV, scene 4. "Music. Here a dance of Shepherds and Shepherdesses".

This must have been a country dance, and the hay at once suggests itself as most suitable. Unfortunately little is actually known of this dance, but it is suggested by some authorities that many features of it survive in the Sir Roger de Coverley, or the Virginia reel (see pp. 238–239) and this would be an appropriate dance, allowing, as it does, for boisterous and clumsy dancing by the rustics and dainty elegance of movement by Florizel and Perdita. Of the latter is said, it will be remembered, "She dances featly".[1]

Music for the Sir Roger de Coverley will be found in *Popular Music of the Olden Time* (CHAPPELL), Vol. II, p. 535.

"Enter Autolycus singing 'Lawn as white as driven snow'."

A contemporary setting for this song by Dr. John Wilson may be found in *Melody and the Lyric* (GIBBON), p. 121, and in *Fifty Shakespere Songs*.

The tune of "Two maids wooing a man", suggested by Autolycus as the one to which they will sing the song for three voices, "Get you hence, for I must go", is unknown, but it can be sung to the air of another popular song, "O mistress mine", which can be found in *Popular Music of the Olden Time*, Vol. I, p. 209, and in *Fifty Shakespere Songs*.

Although "Will you buy any tape" is sometimes indicated as *sung* by Autolycus on his exit, yet since there is only one arrangement that is contemporary and since that is in round form, it might be better for him to "cry" the lines like the huckster that he is.

"Here a dance of twelve Satyrs."

Here is a possible example of a Court antimasque dance that was performed in the public playhouses. Professor Ashley H. Thorndike in his *Influence of Beaumont and Fletcher on Shakespere*, in speaking of Ben Jonson's *Masque of Oberon*, performed at Court on January 1, 1611, says:

> This contains an antimasque of satyrs, and I conjecture that the dance of satyrs in the *Winter's Tale* was directly suggested by the antimasque.[2]

He then goes on to compare the dance and the appearance of the dancers in the masque with the dance and dancers as described in the play. For instance, in the antimasque there are, he says,

---

[1] With graceful agility.
[2] Thorndike, Ashley H., *The Influence of Beaumont and Fletcher on Shakespere*, Press of O. B. Wood, Worcester, Mass., 1901, pp. 32–33.

ten (or twelve) satyrs, 'with bells on their shaggy thighs,'

and he quotes such descriptions as the following from the masque:

an antic dance full of gesture and swift motion,

and

the satyrs beginning to leap and express their joy.

In the play, he points out,

there is a similar antic dance for twelve satyrs . . . [who], like the dancers in the masque, . . . are great leapers and like those are men of hair.

Further confirmation comes from the fact that these "antic" dances in the Court masques were always performed by professional actors, and in the play we have the excited Servant's report that

"One three of them, by their own report, sir, hath danced before the king,"

which might well have been the case.

According to the text, this dance must have been a morris, or a very vigorous galliard, with a good deal of acrobatic display, such as handsprings, somersaults, leaps—"one of them jumps twelve foot and a half"[1]—leap frog, and the Kibby dance step. This last, sometimes called "Cossack dancing" today, consists of squatting and thrusting out alternate legs in rapid succession. Suitable music can be found in *Popular Music of the Olden Time*, Vol. I—for instance, "The Staines Morris Tune", pp. 125–126, "Barleybreak", p. 135, or, if a galliard is preferred, "Galliard, Sweet Margaret", p. 155. This last starts rather slowly in 3/4 time but, changing to 6/8, works up to a very brisk tempo. Again swift lively music is found in "The King's Jig", Vol. II, pp. 495–496, and "Give ear to a frolicsome ditty", Vol. II, p. 554. It goes without saying that, if possible, the accompaniments for the two dances should be played on pipe and tabor.

Act V, scene 3. "Music".

"Music, awake her: strike!" is the cue for the "still" music that accompanies the transformation of the statue to the living Hermione. The "strike" suggests stringed instruments, and an exquisite air such as "Western Wind" played on a dulcimer or harp, off stage, would be very effective. This can be found in *Melody and the Lyric* (GIBBON), p. 33, and in *Popular Music of the Olden Time* (CHAPPELL), Vol. I, p. 58.

---

[1] This would not be difficult for those actors who started their careers as "tumbling boys".

THE TEMPEST

Act I, scene 2. "Re-enter Ariel, invisible, playing and singing".

This song, "Come unto these yellow sands", has a country-dance rhythm, and Ariel may possibly have accompanied himself on a "kit" (a small fiddle), an instrument associated, at the time, with rustic revelling.[1] "Full fathom five", sung a few lines later, must also have been self-accompanied. For modern production, a guitar would be best for these songs. The refrains in both songs are sung by a chorus "within" (off stage), and it would add greatly to the mystification of Ferdinand if some voices came from one window stage, some from another, and some from the minstrels' gallery.

The original musical settings for these songs are lost, but one setting for "Full fathom five", made in 1613 by Robert Johnson, was certainly composed for a Court presentation of the play. This can be found in *Fifty Shakespere Songs* and in *Shakespeare in Music* (ELSON), pp. 187–189. The earliest available setting for "Come unto these yellow sands" is one made by John Banister. This also can be found in *Fifty Shakespere Songs*.

Act II, scene 1. "Enter Ariel (invisible) playing solemn music".

This might very well be a "dump", as the music to a very solemn type of "doleful ditty" was called. One such piece, "My Lady Carey's Dump", can be found in *Shakespeare and Music* (NAYLOR), pp. 199–200. Or a very solemn pavan would be in order, such as any one of the seven to be found in *Lachrymae, or Seven Tears*, or even a song tune such as "When griping grief", in *Shakespeare and Music*, p. 187, or "O Death, rock me on sleep", in *Melody and the Lyric* (GIBBON), p. 34, and also in *Popular Music of the Olden Time* (CHAPPELL), Vol. I, p. 238.

"Re-enter Ariel invisible. . . . Sings in Gonzalo's ear."

Ariel sings, "While you here do snoring lie". The music for this is not known, but it could be sung to "A Gigg" by William Byrd, to be found in *An Elizabethan Virginal Book* (NAYLOR), pp. 43–44.

Act II, scene 2. "Enter Stephano, singing; a bottle in his hand".

This song, "I shall no more to sea", is continued, after two lines of dialogue, with the line "The master, the swabber, the boatswain, and I". (See *Shakespeare and Music* (NAYLOR), p. 185.)

Caliban sings drunkenly,

---

[1] These small instruments, as well as all viols, were not held under the chin, but merely rested against the chest so that self-accompanied singing was not difficult.

"Farewell, master; farewell, farewell!
No more dams I'll make for fish."

The original tune is unknown, but for a later setting, made by John Christopher Smith, see *Fifty Shakespere Songs*.

Act III, scene 2

Stephano drunkenly sings a catch,

"Flout 'em, and scout 'em; and scout 'em, and flout 'em;
Thought is free,"

calling to Trinculo to join him. Caliban, however, stops them by saying "That's not the tune", whereupon the invisible Ariel *"plays the tune on a tabor and a pipe"*. Stephano can, obviously, use any tune for his singing. The correct tune that Ariel plays has not survived, but a catch with these words was composed by Henry Purcell in 1675 and may be based on an old tune. This can be found in a rare book known as Cauldfield's *Collection of the Vocal Music in Shakespear's Plays*.

Act III, scene 3. "Solemn and strange music".

There is an old ballad tune that would justify Gonzalo's description of this music as "marvellous sweet music". It is called "By a bank as I lay", and is to be found in *Popular Music of the Olden Time* (CHAPPELL), Vol. I, p. 63. This could continue for background music through the following business:

"Enter Prospero above, invisible. Enter several strange Shapes, bringing in a banquet: they dance about it with gentle actions of salutation; and, inviting the King, etc., to eat, they depart."

This is no formal or set dance, it seems, but rather light graceful running with deep bows and curtsies and gestures of invitation to the mortals to come to the banquet table and eat. An old tune that was used for the setting of many sad and doleful ballads and songs and known as "Come live with me" would be suitable as background music. This can be found in *Popular Music of the Olden Time*, Vol. I, p. 215, and in *Shakespeare and Music* (NAYLOR), p. 182.

"He [Ariel] vanishes in thunder; then, to soft music, enter the Shapes again, and dance, with mocks[1] and mows,[2] and carrying out the table."

[1] Sport or play.
[2] Grimace.

The same music used for the first part of this "living drollery" can be used here. Again the dance is no more than a mime, but this time there is something sinister and mocking about the gestures and facial expressions.

Act IV, scene 1. "Soft music. Enter Iris".

This music should continue until after Juno enters. Then Juno and Ceres sing a duet, "Honour, riches, marriage-blessing." The musical setting is unknown, but, with careful adaptation, Thomas Giles's setting of "Triumph, now with joy and mirth" might be used, and the same air could be played for the "soft music".

"Enter certain Reapers, properly habited; they join with the Nymphs in a graceful dance."

The *Branle du Haut Barrois* is described by Arbeau in *Orchesography*, p. 118, as being

danced by serving men and wenches, and sometimes by young men and damsels of gentle birth when they make a masquerade disguised as peasants and shepherds, or when they dance merrily among themselves.

Here would seem to be the ideal dance for this particular part of the masque. Moreover, it should not be hard to find music to fit the steps and tempo, for any gay tune in common time will do. The traditional air for this dance will be found in *Orchesography*, p. 119.

Act V, scene 1

Ariel sings "Where the bee sucks", and here we are on safe ground, for a setting by Robert Johnson was composed for a Court presentation of the play. It will be found in *Fifty Shakespere Songs*.

PERICLES

This play is thought to be, in greater part, the work of Fletcher, and the claim is supported, apart from verbal evidence, by the fact that it introduces more continuous instrumental music than any play accredited wholly to Shakespeare. Fletcher consistently used instrumental and vocal music as a theatrical device, and this characteristic is accounted for by his easy access to skilled musicians as a result of his social and professional connections with the Court.

It is a languid and rambling play, and its tainted and decadent themes mark the decline of drama in the public playhouses and the rise of a more sophisticated type of entertainment that catered to the exclusive audience that frequented the private theatres.

Gone are all the hearty flourishes and sennets and the lusty drum and trumpet music, for, with the exception of the traditional three blasts, which, no doubt, heralded the entrance of Gower as Chorus, all the music is soft, insidious, and obviously aimed at theatrical effect.

"*Music*" accompanies the entrance of Antiochus's daughter and, without doubt, continues through the eulogy which follows. The five dumb shows are certainly presented to the sound of music; the masque of Knights and Ladies is danced to music; the visionary Diana speaks to music; the dead Thaisa is restored to life by music; and Marina sings to rouse Pericles from his melancholy.

It is doubtful if there would be any value in a modern presentation of this play, for there is little here to appeal to present-day taste. The introduction of the Chorus and of dumb shows, which were old enough to be revived as historical novelties in 1612, finds no favour today, and the formlessness and grossness of the play as a whole make its revival a very doubtful proposition to any hardy enough to consider such an undertaking. Scenes, notably those accredited to Shakespeare, might be given in an experimental programme—for example, those dealing with the Marina story, especially those in the last act. This would give an opportunity for the inclusion of the song that Marina sings to soothe her father's sad heart. Appropriately enough there is a song written by Fletcher and set to music by Robert Johnson, which is extant and which is so applicable to the situation in the scene that we can almost risk a guess that it was sung in the original performance. It is known as "Care-charming sleep" and can be found in *Melody and the Lyric* (GIBBON), p. 125.

Composers & Their Dates

Anerio, Felice, 1560?–?1614
Arne, Thomas Augustine, 1710–1778
Banister, John, 1630–1679
Bartlet, John, fl. 1606
Bateson, Thomas, 1570?–1630
Bennet, John, fl. 1570–1615
Blow, John, 1648?–1708
Brewster (first name unknown), dates unknown but writing, probably, before 1590
Bull, John, 1562–1628
Byrd, William, 1542?–1623
Campion, Thomas, 1567–1620
Chambonnières, Jacques Champion de, 1602–1672
Cooke, Thomas Simpson, 1782–1848
Corelli, Arcangelo, 1653–1713
Cosyn, Benjamin, fl. 1622–1643
Couperin, Louis, 1630?–?1665
Dowland, John, 1563–1626
East, Michael, 1580?–1648
East, Thomas (printer of music), 1535?–?1608
Farmer, John, fl. 1591–1601
Farnaby, Giles, 1560?–?1600
Ferrabosco, Alfonso (II), 1575?–1628
Fisher, William Arms, 1861–1948
Ford, Thomas, 1580?–1648
Franck, Melchior, 1573?–1639
Frescobaldi, Girolamo, 1583–1643
Gibbons, Orlando, 1583–1625
Giles, Thomas, 1558–1633
Hassler, Hans Leo, 1564–1612
Heywood, John, 1497?–?1580
Hooper, Edmund, 1553–1621
Johnson, Robert, died 1634
Jones, Robert, fl. 1616

Leveridge, Richard, 1670–1758
Locke, Matthew, 1630?–1677
Luiley, William, 1767–1835
Lully, Jean Baptiste, 1639–1687
Lyly, John, 1554?–1606
Marais, Marin, 1656–1728
Mendelssohn, Felix, 1809–1847
Monteverdi, Claudio, 1567–1643
Morley, Thomas, 1557?–?1603
Mundy, William, died 1630
Neusiedler, Hans, 1508 or 1509–1563
Norcome, Daniel, 1576–?1620
Oystermayre, Jehan, 16th century
Palestrina, Giovanni, 1525?–1594
Parsons, Robert, died 1570
Peerson, Martin, 1580?–1651
Pezel, Johann, 1639–1694
Pilkington, Francis, 1562?–1638
Purcell, Henry, 1658–1695
Ravenscroft, Thomas, 1590?–?1633
Rosseter, Philip, 1575?–1623
Schein, Johann Hermann, 1586–1630
Schmid, Bernhard, 16th century
Schubert, Franz Peter, 1797–1828
Smith, John Christopher, 1712–1795
Stevens, Richard John Samuel, 1757–1837
Sullivan, (Sir) Arthur Seymour, 1842–1900
Tomkins, Thomas, 1575?–1656
Tye, Christopher, 1497?–1572
Vautor, Thomas, fl. 1616
Ward, John, fl. 1613
Weelkes, Thomas, 1575?–1623
Wilbye, John, 1574–1638
Wilson, John, 1595–1674
Wither, George, 1588–1667

Books for Reference & Reading[1]

MUSIC

ANDERTON, H. ORSMOND, *Early English Music,* "Musical Opinion", London, 1920. A chronological table of composers and publications from 1265 to 1714. Music in its relation to Court, Church, and stage.

BLOM, ERIC, *Music in England,* Penguin Books, Inc., New York, 1942.

BOYD, MORRISON COMEGYS, *Elizabethan Music and Musical Criticism,* University of Pennsylvania Press, Philadelphia, 1940. An admirable scholarly treatment of the subject. A detailed account of music and composers in Shakespeare's day.

★BRIDGE, (Sir) FREDERICK, *Shakespearean Music in the Plays and Early Operas,* E. P. Dutton & Co., Inc., New York, 1923.

COWLING, G. H., *Music on the Shakespearian Stage,* University Press, Cambridge, England, 1913. Excellent for general information.

DAVEY, HENRY, *History of English Music,* J. Curwen & Sons, London, 1921. Chapter 5, "The Madrigalian Period", has a fine description of the extent and importance of musical composition during the period. The Elizabethan Age is represented as the climax to English music as a whole.

DENT, EDWARD J., "Shakespeare and Music", *A Companion to Shakespeare Studies,* edited by HARLEY GRANVILLE-BARKER and G. B. HARRISON, The Macmillan Company, New York, 1934. Informative and brief.

DOLMETSCH, ARNOLD, *The Interpretation of the Music of the XVII and XVIII Centuries, Revealed by Contemporary Evidence,* The H. W. Gray Co., New York, 1915. Highly technical. Especially recommended to musicians.

★ELSON, C. LOUIS, *Shakespeare in Music,* L. C. Page and Company, Boston, 1914. "A collection of the chief musical allusions in the plays of Shakespeare, with an attempt at their explanation and derivation, together with much of the original music."

GALPIN, (Canon) F. W., *Old English Instruments of Music: Their History and Character,* Methuen & Co., London, 1911. Contains fine photographic reprints of extant Elizabethan instruments.

★GIBBON, JOHN MURRAY, *Melody and the Lyric from Chaucer to the Cavaliers,* E. P. Dutton & Co., Inc., New York, 1930. Shows the influence of popular music on the rhythmic forms of poetry. A fine collection of popular airs and lyrics of the period.

★GROVE, (Sir) GEORGE, *Dictionary of Music and Musicians,* edited by H. C. COLLES, 5 vols., The Macmillan Company, New York, 1934.

★KAPPEY, J. A., *Military Music: A History of Wind-instrumental Bands,* Boosey & Co., London, 1894.

[1] An asterisk indicates books that contain Elizabethan music. See also Elizabethan Music Available for Use in the Plays, pp. 289–291. Some of the items listed contain historical material as well as music.

LAWRENCE, WILLIAM J., *The Elizabethan Playhouse and Other Studies*, Shakespeare Head Press, Stratford-on-Avon, 1912. See Chap. 4, "Music and Song in the Elizabethan Theatre", and Chap. 10, "Who Wrote the Famous *Macbeth* Music?"

——, *Old Theatre Days and Ways*, George G. Harrap & Co., Ltd., London, 1935. See Chap. 11, "Calling for Tunes".

——, *Shakespeare's Workshop*, Houghton Mifflin, Boston, 1928. See "A Plummet for Bottom's Dream", conclusions in regard to the music in *As You Like It* and *A Midsummer Night's Dream*.

——, *Those Nut-cracking Elizabethans: Studies of the Early Theatre and Drama*, Argonaut Press, London, 1935. See Chap. 7, "Bells in the Elizabethan Drama".

MONCUR-SIME, A. H., *Shakespeare: His Music and Song*, Routledge & Kegan Paul, Ltd., London, 1917. Contains every allusion to music in the plays. Useful for quick reference.

*NAYLOR, (Dr.) EDWARD W., *An Elizabethan Virginal Book, being a critical essay on the contents of a manuscript in the Fitzwilliam Museum at Cambridge*, E. P. Dutton & Co., New York, 1905. "A guide to what is most worthy in the great size and variety of the published *Fitzwilliam Virginal Book*. [Of special interest] to students of Elizabethan and Jacobean drama looking for suitable music in the presentation of the plays."

*——, *Shakespeare and Music*, rev. ed., J. M. Dent & Sons, Ltd., London, 1931. One of the most important books on the subject, being a full and concise account of every aspect of music in the performance of the plays.

*NOBLE, RICHMOND, *Shakespeare's Use of Song with the Text of the Principal Songs*, Oxford University Press, New York, 1923.

*READ, CHARLES, *The Elizabethan Jig and Related Song and Dance*, Baskerville, Chicago, 1929.

SQUIRE, W. BARCLAY, "Music", *Shakespeare's England*, Vol. II, Chap. 17 (2).

TURNER, W. J., *English Music*, Britain in Pictures, Ltd., London, 1941? See Chap. 2 for an interesting account of the development of secular music in England. Illustrations of Elizabethan musicians.

DANCE

*ARBEAU, THOINOT (pseudonym for Jehan Tabourot), *Orchesography, a treatise in the form of a dialogue whereby all manner of persons may easily acquire and practise the honourable exercise of dancing*, translated from the original edition published at Langres, 1588, by Cyril W. Beaumont, C. W. Beaumont, London, 1925. Excellent source for Court dances of the Elizabethan period. The French forms are described but since the English court danced the imported dances, the descriptions are undoubtedly apt. Very detailed delineation of steps, movements, music, and deportment.

*DOLMETSCH, MABEL, *Dances of England and France from 1450–1600, with Their Music and Authentic Manner of Performance*, Routledge and Kegan Paul, Ltd., London, 1949. This book is indispensable for the student and performer of Elizabethan dances, containing as it does detailed descriptions of the steps, figures, and authentic manner in which they should be performed. Very beautiful contemporary music together with fine illustrations makes this a most valuable text.

DOUCE, FRANCIS, *Illustrations of Shakspeare and of Ancient Manners: with Dissertations on the Clowns and Fools of Shakspeare; on the Collection of Popular Tales Entitled Gesta Romanorum; and on the English Morris Dance*, Longman, Hurst, Reese and Orme, London, 1807. Vol. II, Dissertation; Vol. III, Ancient English Morris Dance.

*HORST, LOUIS, *Pre-classic Dance Forms*, The Dance Observer, New York, 1937. Brief but excellent histories of the Court dances; bibliographies of suggested music, classified according to specific dances. Instructions for a number of the dances.

LAWRENCE, WILLIAM J., *Pre-Restoration Stage Studies*, Harvard University Press, Cambridge, Mass., 1927. See Chap. 4, "The Elizabethan Stage Jig".

*NAYLOR, (Dr.) EDWARD W., *An Elizabethan Virginal Book*, E. P. Dutton & Co., Inc., New York, 1905. Excellent descriptions of steps of the Elizabethan dances together with music for their performance.

——, *Shakespeare and Music*, J. M. Dent & Sons, Ltd., London, 1931. See Chap. 5, "Dances and Dancing".

*PLAYFORD, JOHN, *The English Dancing Master, now reprinted for the first time from the edition of 1650, with the tunes in modern notation*, edited by Leslie Bridgewater and Hugh Mellor, Hugh Mellor, London, 1933. Airs, steps, and figures of traditional country dances.

SACHS, CURT, *World History of the Dance*, translated by Bessie Schonberg, W. W. Norton & Company, New York, 1937. Background material for practically every known type of dance may be found by means of the index of this extremely useful and interesting book.

SHARP, CECIL J., and A. P. OPPÉ, *The Dance: An Historical Survey of Dancing in Europe*, Minton, Balch & Co., New York, 1924.

Elizabethan Music Available for Use in the Plays[1]

Ayres by Alfonso Ferrabosco the Younger, The English School of Lutenist Song Writers, Second Series, edited by Rev. EDMUND H. FELLOWES, Stainer & Bell, Ltd., London, c. 1925.

The Celebrated Music to Macbeth in Complete Score with Accompaniment for the Pianoforte by Matthew Lock, modern arrangement for piano by E. J. LODER, Angener & Co., London, n.d. For a discussion of the composer, see page 258.

The Collected Works of William Byrd, edited by Rev. EDMUND H. FELLOWES, London, 1937.

A Collection of the Vocal Music in Shakespear's Plays, including the whole of the songs, duetts, glees, choruses, etc., edited by John Cauldfield. Engraved from original manuscripts and early printed copies, chiefly from the collection of W. KITCHINER; revised and arranged with an accompaniment for the pianoforte by Mr. ADDISON. Very rare, but can be found in some music libraries. Boston Public Library has one copy.

Dances Grave and Gay, edited by MARGARET H. GLYN, Winthrop Rogers, London, n.d.

Easy Elizabethans, edited by HAROLD CRAXTON, Oxford University Press, New York, n.d.

Elizabethan Suite, arranged for two pianos by ETHEL BARTLETT, Oxford University Press, New York, 1947.

English Ayres: Elizabethan and Jacobean, edited and transcribed from the original edition by PETER WARLOCK and PHILIP WILSON, Oxford University Press, New York, 1927. Love lyrics with settings composed by the most famous musicians of the time. Arranged for piano.

English Instrumental Music in the 16th and 17th Centuries from MSS in the New York Public Library. Part IV, No. 2, four *In Nomines* by WILLIAM BYRD, ROBERT PARSONS, ALFONSO FERRABOSCO, and BREWSTER (first name unknown); No. 6, eight suites in four parts for consort music by MATTHEW LOCKE; pavans, galliards, almaines, and other short airs in five parts for viols, violins, and wind instruments. These can be purchased from the New York Public Library, 42nd Street, New York.

The English Madrigal School, edited by Rev. EDMUND H. FELLOWES, Stainer & Bell, Ltd., London, 1913-1924. Vocal scores with pianoforte accompaniment.

The English School of Lutenist Song Writers, Series 1 and 2, edited by Rev. EDMUND H. FELLOWES, Stainer & Bell, Ltd., London, 1920-1932. Each series, 16 vols.

Fifty Shakespere Songs, edited by CHARLES VINCENT, Oliver Ditson Co., Boston, 1906. Part I. Songs mentioned in the plays. Part II. Songs possibly sung in the

---

[1] See also Books for Reference and Reading, pp. 286-288, in some of which music is included; and Recordings Available for Use in Elizabethan Stage Production, pages 292-298.

original performances. Part III. Settings composed since Shakespeare's time to the middle of the 19th century. Part IV. Recent settings.

The First Book of Elizabethan Songs, The Second Book of Elizabethan Songs, The Third Book of Elizabethan Songs, originally composed for one voice to sing and four stringed instruments to accompany, transcribed from 16th and early 17th century MSS by PETER WARLOCK, Oxford University Press, New York, 1926. Separate scores for each instrument are included in the volumes. Here may be found many of the songs sung by the Children of the Chapel Royal, some of which are presumably from their plays.

The Fitzwilliam Virginal Book, edited from the original manuscript with an introduction and notes by J. A. FULLER MAITLAND and W. BARCLAY SQUIRE, London, 1899. Rare and very expensive. For what is best in this collection for use in stage production, see *An Elizabethan Virginal Book* (NAYLOR).[1] See also reprint edition and *Select Pieces from the Fitzwilliam Virginal Book* listed below.

The Fitzwilliam Virginal Book, reprint edition, Broude Brothers, New York.

Forty Elizabethan Songs, edited and arranged, with the original accompaniments, by Rev. EDMUND H. FELLOWES, Stainer & Bell, Ltd., London, 1921. Four song albums of "a choice selection from the famous school of song writers who were contemporaries of Shakespeare". Arranged for piano accompaniment. Available in two keys—high and low.

Forty-five Pieces for Keyboard Music Composed by William Byrd, edited by STEPHEN TUTTLE, editions de l'Oiseau-Lyre, Paris, n.d.

The Golden Treasury of Piano Music: a Collection of Pieces Written for the Virginal, Spinet, Harpsichord, and Clavichord, by composers of the 16th, 17th, and 18th centuries, edited by LOUIS OESTERLE, 2 vols., G. Schirmer, Inc., New York, 1904. Volume I contains music of Shakespeare's time.

The Handbook of Shakespeare Music, being an account of three hundred and fifty pieces of music set to words taken from the plays and poems by Shakespeare, the compositions ranging from the Elizabethan Age to the present time, by ALFRED ROFFE, Chatto & Windus, London, 1878.

John Bull, selected edition, transcribed and edited from MSS by MARGARET H. GLYN, 2 vols, Stainer & Bell, Ltd., London, n.d.

Lachrymae, or Seven Tears, figured in seven passionate pavans with divers other pavans, galiards and almands, by JOHN DOWLAND, transcribed from the original edition of 1605, Oxford University Press, New York, 1927. "Score and separate parts for violin 1, violin 2, viols, cello 1, cello 2, and lute."

Old English Composers for the Virginals and Harpsichord: A Collection of Preludes, Galliards, Pavanes, Grounds, Chaconnes, Suites, Overtures, Sonatas, etc., Selected from the Works of William Byrd, Dr. John Bull, Orlando Gibbons, Dr. John Blow, Henry Purcell and Dr. Thomas Augustine Arne, revised and edited by E. PAUER, G. Schirmer, Inc., New York, n.d. This collection includes all the *Parthenia* music.

Old English Suite, by GILES FARNABY, edited by GRANVILLE BANTOCK, Novello, London, n.d.

---

[1] For bibliographical details, see Books for Reference and Reading, p. 287.

Orlando Gibbons: Complete Keyboard Works, transcribed and edited by MARGARET H. GLYN, 5 vols., Stainer & Bell, Ltd., London, 1925.

The Oxford Choral Songs from the Old Masters: The English Lutenists, twenty-six transcriptions from lute tablature by PETER WARLOCK and PHILIP WILSON, edited by W. G. WHITTAKER, Oxford University Press, New York, 1927. "A scholarly edition of airs, mostly Elizabethan, for choral singing."

Pammelia and Other Rounds and Catches, by THOMAS RAVENSCROFT (1609–1611), transcribed and edited from the original editions by PETER WARLOCK, Oxford University Press, New York, 1929.

Parthenia, or The Maydenhead of the First Musicke That Ever Was Printed for the Virginals, by WILLIAM BYRD, Dr. JOHN BULL, and ORLANDO GIBBONS, The Harrow Replicas, No. 3, W. Heffer & Sons, Ltd., Cambridge, England, 1943. These replicas are fine facsimiles of memorable books, autographs, and documents.

——, a modern reprint, edited by MARGARET H. GLYN, London (?), 1927.

——, edited by KURT STONE, with historical notes and facsimiles, Broude Brothers, New York, 1952. The first American edition of this collection. See also *Old English Composers for the Virginals and Harpsichord* listed above.

Popular Music of the Olden Time, by W. CHAPPELL, 2 vols., Chappell Company, London, n.d. A famous collection of popular song and dance music together with historical background and derivations. Special sections on Elizabethan music and music "illustrating Shakespeare", Vol. I, pp. 98–243.

Select Pieces from the Fitzwilliam Virginal Book, edited by J. A. FULLER MAITLAND and W. BARCLAY SQUIRE, Chester, London, n.d.

Six English Tunes from the 16th and Early 17th Centuries for String Quintet (from a MS in the British Museum, about 1625), transcribed and edited by PETER WARLOCK, Oxford University Press, New York, 1929.

Thirty Virginal Pieces, transcribed by ELINOR GLYN, Stainer & Bell, Ltd., London, 1927.

Tudor Church Music, 10 vols., Oxford University Press, New York, 1923–1929.

Twenty-five Pieces for Keyed Instruments from Cosyn's Virginal Book, by JOHN BULL, WILLIAM BYRD, BENJAMIN COSYN, and ORLANDO GIBBONS, published by Chester, London, n.d.

For further information on available Elizabethan music, both secular and liturgical, it is suggested that application be made to Stainer & Bell, Ltd., 58 Berners Street, London, W.1, for their *Catalogue of Elizabethan and Jacobean Music.*

Recordings Available for Use in Elizabethan
Stage Production

The modern producer is faced by greater difficulties than were ever dreamed of by the Elizabethan stage manager for, added to the lack of musical ability among actors, he has to take into account the fact of the Musicians Union, which makes the hiring of even a trio far beyond his limited budget. Fortunately, however, there is a solution to this problem of supplying a suitable musical background for the plays—although the producer will resort to it with reservations. It is possible that, given a fine gramophone with perfect amplification, he can supply incidental music, and even songs, by means of recordings. Not only are many fine recordings of Elizabethan music available, but, in many cases, it is played on authentic instruments of the period.

New records are made and old records are discontinued so rapidly that it is impossible to present an accurate up-to-the-minute list of available recordings of Elizabethan music that might be of use to the producer of a Shakespearean play. The list following should, therefore, be considered as suggestive only.

Most of the records mentioned can be purchased from distributing agencies that specialize in early music, among which are The Gramophone Shop, Inc., New York, and His Master's Voice, London.

Those records which were known to have been discontinued at the time this list was compiled have been indicated by a solid circle (●) preceding the record number. These records may often be procured from music libraries or from distributors who deal in rare and discontinued records, such as The Rudolph Wurlitzer Company, 121 East 4th Street, Cincinnati, Ohio; G. S. Falkenstein, 1118 Walnut Street, Philadelphia 7, Pa.; and The Record Collector's Exchange, 1329 Sixth Avenue, New York 19, N.Y.

The full addresses of the record manufacturers represented in the list are given below, together with abbreviations and short titles.

Allegro (Allegro), 2 Columbus Circle, New York 19, N.Y.

L'Anthologie Sonore (AS), records obtainable from The Gramophone Shop, Inc., 18 East 48th Street, New York, N.Y.

Columbia Graphophone Company, Ltd. (Columbia), Hayes, Middlesex, England

His Master's Voice Records (HMV), The Gramophone Company, Ltd., Hayes, Middlesex, England

Major Sound Effect Records (MSER), distributed by Thomas J. Valentino, Inc., 1600 Broadway, New York 19, N.Y.

R.C.A. Victor Records (Victor), R.C.A. Victor Division, Radio Corporation of America, Camden, N.J.

Vocal Music

ECCLESIASTICAL SELECTIONS

Gregorian Chants, sung by the Monk Choir of Saint-Pierre de Solmes Abbey. [HMV ● Album M-87, Records 12538–12549.]

——, "Requiem aeternam" (introit), "Absolve Domine" (tract), and "Domine Jesu Christe" (offertory) from the *Mass for the Dead*. These could be used for background music for the closing lines of *Richard II*, when the coffin is brought in; for the opening of *Richard III*, I, 2; for the exit at the end of *Henry V*, IV, 8; and for the opening scene of *1 Henry VI*.

——, "Sanctus" and "Agnus Dei" from the Mass *Cum Jubilo*. This could be used before and during the chorus speech that precedes Act V in *Henry V*.

The Masterpieces of Gregorian Chant, sung and recorded in the monastery chapel by the Choir of Saint-Benoit-Du-Lac, Saint-Benoit-Du-Lac, Brome County, Province of Quebec, Canada. Obtainable direct from the monastery.

——, "Kyrie" from the Mass *Clemens Rector*. [G–8A.]

——, "Alleluia: Emitte Spiritum." [G–9B.]

——, "Alleluia: Veni Sancte Spiritus." [G–9B.] Suitable for the coronation or christening in *Henry VIII*.

——, "Sanctus" from the Mass *Cum Jubilo*. [G–11A.] Appropriate for *Henry V*, IV, 8, after the Battle of Agincourt.

——, "Requiem aeternam" (introit). [3003–A.]

——, "Requiem aeternam" (gradual). [3004–A.] Appropriate for funerals.

Medieval and Renaissance Choral Music, sung by the Choir of the Pius X School of Liturgical Music, Manhattanville College of the Sacred Heart. [Victor ● Album M–739.]

"Introitus" from *Missa pro Defunctis* (ANERIO), sung by the Sistine Choir. [HMV DB1572.] Could be used in place of "Non Nobis". (See *Henry V*, p. 244.)

"Nunc dimittis" (PALESTRINA), sung by unaccompanied choir, conducted by Sir Richard R. Terry. [Columbia 5711.]

"Sanctus" and "Hosanna" from *Missa Papae Marcelli* (PALESTRINA), sung by unaccompanied choir, conducted by Sir Richard R. Terry. [Columbia 5712.]

"O come, ye servants of the Lord" (TYE), sung by the Choir of Westminster Abbey. [HMV RG8.] Suitable for the coronation scene in *Henry VIII*.

SHAKESPEAREAN SONGS

Shakespearean Songs, sung by Leslie French, tenor, as sung in the Shakespearean Plays at London's Open Air Theatre: "It was a lover and his lass"; "Under the

greenwood tree"; "Sigh no more, ladies"; "When daisies pied". [Columbia ●
DX927.]

Shakespearean Songs, "Come away, Death" (BARRATT); "When that I was a little tiny
boy"; "Come unto these yellow sands"; "Full fathom five"; "Where the bee
sucks". [Columbia ● DX928.]

Songs from Shakespeare's Plays, sung by Marie Houston, soprano; Frank La Forge at
the Harpsichord: "Willow, willow" (from *Othello*); the Airs sung by Ophelia.
[Victor Album P–39, Record 26706.] Authentic traditional tunes.

——, "Where the bee sucks" (ARNE); "When daisies pied"; the Cuckoo Song from
Love's Labour's Lost, with flute. [Victor Album P–39, Record 26707.]

Songs from Shakespeare's Plays: "Blow, blow, thou winter wind" (ARNE); "Under
the greenwood tree" (ARNE). [HMV ● B4199.]

——, "O mistress mine" (MORLEY); "Farewell, dear heart" (JONES); "Come away,
Death" (traditional); "I am gone, Sir" (traditional); "When that I was a little tiny
boy" (traditional). [HMV B201.]

Songs from Shakespeare's Plays, sung by Max Meili, with lute accompaniment: "It
was a lover and his lass". [Victor Album M–495, Record 11–0012.]

OTHER ELIZABETHAN SONGS

Columbia History of Music, Vol. I, to the opening of the 17th century: "Awake, sweet
love" (DOWLAND), sung by Cecilie Dolmetsch, soprano, with lute and viol
accompaniment; "Sumer is i-cumen in" (A.D. 1240), sung by St. George's Singers,
unaccompanied. [Columbia 5715.]

——, "Rest, sweet nymphs" (PILKINGTON) and "Sing we and chant it" (MORLEY),
sung by St. George's Singers, unaccompanied, directed by Dr. Edmund H.
Fellowes. [Columbia 5716.]

——, "As Vesta was descending" (WEELKES), "The Silver Swan" (GIBBONS), and
"Fair Phyllis" (FARMER), sung by St. George's Singers. [Columbia 5717.]

Early English Composers, 16th Century Songs, edited by Rev. EDMUND H. FELLOWES,
sung by St. George's Singers unaccompanied. [Album]. Appropriate for incidental
music.

——, "Lightly she whipped" (MUNDY); "Ah! dear heart" (GIBBONS); Sister, awake"
(BATESON). [Columbia 9876.]

——, "I follow, lo, the footing" (MORLEY); "Trio, how merrily we live" (EAST);
"O care, thou wilt dispatch me" (WEELKES). [Columbia 9877.]

——, "Lullaby, my sweet little boy" (BYRD). [Columbia 5546.]

——, "Lady, when I behold" (WILBYE); "Fire, fire, my heart" (MORLEY). [Columbia
5548.]

——, "Sweet Suffolk owl" (VAUTOR). [Columbia 5549.]

English Madrigals, sung by the Cambridge University Madrigal Society:
Set 1. Madrigals by JOHN BENNET, WILLIAM BYRD, JOHN DOWLAND, ORLANDO
GIBBONS, THOMAS MORLEY, THOMAS TOMKINS, THOMAS WEELKES, JOHN
WILBYE. [AS Album G–C3739/44.]

Set 2. Madrigals by THOMAS BATESON, THOMAS TOMKINS, JOHN BARTLET, JOHN WARD, JOHN WILBYE, THOMAS VAUTOR, ORLANDO GIBBONS, THOMAS WEELKES, FRANCIS PILKINGTON, THOMAS MORLEY, JOHN FARMER, GILES FARNABY, JOHN BENNET. [AS Album G–C3745/50.]

English Madrigals circa 1600, motet and madrigal choir (unaccompanied) conducted by Heinrich Opienski. [AS Vol. VI, No. 58.]

——, "Since my tears" (MORLEY). If played very softly, this could be the "still" music for the vision in *Henry VIII*.

——, "Farewell, deare love" (JONES). This could form part of a theme song for *Romeo and Juliet*, to be played as part of the overture and entr'acte music.

——, "Go, crystal tears" (DOWLAND). If played softly, this would be very effective for the tomb scene in *Much Ado about Nothing*.

Folk Songs and Ballads, Vol. II, including "Greensleeves" arranged and sung by SUSAN REED to an accompaniment played on the zither and Irish harp. [Victor Album DM–1107.]

Music of the Renaissance, sung by Max Meili; lute accompaniment by Fritz Wörsching: "Come, deep sleep" (DOWLAND); "Come again" (DOWLAND); *also* "It was a lover and his lass" by Shakespeare (MORLEY). [Victor Album M–495, Record 11–0012.]

"Ah, dear heart" (GIBBONS) and "Sweet honey-sucking bee" (WILBYE), sung by The London Madrigal Group. [Victor 4317.]

"Come again, sweet love" (DOWLAND), sung by Gladys Swarthout, mezzo-soprano. [Victor Album M–679, Record M16778.]

"May sweet oblivion lull thee" (MONTEVERDI), sung by Doris Owen, contralto, with harpsichord accompaniment. [Columbia DB500.]

"There is a lady" (FORD) and "Bring us in good ale" (WOODGATE), sung by Stuart Robertson, bass-baritone. [HMV B4255.]

"There is a lady" (FORD), sung by Robert Wilson, tenor, [HMV BD1103.]

Instrumental Music

WIND INSTRUMENTS

Brasses

German Municipal Music of the Late 17th Century (JOHANN PEZEL), played on five brass instruments. [AS Vol. I, No. 2.] Could be used for incidental music for *A Midsummer Night's Dream* as follows: Intrada—Clowns; Allemande—Courtiers; Courante and Allemande—Lovers; Gigue—Fairies. The first allemande could also be used for the dance in *Henry VIII*.

The Instrumental Suite at the Beginning of the 17th Century: MELCHIOR FRANCK—Pavana, Tantz, Intrada; JOHANN HERMANN SCHEIN—Paduana, Gagliarda, Courante, Allemande, Tripla. Brass ensemble conducted by Curt Sachs. [AS Vol. VI, No. 57.] Ceremonial and courtly dance music.

Clarinet

"Gigue" (Corelli), played by Reginald Kell, with piano accompaniment. [Columbia DB2189.]

Pipes

"La Volta" (Byrd); "Ayre" (Rosseter); "Tower Hill" (Farnaby)—played by the Pipers' Guild Quartet. [Columbia DB2282.]

Recorders

"Green Sleeves to a Ground" (English tune, 16th century; variations, 17th century), played by the Dolmetsch family (with virginals). [Columbia DB1062.]

Stringed Instruments

Viola da gamba, Viols, etc.

Anonymous German (17th Century), sonata for violin, viola d'amore, and bass. Ensemble of viols with harpsichord. [AS Vol. II, No. 19.] Suitable for the overture and for the entrance of the Prince of Morocco and his train in *The Merchant of Venice*; and for processional music in *Henry VIII*.

French Dances of the 16th Century. [AS Vol. I, No. 6.] The fourth item is a pavan and galliard. Both are admirable for the dance in *Romeo and Juliet*, and the rest of the record can be continued very softly throughout the dialogue (see page 253).

Piece for Two Viols: Prelude, Allemande, Sarabande, Gigue (Marin Marais), played on viols and harpsichord. [AS Vol. VIII, No. 78.] Delightful for gay dances.

Sixteenth Century Spanish Instrumental Music: (a) three pavans; *(b)* ricerda for viola da gamba. [AS Vol. IV, No. 40.] The pavans, *(a)*, could be used for background music for the casket-choosing scene in *The Merchant of Venice*. The second part, *(b)*, is splendid for the entrance of the Prince of Arragon.

"Divisions on a Ground" (Norcome); "Fantasy for a Chest of Six Viols" (Weelkes) —played by the Dolmetsch family. [Columbia 5714 (from the Columbia History of Music).]

Lute

Renaissance Music for the Lute, selections by Neusiedler, Stralock, Fiorento, *et al.* [Allegro AL6.]

Sixteenth Century Lute Music, including villanelle, branle gay, and English dance by John Dowland. [AS Vol. IV, No. 36.] Suitable for entr'acte, incidental, or dance music.

Virginals

English Virginalists: Byrd ("The Bells"); Farnaby ("The New Sa-Hoo" and "A Toye"); Peerson ("The Fall of the Leafe"). [AS Vol. II, No. 14.] "The Bells" would be exquisitely appropriate for the entrance to the wedding in *Much Ado about Nothing.* "The Fall of the Leafe" is beautiful for "still" music, especially for the garden scene in *The Merchant of Venice.*

Music for the Virginals (from the *Fitzwilliam Virginal Book*), selections by FARNABY, BYRD, GIBBONS, BULL, MUNDY, PEERSON, TOMKINS, *et al.* Played on virginals. [Allegro AL28.]

"Earl of Salisbury", pavan and galliard (BYRD), played by Rudolph Dolmetsch. [Columbia 5712 (from the *Columbia History of Music*, Vol. I).]

"The King's Hunt" (BULL); "His Toye", "His Dreame", and "His Reste" (FARNABY), played by Rudolph Dolmetsch. [Columbia 5713 (from the *Columbia History of Music*, Vol. I).]

Harpsichord

Eight Suites for Harpsichord (PURCELL). [GSC Album GSC–2.]

Kirkpatrick Harpsichord Recital. [Victor Musicraft Album No. 25.] See especially "The Lord of Salisbury, his Pavin" (GIBBONS); "The Queene's Command (GIBBONS); "Goe from my window" (MORLEY).

Three Dances; Branle de Basque, Pavanne, and Passacaille. (LOUIS COUPERIN). [AS Vol. X, No. 92.] This music could be used for the Island music in *The Tempest* with beautiful effect.

A Treasury of Harpsichord Music, played by Wanda Landowska. [Victor.] Music by PURCELL, CHAMBONNIÈRES, and COUPERIN is included.

"Wolsey's Wild" (BYRD), played by Wanda Landowska. [HMV DA 1014.]

Piano (Duets)

Elizabethan Suite in Four Parts, arranged by ETHEL BARTLETT, played by Ethel Bartlett and Rae Robertson: (1) Variations on "John, come kisse me now" (BYRD, *Fitzwilliam Virginal Book*, No. 10); (2) "His Conceit" (FARNABY. *Fitzwilliam Virginal Book*, No. 273); "Earle of Salisbury's Pavan", from *Parthenia* (BYRD); "A Toye" (FARNABY. *Fitzwilliam Virginal Book*, No. 268. [Columbia DX1340.]
——, (3) "The Falle of the Leafe" (PEERSON); "Tower Hill Jigge" (FARNABY); "Tune for Two Virginals" (FARNABY. *Fitzwilliam Virginal Book*, Nos. 272, 245, 55); (4) "His Dream" (FARNABY. *Fitzwilliam Virginal Book*, No. 194); "The King's Hunting Jigge" (BULL. *Fitzwilliam Virginal Book*, No. 135). [Columbia DX1341.]

Sound Effects

BELLS AND CHIMES

Bells: Midnight; Angelus; Peals. [Columbia YB8.]

Bow Bells, actual chimes rung at St. Mary-le-Bow Church, Cheapside, London, by the Ancient Society of College Youths. [Columbia DB1627.]

Cathedral Bells. [MSER 4029A, 5005B.]

S.S.P.—U

Changes on Bells of St. Margaret's, Westminster (Stedman Caters and Grandsire Caters) [HMV C2098.]

Changes on the Peal of Twelve Bells, introducing Great Peter, 10¾-ton Bourdon bell, rung by York Minster Society of Change Ringers. [HMV B2691.]

Clock Chimes. [MSER 5024A.]

Clock Chimes and Bells. [Columbia YB1.]

Clock Chimes and Bells: quarter-hour; half-hour; three-quarter hour; twelve o'clock (household clock); Big Ben chimes and twelve o'clock. [HMV E575.]

BUGLES AND TRUMPETS

Bugle Calls; fanfare; reveille; rouse. [HMV E582.]

Bugle Calls of the Army. [Victor 27675, 27676.] The last three numbers on Record 27676 are flourishes.

Fanfares. [MSER 5010B, 5011B, 5019A.]

Trumpets and Bugles: fanfare, reveille; bugle call. [Columbia YB9.]

DRUMS

Continuous Drum Roll; Tympani Roll; Cymbal Roll. [Columbia YB16.]

Drum Rolls. [MSER 5029A, 5030B.]

Index